# WANTING A CHILD

"*Wanting a Child* contains the best writing I have seen on infertility, treatment by reproductive technology, and adoption . . . By all means run don't walk to buy this book . . . *Wanting a Child* is a powerful read that will resonate with the increasing numbers who experience difficulty becoming a parent (some six million at last count)—and for the general reader, the first-rate writing in these quests will enlighten and reward."    —KAREN PROPP, *The Women's Review of Books*

"The editors of this remarkable anthology know first-hand the pain and grief of miscarriage and neo-natal death, yet this is mostly an inspirational (and occasionally humorous) survey of what it is like to want a child more than anything and how that desire is changing the look and character of U.S. families."    —*Miami Herald*

"This collection of essays explores the emotional minefield of miscarriage, infertility, surrogacy, in vitro fertilization, and adoption. Even those fortunate enough to have escaped these experiences will find the book a compelling read. If you've known the deep desire to have a baby, you'll understand."    —PAMELA ABRAMS, *Child*

"*Wanting a Child* should make those who want children less lonely, but it will also make parents like me more grateful."
                               —DANIEL AKST, *Civilization*

"In the inspiring and heart-wrenching *Wanting a Child*, writers share the unspoken truths of infertility, adoption, and miscarriage in their quest for parenthood by any means necessary."
                               —ELISSA SCHAPPELL, *Vanity Fair*

"These intensely moving accounts delineate most eloquently the infinite varieties of pain the childless endure and the unbelieving, joyful redemption they experience when, at last, a child enters their lives."
                               —KATHRYN CARPENTER, *Booklist*

"For those in prime parenting years who have faced such trials, these are voices of comfort and wonder." —*Kirkus Reviews*

"What makes [this] book so compelling and valuable is that [it] fill[s] a very real need for a dialogue that is specific to the situations and lifestyles of this day and age."
—MARI NAMA-ANA DANQUAH,
*Washington City Paper*

"[A] hauntingly written and heartfelt collection." —*Publishers Weekly*

"The experiences detailed in this terrific book take us straight into the territory of love, heartbreak, and endurance. We can't help but be pulled in by both the drama and the familiarity of these affecting tales." —MEG WOLITZER, author of *This Is Your Life*

"The desire for a child is achingly told in these essays that remind us of why we have writers in the first place. To move us with the tales they spin and dazzle us with the words they weave. These pieces will break your heart because they are true and because they are so exquisitely rendered." —MARY MORRIS, author of *The Lifeguard*

"*Wanting a Child* beautifully illuminates life's deadly meanings encased in too fragile flesh. Its byways are not only hospital corridors and high-tech labs and distant shores, but the torturous and miraculous path of the heart to its source where love beyond reason lies, where unfathomable blessings reside."
—GWENDOLYN M. PARKER, author of
*These Same Long Bones* and
*Trespassing: My Sojourn in the Halls of Privilege*

JILL BIALOSKY, author of *The End of Desire*, is an editor at W. W. Norton. HELEN SCHULMAN, author of *The Revisionist*, teaches in the M.F.A. program at Columbia University. They both live in New York City with their families.

# WANTING A CHILD

EDITED

AND WITH

AN INTRODUCTION BY

# JILL BIALOSKY
AND HELEN SCHULMAN

Farrar, Straus and Giroux / New York

Farrar, Straus and Giroux
19 Union Square West, New York 10003

Distributed in Canada by Douglas & McIntyre Ltd.
Printed in the United States of America
Designed by Abby Kagan
First published in 1998 by Farrar, Straus and Giroux
First paperback edition, 1999

Library of Congress Cataloging-in-Publication Data
Wanting a child / edited and with an introduction by Jill Bialosky and
Helen Schulman. — 1st ed.
    p.    cm.
    ISBN 0-374-52594-3 (pbk)
    1. Parents — United States — Case studies.   2. Childlessness — United
States — Psychological aspects — Case studies.   3. Human reproductive
technology — United States — Case studies.   4. Adoption — United
States — Case studies.   I. Bialosky, Jill.   II. Schulman, Helen.
HQ755.8.W367   1998
306.874 — dc21                             97-32348

Grateful acknowledgment is given for permission to reprint the following: "The New Life"
by Marie Howe. First published in What the Living Do. Copyright © 1997 by Marie Howe.
Reprinted by permission of W. W. Norton & Company. "Missing Children" by Bob Shacochis. First published in Harper's. Copyright © 1996 by Bob Shacochis. Reprinted by
permission of Brandt & Brandt Literary Agents, Inc. "A Small Memorial" by Peter Carey.
First published in The New Yorker. Copyright © 1995 by Peter Carey. Reprinted by permission of International Creative Management. "Bringing Home Baby" by Tama Janowitz.
First published in Vogue. Copyright © 1996 by Tama Janowitz. Reprinted by permission
of the author. "Death Before Life" by Kevin Canty. First published in Vogue. Copyright
© 1995 by Kevin Canty. Reprinted by permission of Georges Borchardt, Inc. "The Ghost
Mother" by Marly Swick. From The Summer Before the Summer of Love. Copyright ©
1995 by Marly Swick. Reprinted by permission of HarperCollins Publishers, Inc. "Pretty
Story" by Amy Hempel. From Salmagundi. Copyright © 1997 by Amy Hempel. Reprinted
by permission of the author. "Swimmer in the Secret Sea" by William Kotzwinkle. First
published in Redbook. Copyright © 1975 by William Kotzwinkle. Reprinted by permission
of Harold Ober Associates, Inc.

TO LUCAS AND ZOË

For their assistance, encouragement, and support, the editors of this anthology would like to pay tribute to: Cheryl Sucher, Ellen Levine, Elisabeth Kallick Dyssegaard, Helen Eisenbach, Sarah Chalfant, Sloan Harris; and to our families, especially David Schwartz and Bruce Handy. We would like to thank our contributors for sharing their daring, honest, and beautifully written stories with all of us.

# CONTENTS

# THE NEW LIFE

*This morning, James still deep asleep under the embroidered white sheets*
*a heavy heavy rain*

*the city still dark and the rain so loud the city was quiet,*
*a shhhh in the streets, as I drove up First Avenue happy, from Twenty-first Street*

*to Fifty-seventh Street without a light to stop for, a deep privacy in the car,*
*and nobody, for once, beeping —*

*the sky behind the falling rain lightening from dark to heavy gray —*
*and why shouldn't I be happy, and why shouldn't we argue*

*and sit in the two kitchen chairs, our faces downcast, after I get home*
*after what we've done, what we have allowed ourselves to long for?*
                                                                    *— Marie Howe*

# WANTING A CHILD

# INTRODUCTION

We'd met several times at dinner parties, but we weren't friends. It was the novelist Cheryl Sucher who brought us together, several weeks after Helen's second miscarriage, a year after Jill's second loss. Jill left a message on Helen's machine: "You may not be ready to talk now, but when you are, I'd like to meet for coffee." This gesture was the start of a friendship that nourished and sustained us during the bleak years we both spent wanting a child, years that taught us about desire and hope, suffering and grief, years that were suffused with loneliness. Huddled together in our local Starbucks, we would watch with jealousy and awe as parents with strollers came and went. Some of these families appeared to be "traditional," that is, a mother, a father, and a biological child. Others were same-sex couples with kids, single parents, or parents with children of a different race. Whatever the configuration, we lusted after these babies, and we'd confess to one another our anger and bewilderment at the hand that fate had dealt us.

The power of shared experience brought comfort and consolation at a time when no one else in our lives could reach us; neither friends nor families nor even our partners. In a culture determined to spill the beans on just about every aspect of private life—incest and sexual compulsions and affairs—in a culture where no subject felt taboo any longer, infertility and pregnancy loss seemed like the single area no one wanted to talk about.

Our losses *were* painful to talk about. It was hard to convey the breadth of our grief and longing to those who hadn't experienced it firsthand. We were also afraid and often amazed at the extent and power of our own suffering. Somehow the messages that we received regarding our miscarriages and pregnancy losses were that this child wasn't meant to be, and in that message was also the fallacy that they weren't to be mourned. And when something can't be mourned, talked about, allowed to be real, the experience becomes ensconced in a cloud of shame.

Only when we were in the company of each other, and of others who had also experienced hardship in their quest for a child, did we feel we were understood. When we were together, we were free to be ourselves—we could whine and complain and laugh about our situations. Together we could be ugly and honest. We could divulge the feelings of displaced anger and jealousy we harbored over a friend who was pregnant, a cousin who had popped out baby number two. We could talk about our burning desire to have a child, and our fears that we wouldn't, without expecting easy answers or pacifying reassurances. We both knew that the only thing that would save us was a child, finally, and that what we had to offer each other was ways to bear the time we would have to endure until that day came. When we both suffered subsequent disappointments, we called upon each other. Through the long, exciting, frightening, and difficult process of Jill's adoption and Helen's pregnancy, we held each other's hands, and when our babies finally came home, we each held our friend's child in our own arms.

Our kids have brought us the joy of which we had long dreamed and, surprisingly, more joy even than that; but they did not erase our painful pasts, nor was it ever their job to do so. Several weeks before the birth of Helen's daughter, we sat in Jill's living room talking. How could we turn our experiences into something positive? How could we honor the children that we'd lost?

We are both avid readers. We are writers by profession. Jill is also a book editor, and Helen is a teacher of writing and literature. We are, by nature, both people who turn to books for comfort and solace. Yet when we skulked the stacks of our local bookstore, there were plenty of how-to books on adoption and infertility, on pregnancy loss and miscarriage, written by doctors and shrinks and professionals, but there was very little written by the women and men who were experiencing the emotionally trying crossroads we had entered—people who desperately wanted a child, and believed that having a child was their God-given right but were finding, in fact, that having a child was damn hard. We needed to hear the stories of the ways in which these people finally did or did not realize their dream. We needed to hear these voices, but we couldn't find them. We felt as if we were the only two parent wannabes who still didn't inhabit an *Ozzie and Harriet* world, yet we knew in our hearts that we were not alone. For decades and centuries we had not been alone. When we found a paucity of intelligent, well-written material on the subject that most obsessed us, we became each other's library. That is, we shared anecdotes and information—about everything from infertility treatments to adoption—and we were still hungry.

We decided to put together an anthology. We quickly counted up the number of accomplished poets and novelists that we knew who wanted children and had taken a variety of different journeys to achieve their goal. We counted them up on all four hands, and then we counted them up on our toes. Some of these writers had been successful, some were still in the throes of their quest, some had made peace with the fact that they wouldn't become parents, and some had realized that they wanted to remain child-free after all.

The world is changing. Medical and technological advances have given our friends and acquaintances choices they would not have had ten years ago, while for others, these same scientific advances have kept them in a perpetual state of hope. Different attitudes about parenting and a growing acceptance of who we are, both in the world and within ourselves, allow some of us to realize a dream that others may think we do not deserve to conjure even in the privacy of our own hearts: now same-sex and single parents raise biological children, brought into the world through sperm and egg donation and surrogacy. More and more people we know are finding their children through adoptions, some that take them halfway around the world, while others reconnect in midlife with a child from whom they parted in its infancy. Our friends and colleagues are also becoming parents by proxy, by falling in love with someone who already has a child or ending up with a mate who passionately wants one. And because so many couples have split up, many co-parents now end up raising children alone. Many women we know have come to realize in their forties that the choices they made earlier may now jeopardize their chances for biological parenthood. Some have decided they don't want a child at all. We are moved by the stories of parents who expected a healthy child but found out their child would be or was born with health problems and disabilities; how some parents made the difficult choice to terminate such a pregnancy and others carried these children to term; and how these children won the hearts of their parents all the same. We have been reminded again and again how, even though we wouldn't wish these difficult experiences on anyone, often out of hardship one also finds unexpected joy. The traditional American family no longer seems to exist—but did it ever really, we wondered, when our own parents came from families that included orphaned refugees and stray survivors of world wars? A parent is a person who raises a child. This anthology is full of their stories.

When we initially spread the word about this project, the writers we approached seemed extremely eager to be a part of it. These are stories people burn to tell. As we began to curate and commission these essays, every effort to be inclusive and to celebrate the diversity of these new families—affluent and working class, and of a variety of ethnic backgrounds—was made and, we thought, met. But as the months between assignment and delivery passed, and even (sigh) long after our deadlines came and went, our fax machines stayed quiet and our mailboxes remained half-empty. What was going on? we wondered, as we made our at first polite, then more nudgey, follow-up calls. Are writers just erratic, anxious, or overextended folk by nature? Or were we, as editors, discovering a problem inherent in our project?

As uplifting, funny, courageous, and hopeful as many of these personal histories may be they are also full of pain and yearning. We lost several writers over the issue of privacy—people who were happy, even eager, to discuss the peculiarities of their adoption process, the termination of a pregnancy, or the specter of the "ghost" (biological mother) over the phone but who couldn't bear to bring pen to paper. Suddenly the privacy issues of their lovers, their children, even their ex-spouses, became obstacles they could not overcome. In three cases—Hempel, Swick, and Kotzwinkle—we collected pieces of short fiction to fill some of the gaps. We regret the gaps that still remain. For some of our writers, the memories themselves were just too painful to explore. And yes, some of our writers were just being plain old overextended, neurotic writers. They didn't have the time or the confidence to step up to the plate.

Now that we are mothers, finding a few hours to put together the loose ends of this project, between feedings, diapers, play groups, work schedules, and writing, was not easy. One day not too long ago, we sat in Jill's living room and, as tired mothers are somewhat reluctant to do, popped in a video of *Dumbo* so we could have a few minutes to talk without interruption. At the beginning of the video, a flock of storks fills the sky, each carrying a Santa Claus–like bundle in its beak. The storks fly over a circus in Florida, then one by one drop down. The first stork delivers newborn cubs to the expectant mother in the tiger's den, the second lands among the giraffes, the next among the kangaroos. Each expectant mother animal greedily searches the sky, and when the stork lands in her cage and the bundle unfolds, revealing her baby, her face fills with joy and contentment. As the newborn nuzzles up to her, the music becomes lighter, uplifting.

Suddenly the tone of the music darkens. An expectant elephant looks up in the sky with longing and anticipation. Each time she sees a stork flying overhead, a glint of hope appears in her eyes, and each time, as the stork lands in another animal's cage, it is crushed. Day turns to night. The storks vanish from the sky. Tears stream down the elephant's face.

Eventually, even the mother elephant is united with her baby, but not in the way she initially imagined.

Now that we have our children, the moral of this message seems simple: There are always those for whom things don't come as easily or as quickly as they once imagined they would. What becomes clear, as our young children watch this familiar story, is how early these desires—this desire for a child—is imprinted in our minds and hearts and imaginations, and how necessary it is for new stories to be told.

We are extremely proud of the essays in this anthology. They are brave, important stories, honestly told, that reflect realistic ways in which men and women become parents, and children are born and cared for and loved. When we read and reread them, both of us catch our breath. We are moved as we come to know the families of our writers, in the flesh and through their work; for whatever their con-figurations, these families of one, two, three, or more are made up of brave people, eager to live their lives, fully embracing what it means to be human. This is what we want for our two children. We want them to have the self-confidence, the courage to go after what they want, to love freely and furiously.

In the middle of our private screening of *Dumbo*, Jill's son leaned over and kissed Helen's daughter. No matter that in the next five minutes one child would steal a toy out of the other child's hand; no matter that the second child would then whack the first kid over the head. In that one moment our dreams felt fulfilled. Our children were in the world.

Jill Bialosky<br>
Helen Schulman

# H E E D L E S S   L O V E

BARBARA JONES

This is a story that never changes. I've told it over business
lunches, at cocktail parties, in my gynecologist's office. I've
told it in letters, in a magazine article, live on national television. First, I told it to family and friends; soon I'll be able to tell it
to my daughter. Every time I tell this story, my listener's eyes
brighten—it is a happy story—and this brightness in the eyes eggs me
on; I tell the story again and again. But each listener also looks at me
as if I'm speaking of something odd—happy but odd—and this is a
true story about my life that I didn't experience as an oddity. To me,
this story is commonplace, a story about ordinary love.

I was thirty-four years old, divorced, happy. I lived in a two-
bedroom, two-bath apartment in Manhattan with a likable and almost
always absentee roommate. I jogged alone in Central Park, went to
afternoon movies with writer and actor friends, showed up at art openings, hung out in bookstores, bought designer clothes at sample sales,
danced the AIDS Danceathon, fished for blues from the North Fork
of Long Island, flew to Italy for a long weekend. I went on dates; I

liked dating. I made my living as a freelance writer; I had $20,000 in the bank from a book I'd ghostwritten. On the telephone I told my brother, "If I get hit by a bus or anything, please know that I'm happy; whatever happens from now on, it's all right with me, because I've known happiness." I suppose I don't like to think of the nag I was during my marriage as me; in any case, as a devil-may-care divorcée—reading Boccaccio's *Decameron* with friends, eating Thanksgiving dinner in a Polish diner with a lover, greedy and generous, content and desiring—I was the person I think I am.

One Sunday morning in April, I happened to be alone in my apartment reading *The New York Times*, and the *Times Magazine* cover story was about a couple who had adopted a baby girl from China. The article mentioned that the Chinese government allowed single women to adopt Chinese infants. The article also mentioned that these babies were all girls. In China parents are allowed only one child, and most parents dearly want a boy (they *need* a boy, they feel, because sons and daughters-in-law take care of elderly parents— without a son, a Chinese citizen has no pension); in China about a million newborn girls are killed or abandoned every year. As soon as I read the *Times* article, I was done for, although I didn't realize it then. Reading the paper I only thought, "Well, *I* want a daughter" and "If I don't remarry in a few years, this is what I'll do: I'll adopt a baby girl from China." I saved the magazine, set it aside just in case—in case, in six or eight years, I might need to refer to it. But only a month later, while cleaning off my desk, I happened across the article and reread it. On this read, I saw something I'd missed the first time: If I remarried and had a biological child, I would no longer be eligible to adopt a daughter from China. The Chinese government was offering children only to the childless. In May, as in April, to adopt a daughter from China and have no biological children seemed like a fine possibility, but in May, suddenly, to have biological children but no child from China felt unbearable.

Why?

That's what everyone wanted to know.

Was something "wrong" with my reproductive system? Didn't I want a biological child? Didn't I want to wait for a partner? Why wasn't I waiting until I was a more established writer? Why a Chinese baby? (Was I a racist—why not an African-American baby, a Mexican baby, a Caucasian baby?) Some friends, some dates, even some gossipy acquaintances had questions for me. But my own only question was asked by a gleeful voice in my mind: "You're going to do *what?*" I never had a doubt. From the day I reread that magazine story, I thought, "I'm going forward with this. Maybe someone or something outside of me will to try to stop me, but I am not ever going to stop."

I contacted one of the two adoption agencies mentioned in the *Times* article. I went, accompanied by my roommate and by another male friend, to a required introductory meeting at the agency. I learned that to adopt an infant from China, I needed to have a plan for who would take care of the child if I died and I needed to earn at least $30,000 a year. The cost of the adoption, including all expenses for travel to and from China, was $20,000. After the introductory meeting, I signed up for an "intake interview" at the agency. After the interview, a committee at the adoption agency decided to take my case. After the committee decided to take my case, I fell in love with my friend Steve. Two weeks later, Steve moved in with me.

Why would a woman who was with a man and who could bear a child want to adopt? At the adoption agency, I said, "I'm seeing a man I might end up marrying. Do you want to know about this?" The agency said, "If you were in a permanent relationship, we would recommend that you and your partner pursue biological parenthood first." "Okay," I said, and I didn't tell them about Steve.

I went through a physical, a fingerprinting session at my neighborhood police station (so I could be checked out by the FBI), a social worker's visit to my home. I collected my birth certificate, my divorce decree, tax forms, a financial statement from my accountant, recommendations from friends; I wrote an autobiography, and I filled out dozens of government forms—immigration forms for the baby, forms testifying to the expertise of my social worker; I signed a paper swearing to the Chinese government that I would love the child forever and that I would put her through college.

Steve started seeing a therapist. He loved me, and he liked the idea of my adopting a baby, but he was worried because he just wasn't picturing a baby in his daydreams about our future together.

In August my papers were in order, and the adoption agency sent them to China. In September the social worker phoned to say she had received a medical report on and photograph of a three-month-old baby. Did I want the baby? Briefly, in the hour before I saw the picture, I had imagined this infant might be a delicate flower: exotic and wan. In fact, she looked like a Chinese Winston Churchill, deeply skeptical about the merits of the photo session, powerfully irritated—as if someone had just taken away her cigar.

At a birthday party for a friend who is a poet, we gather in her step-children's bedroom because that's where the upright is. We sit on the bunk beds, on the changing table, on the dollhouse roof, on the floor. A composer has set one of the poet's sonnets to music, and a soprano will sing this love song while the composer accompanies her on the piano. As soon as the music begins, the poet and her lover begin to weep. My daughter, Maria, is now two and a half and lushly beautiful, a Chinese-American Sophia Loren. The composer begins to play, and Maria, clutching a cache of tiny stuffed animals, climbs onto the piano bench alongside the composer and begins to throw the toys, one by one, at the composer's head. The composer ducks and bobs and somehow keeps playing. The poet and her beloved continue to weep. I manage to step between and climb over party guests to reach Maria, grab her, swing her above my head and across the room, and plunk her down amidst other children on the top bunk; immediately, she stands and shouts repeatedly, "I'm up here! Look everybody!" When the song ends, the composer, the singer, the poet, and the poet's lover collapse in tears; Maria demands and has her turn at the piano, banging out an overture, lifting her hands in a melodramatic caesura, before launching, singing, into "Someday My Prince Will Come."

Oh, I hear the other mothers talk about Maria. They call her a "buster," a "pistol"; they say she's "like a boy." One mother greets her, "Hey, *girlfriend*," as if Maria were thirty-five years old. Another mother, pregnant with her second daughter, leans to me at one of the kiddie birthdays and says out of the corner of her mouth, "For your second child, *you deserve an easy one*." My daughter's grand-mothers send her dresses and toys and phone us cooing at her beauty in the photographs we send, but both have told us outright that they will not baby-sit her by themselves: she's just too much to handle.

After the scene at the poet's birthday, two friends, independently, tell me that I look at Maria with "a look of helpless love." It's interesting that two people say this exact same thing, so I consider what they've said. But I do not love her with a helpless love; I have help.

Once, when Maria was eight months old, Steve and I walked with her six blocks along the river on iced-over sidewalks in subzero winds. We were going from a party to our home, and it seemed silly and impractical to find a taxi for such a short distance. We pushed home on foot, against the kind of wind that makes your eyes tear and in the kind of cold that freezes those tears to your face. Steve had Maria against his chest, inside his coat. Four blocks from our building, on the overpass above West Ninety-sixth Street, crosswinds began to slam us from the side. Later, Steve told me Maria began to scream a desperate scream then that he'd never heard before and could never have imagined. I was less than a yard behind him, but I didn't hear a thing because of the winds. I struggled to stand, to inch forward, to not slide into the street. In the street a car spun around. Suddenly Steve took off. He squiggled. He shimmied. All of the great effort he'd summoned looked, from behind, as if he were merely doing a little dance. Still, he had sped up; he departed from me. He and Maria moved up the hill and around the corner, out of sight. In our lobby, panting, our cheeks aflame, Steve said, "Well, I hate to say this, but I've made my choice." If it were between me and Maria, he'd have to save Maria now, he meant, because she was his daughter.


The irrevocable moment in becoming a parent is not the moment you conceive a child; it's the moment you conceive of her. Maybe in your mind she looks partly like you and partly like your husband. Maybe she looks partly like you and partly like some handsome, genius sperm-bank stranger. Maybe she is coffee brown and Peruvian; you are albumen white and Swedish. Maybe she is a he. But whatever your idea of your child, once you have it, once you have thought of her as yours (which may happen ten years before she's born, or four months into your pregnancy, or six weeks after you meet her), nothing can stop you from wanting her. And only some terrible force outside of your control will prevent you from having her. You will run through icy winds for her. You will leave your wife for her. You will quit your job for her, take two jobs for her. You will lie slant, almost upside down, for forty-eight hours so she can be born two fewer days premature. You will let your bones crack apart for her. If the adoption agency says you are too old to adopt her, you will find another agency. If the first in vitro insemination fails to produce her, you will shoot hormones into your butt for another month. And if you miscarry, your child has died. If the birth mother changes her mind, your child has been torn from you.

I traveled to China with my mother and seven other adopting families. We spent our first day in Beijing, sightseeing in Tienanmen Square and at the Great Wall. Our second day, we flew south to an industrial city called Hefei, and while we were flying, our babies were traveling too—four bumpy hours in a van from Wuhu City to Hefei. Only an hour after we checked in to our hotel, our guide, Xiong Yan, told us to go to our rooms: the babies were coming. Each baby would be delivered to its parents in their room. At first we were all too excited to obey Xiong Yan. We gathered in the hotel hallway, giggling, whispering. Every time we heard the whirr of the elevator, we raced back to our rooms and stood in the doorways, peeking out. Finally we heard the elevator stop on our floor; we heard the elevator doors open; we scrambled to our rooms. My mother and I, looking down the hall, saw a beautiful infant in a yellow jogging suit. "Is that ours? We'll take her," my mother said. But she wasn't ours. "*This* is your baby," Xiong Yan said. A stocky woman was in our doorway, holding a fat-cheeked five-month-old in a pale blue sweat suit. The baby fixed a long serious look on me, frowned, and started to bawl. My mother started to bawl too. And eight days later, when I carried Maria out of international customs and through the revolving doors at Kennedy Airport, there was my father, holding a huge posterboard sign that read "Welcome Maria" and sniveling. And there was Steve, weeping—I'd never seen him weep before. But when I first lifted my daughter from the stocky arms of the woman who had been her night nurse and looked into her furious face, I did not cry.

# THE HABITUAL ABORTER

## HELEN SCHULMAN

'

At night, in Venice, while my husband dreamed, I designed a
yellow dress. For the first half hour or so of sleeplessness, I
imagined it as a pale silk chiffon, cut close, strapless, with a
band of satin piping below the collarbone. The back was adorned
with tiny cloth-covered buttons that mimicked the spine; below the
knees, a mermaid skirt fanned out in a little triangular tail of knife
pleats. As the evening waxed, the dress grew sleeves, cap length with
opera gloves, and then the sleeves elongated, kissing the wrists. Mer-
curial, the dress was sometimes fashioned from yards and yards of silk
charmeuse, then linen, then organza, and even, in a misguided moment, spandex. These fabrics came in orangey yolk yellows, in neurotic electric yellows, in the palest, whitest, clear yellow of an infant's
pee.

That was the only way I could get through a night, stitching up
and tearing apart the yellow dress inside my mind. I designed and
redesigned that formal, silly thing every night, all night for a week.

Since it kept me from thinking about my pregnancy, the yellow dress was a godsend.

It had taken us three years, three miscarriages, five doctors, two surgical procedures, a blood transfusion, infertility drugs, four months of progesterone shots, endless, endless testing, and a partridge in a pear tree to achieve this pregnancy. The legacy of those three miscarriages was that as soon as the test had come back positive, I started ducking into bathrooms, in coffee shops, in museums, in the Starbucks that thankfully (at that moment in my life anyway) popped up on every corner. I ducked into bathrooms in order to check my underwear for blood. But with this pregnancy, my fourth pregnancy—the final try, my husband said—my last hope, there was no little brown scratch on my panties. This time the blood had come in torrents, on my way home from my therapist's office no less, so much blood that I stopped for once worrying about the baby and worried instead for my own life.

How was it that I could bleed so much and still my baby's heart was beating? After rushing from one doctor's office to another, the pregnancy was termed fragile but viable. The two layers that made up the uterine sac had for some unknown reason chosen to separate, and I was confined to bed in order for them to knit back. I almost literally did not move for four months. For four months my students, those guardian angels, came to my house, and I held court from my living room sofa. For four months, my husband, that reluctant caretaker, brought me food, drink, and trashy magazines. For four months, I did little but worry and hyperventilate and cry.

So when the doctors finally said, "Time's up, you're fine, get out of bed," my husband said, "Great, we deserve a vacation, this is our last chance for adventure." But I was afraid to leave our bed's soft confines, the down comforter and tray table permanently set up as if for a consumptive. Our bedroom's dusty floorboards, the endless array of half-empty tea mugs, a stained Indian schmata covering our windows as if we were still in college, even the cracker crumbs that stuck to my skin and sheets, all spoke of safety to me. For the sixteen weeks that I had lain on my left side in that bed and had not moved, my baby had remained alive. What would happen to her now, if I ventured out into the world?

But I sensed the undertext to my husband's hit-the-road cheer. If we didn't have some fun, and soon, our marriage would be in serious trouble. Having lost three babies, I wasn't in the mood to lose my husband as well. So we went to Italy, romantic, romantic Italy. To eat and eat, and look at art, and buy me great outfits for later.

We stayed right next door to La Fenice, the opera house that had caught fire and burned down to its graceful hulk just a week before our arrival. You could still smell the ash in the air, in the drapes and bedspread, and after a few days of not-sleeping there, I could smell it on our clothes and hair. Each morning my husband woke up dreaming that our hotel room was on fire. In Venice I didn't sleep, and so I didn't dream. I lay still and worried. Mostly I worried that my baby would die—that she would die and that I would live—so I ate cornettos and regina all night and drank sugary orange and lemon sodas in the hopes of getting her so juiced up she'd be forced to kick inside me, a sure sign that her tiny heart, that flickering light, kept beating; and I designed and redesigned that yellow dress while I listened for the clang of the hammers that signaled morning. There were just two workmen on the shaky scaffolding that hung right outside our window, two workmen to set that decimated, beautiful, and complex opera house to rights. At around 7 a.m. they would begin banging away desultorily on what seemed to me would probably go down in history as the world's longest restoration project. There was nothing left of the insides of La Fenice.


My husband was not keen on becoming a father. I, on the other hand, wanted a baby. We had lived together five years before we married, and then it took another twelve months of cajoling to get him to throw away the birth control. I immediately got pregnant. I had never been pregnant before—even in high school I was scrupulously careful—and my gynecological life had been uneventful. After all those years of controlling my fertility, I never doubted I would be able to have a child. I believed it was my God-given right. So it wasn't that I wasn't grateful that I had gotten pregnant easily—I was very grateful. But I wasn't surprised. Our first year of marriage was the best year I ever had. I guess the truth was, I was used to feeling blessed.

We told our parents I was pregnant and no one else, because doctor number one had instructed us not to announce my pregnancy until the first trimester was over and at that time in my life I still put my faith in doctors.

About a month later I began to bleed. Doctor number one called me into her office. Finding no little sac on the sonogram of my uterus, she reversed her diagnosis.

"I don't understand," I said to doctor number one, a phrase I would use over and over again during the next three years, a phrase I repeat to myself to this day when I'm trying to get a grasp on all that transpired during our quest to have a child. My blood and urine tests had been positive. I'd missed a period, and my body had already begun to change. Besides, doctor number one had told me I was pregnant. I'd already told my husband. How could I not be pregnant?

"Perhaps," she said, "your pregnancy is hysterical."

I felt so ashamed when I left her office. Was I crazy? I sobbed in my husband's arms. And then I confessed to him. I had imagined the whole thing, I said. The baby existed only in my mind. Good thing we never told anyone, we said to each other, my husband looking at me with a worried eye.

Later that evening, doctor number one called me at home to say that perhaps she had been mistaken. After receiving the results of my blood tests, she now thought I had had a pregnancy in my tubes. Had I ever had chlamydia?

"No," I said, "not that I'm aware of," but maybe that was the problem, maybe I had an STD and I was too stupid to know it. I was rushed to the hospital the next morning, and the radiologist said that yes indeed I'd been pregnant, he could see that little blighted ovum. Did I know that I had two uteruses?

That afternoon, back at her office, doctor number one told me that the radiologist had misread my sonogram. I had only one uterus after all, but she concurred with his prognosis that the pregnancy had failed. My husband had a magazine writing assignment, and we were scheduled to take a trip to Florida. "Go," said doctor number one. "Don't let this stop you." And I didn't. I didn't let it stop me. I began to hemorrhage in the taxi to the airport. Codeine and Scotch got me through the flight, most of which I spent curled up in agony on the floor of the tiny airplane bathroom. The remains of our baby were flushed down a toilet in a motel in Disney World. "Don't let this stop you," said doctor number one.

Right.

Even now I have trouble explaining why it was I so desperately wanted that baby. After all, as these things go, my first miscarriage happened blessedly early. I required no cleanup surgery, and in a matter of weeks my body returned to normal. But after spending most of my adult life dreaming about having a child, from the moment that store-bought dipstick turned blue, this baby had been real to me. I dreamed about her tiny fingers, the fragrance of her small, damp head. I loved her, and I was dying to be a mother. More. I needed to be her mother. The person I saw myself as was a person who took care of a child—as dangerously reactionary as it may sound, I needed a child to complete myself. So when I look back on it, I think that much of my mourning came not only from the loss of this one special, specific potential person but also from the damage it wreaked on my own vision of myself. As far as I was concerned, I was a childless mother.

When we got home from Disney World, it seemed that no one understood my devastation. My husband was bewildered by the ferocity of my reaction, and I by his relative lack of one. "Is that all? When I heard your voice, I thought someone had died," said one of the two people I had told. Someone did die, I thought, but I said nothing. "How will you react when you have a real problem?" asked a family member. And so I kept quiet, ashamed of the volume of my grief.

A series of tests ensued, some painful, some not, some covered by health insurance, some not. I was STD-free, and I had physiologically normal reproductive organs. But months and months went by, and I didn't get pregnant again. We went to another doctor. He performed a postcoital test and told me my husband had no sperm.

Suddenly my husband began to take the whole endeavor seriously. Before then, just like my family and friends, he'd thought I was overreacting. If I just relaxed, he said, everything would be fine. Now, for the first time, the problem, if there was a problem, could have originated with him. It would be easy now to poke fun at him, to say that once we were talking about his gonads instead of mine, the alarms could go off. But in truth, wasn't that exactly what was happening to me? I knew intellectually that being a woman had nothing to do with procreating, that being a good parent had to do with just about everything but, but on a primal level I felt differently. I was failing him, I was failing me, I wasn't doing my job. I was defective.

The next round of tests confirmed my self-doubts. My husband *did* have sperm, but something was wrong with my cervical mucus. I began to read up, eager to correct myself. I took out medical journals, bought and borrowed books on herbology and flower essences. Anything I could get my hands on. Robitussin, said one women's health guide, will thin your cervical mucus. For two weeks I guzzled so much Robitussin, I got drunk.

And exactly a year after my first miscarriage, I got pregnant.

"It was the Robitussin," I said.

"It was the Robitussin," said my husband.

We didn't tell anyone.

My second pregnancy proceeded normally. At week seven we saw a heartbeat on the sonogram. At week nine we could make out a head, hands, legs, and always that beautiful flickering light of our baby's heart. When I looked at my child up on the screen, I instantly knew her name, a name so beautiful and precious to me that I dare not write it down. As the days went by, I talked to her, I read to her, I was completely enthralled by the mysterious budding flower of her personality. I waited breathlessly for her to reveal herself, to enter the world, to rest in my arms.

In the meantime I started rewriting a screenplay with a director I had long admired. One of the main characters in the screenplay was a pregnant teenage girl. As part of our research, I spent a month going back to high school, sitting in on "parenting" classes, talking to teenage mothers. "I'm pregnant too," I wanted to say to the girls I had befriended, girls whose own mothers were younger than I was, but I didn't. It would have been inappropriate. I didn't tell the director. It would have been unprofessional. We were waiting for the first trimester to be over.

When I entered doctor number three's office in my twelfth week, the nurse said to me, "I guess you're getting ready to announce your good news." And I thought yes, yes, yes, now I can tell the world about her. But that day there was no little flickering light on the sonogram.

I was in surgery the next morning. I stayed in bed the following day. On the third day I was back at the high school watching fifteen-year-old mothers feed their babies Coca-Cola instead of formula.

I didn't say a word about my losses to anyone but my closest friends. I kept quiet and felt ashamed and blamed myself. I shouldn't have tempted fate by taking the screenwriting job. I shouldn't have eaten sushi, taken a train trip, worked out. I'd had a wild, sexy youth, and I was paying for it. I'd done drugs. Failed someone when he needed me most. God was punishing me for marrying a gentile. Whatever it was, I'd cursed myself.

Again, I tried to get pregnant. One month, two months, three. Again, the ovulation kits, the basal temperature thermometers. I don't know why, since I had been pregnant twice before, but I was convinced that I would never get pregnant again. I was convinced, and a depression like none other I had known before began to envelop me. I felt like I was living inside a murky, veined membrane, impossible to navigate. I spent most of my time going to doctors, testing my urine, and crying. And when my period came each month, when I saw my own blood, I would relive the previous loss. When I began to think about what life would be like without ever having a child, survival felt impossible. I seriously contemplated suicide.

Doctor number three suggested another exploratory surgery.

I leaped at the opportunity.

By this point most of my friends had babies. They were in one world, and I was in another. It hurt too much to be on the outside, nose pressed up to the glass. So I ducked when I saw them pushing their strollers up and down Broadway, and I begged doctor number three to do something to alleviate my pain.

He prescribed a fertility drug called Clomid. It thinned out my uterine lining. I lost another month. We changed the dose. Still no dice, and I lost another month. Every day was one day closer to ovulation, every day after ovulation I would hold my breath, praying for the onset of nausea. Every period felt like another loss. We increased the stakes, and I started taking Metrodin intramuscularly. Each morning my husband gave me another reluctant shot in the butt.

I got pregnant.

Three days after I learned I was pregnant, I began to bleed.

After I had spent ten days in bed, doctor number three determined that this pregnancy, like all the others, had gone South.

I began knocking wood. It started as a gesture. My dad said, "by this time next year, you'll have a baby"—and I'd knock. On the table. On the sole of my boot. On my cat's forehead. My husband would say, "When we have a kid . . ." and I'd knock, on a tree, on a chair in a restaurant, on any available doorframe. I'd read a story in the paper —woman survives car accident but loses baby—and I'd knock. An ad from Baby Gap would swoosh by on the side of a passing bus. I'd knock. I'd pass a maternity shop. Knock, knock, cross the street. I couldn't walk on the same block as the offices of doctors number one, two, and three. I couldn't wear the outfit I'd worn the day of miscarriages one, two, and three. I bought a wooden bangle bracelet. I bought a bed frame. Wood. A picture frame. Wood. "Please, honey," said my husband. "Stop knocking, or I'll kill you."

I'd always felt I had some semblance of control over my life. If I did badly in school, I worked harder. If I wrote something that didn't work, I rewrote it. Relationships floundered, I resurrected them. We had no money, I got another job. And when the mundane, earth-shattering tragedies of life came my way—death and disease and heartbreak—I mourned, made my peace, and moved on. There was nothing that I couldn't accomplish, at least to some degree, if I really put my mind to it.

But not this. Not with douches and antibiotics. Yoga. Acupuncture. Thinking positively. The more obvious it became that I had no control over what was happening to me, the more I tried to control it anyway. I did more research. Joined a support group. Went to doctors and doctors and doctors. Still I could make no peace.

Night after night I dreamed that I had never married, never written a word, never had a boyfriend. I was still living at home with my parents.

What happened to me? I'd ask myself over and over in my dreams. How had I ruined my life?

A week after my third miscarriage, during a killer bout of the flu, I vomited my way into a full-fledged delirium. My temperature hovered around a hundred and four, and my kidneys had begun to shut down. Still I made my husband give me my fertility shots. I hadn't eaten in five days. In another twenty-four hours, I would probably have gone into a coma. When the ER doctor, not George Clooney, told me I might have died, I thought death, a coma, neither one would be so bad, it was being awake that felt so terrible. A friend sent flowers and a note: "What's with your karma? In another life were you Genghis Khan?"

And I thought no, in another life, I was young and in love, happily married, friend to many, a writer. It is only in this nightmare life that I am lonely and old and half-dead, selfish and mean and jealous, friendless and on the verge of a divorce. It is only in this life that I am Genghis Khan, because all that is left of me is this fruitless pursuit, and I hate everyone.

They placed me on the maternity ward. I lay in my hospital bed and watched the beginning of the O.J. murder trial. I hated every single newborn baby sleeping down the hall. I hated the doctors who came into my room, my parents, my husband, everyone who told me to take a break, to give up trying. "You're a wreck," my doctor said. "You couldn't carry a pregnancy now." The hospital gynecologist intimated that I'd been malpracticed. "Why the fertility drugs?" she said, her eyes focusing in on Denise Brown. "You've been vomiting for days, and you've just had a miscarriage. You're supposed to take off a couple of months. What are you, nuts?"

Yes, I thought, I am nuts. I am nuts, and I'm Genghis Khan. I will stop at nothing. I will ruin my health, take drugs that may give me cancer, cheat on my husband, spend all our money, give up my work, whatever it takes to have a child.

"I'm not doing it anymore," said my husband, before he left my hospital room that night.

Over the din of my TV set, I could hear the nurses out in the hall gossiping over my chart.

"Schulman? She's a habitual aborter."

———

Was it true? Was I addicted to loss and grief? Was I perpetually bringing all of this down upon myself, my own body failing me, killing
my desires and dreams? To prove to my husband that I could still
live my life, I agreed to go to Italy. We'd decided on Venice in mid-
February because we thought it would be down season, cheaper, terrifically gray and wet and quiet. What we didn't count on was
Carnival. The narrow winding streets, the fetid, stinking canals—those
petri dishes—the cafés, the restaurants and vaporetti, Harry's Bar were
all stuffed to the gills with elaborately costumed, drunk, insane Eu-
ropeans. They wore long wide gowns and courtiers' suits and these
frozen white masks that made every single one of them look dead. I
was not prepared for this. I would walk with my hands out in front
of me, to fend off the crowds, to keep a stray arm or bag or bustled
derriere from knocking into my belly. I would shut my eyes whenever
one of those masked, well-dressed corpses passed by. The streets were
teeming with them, with jugglers and musicians and pickpockets, and
all of them looked ominous to me. I felt like I had cursed myself just
by being there.

I took to designing the dress in my head all day as well as during
the night. We'd enter an open-air market—cockles and mussels and
octopus and eel and the dark inky cuttlefish that makes Venetian
risotto so famous. Three kinds of artichokes, whole and small, large
and pared down, hearts bobbing in acidulated water. Big black egg-
plants and globular white ones, bright green squash with yellow
squash blossoms, and trussed-up, plucked baby birds, and I'd shut my
eyes and knock on my wooden bangle and design. Long sleeves, short
sleeves, a pouf skirt, a wasp waist. My husband had no idea what was
going on. As far as he was concerned, we were out of the woods and
celebrating. We were in Italy. Great food. Great art. Having fun. But
in every museum, every church, in every restaurant and café bar, even
above the double bed in our room in the hotel next to La Fenice,
hung the same image: a mother and child. There was no escaping
them. So I designed and designed, and I knocked and I knocked. I
couldn't bear to hope.

Throughout the course of our marriage and our trip through the
land of infertility, stupid as it sounds, it had never ceased to amaze
me how close two people can be and how far apart. In Italy my
husband was in heaven, he was convinced that the nightmare was

over, the nightmare that both of us secretly believed I had inflicted upon us through the strength of my will. Certainly he wouldn't have volunteered for all the medical intervention we'd gone through, the tests and prodding, the endless jerking off into a cup, the whole humiliating, desexualizing affair.

There were many times throughout our journey when my husband wanted to give up. Still he accompanied me along every excruciating, bloody step; he'd even gone with me to Philadelphia to Thomas Jefferson Hospital where, in a painful and highly experimental procedure, I was immunized with white cells from his blood in an effort to keep my body from rejecting his child. I remember watching his blood flow into my body and thinking is this the ultimate union or an act of medical madness? Had whatever Stealth bombers that might have been circling around his bloodstream just entered mine? What were we doing really? Taking advantage of the gifts medical technology could miraculously bestow, or trying to fight the will of God? My husband had done everything a person could do to stand by me, to support me, happily, stubbornly, reluctantly, and at knifepoint. I loved and hated him for it. I hated him for not wanting this as much as I did, for making the burden of continuation mine. He didn't have the same hole to fill inside him; he didn't need another human being to complete his own vision of himself. When we left Philadelphia, him holding ice packs around my swollen and useless right arm, I saw beyond the anger in his eyes to a look I had never seen from him before. It was pity.

I think about how close we came to breaking up and how far we have come from that horrible time now as I write at my desk in New York City. Three and a half months after our trip to Venice, I went into labor on my due date. The labor continued without progression, every five to ten minutes for three days. During those three days I watched one Woody Allen movie after another, pressing the stop-motion button on my remote control whenever I was hit by my next contraction, and of course, I couldn't eat or sleep.

When my doctors finally thought it was safe to induce me, they broke my water, and an infection spiraled. In their efforts to get the baby out quickly, my contractions were hastened by medication, and the pain meds were turned off. We were wheeled into the OR flanked by a surgical and pediatric team because an emergency C-section was now in order. As I went shrieking down the hall on my gurney, I kept thinking about that yellow dress, lowering and loosening the waist, shirring the neckline, I kept thinking about it because I couldn't allow myself to think about what I was afraid of most: that we'd come this far and still I would lose her.

A crowd gathered in the OR. Our baby was transverse, her head was pointed at an angle, and basically she was banging against my uterine wall. My doctor was going to attempt one last try at a vaginal birth. A group of interns and residents had come to observe. The anesthesia was turned back on, the anesthesiologist herself had her arms around me, and my husband held my hand as my ob-gyn used forceps to flip the baby around—a daring process that saved us from the emergency C but also broke my tailbone.

Even with the anesthesia, I felt her turn.

I shouted, "Whoa." And then, "Get that baby out of me!"

And they did.

And she was fine, thank God. She was perfect.


I keep a photograph of us from that trip to Venice in a drawer in my desk, and every once in a while I look at it, see the fear in my face, see the hope in my husband's. Above my desk there is another photograph, a family portrait, taken by a good friend of my husband's who is a wonderful photographer. The picture was taken less than three months after our baby's birth. It's of the three of us on our sofa, and I love it for many reasons. One, because it is a single-image photo-collage, the photographer's specialty; two, because it captures the heaviness and exhaustion and pride that rule you when a baby has just been born (my husband calls the photo "Upper West Side Gothic"); but mostly, because our daughter sits in the center of the picture like a little sunflower, her eyes couldn't be any bigger or wider, she looks shocked but pleased to find herself in the living, breathing world.

Even though I look at the photo every day, I've never noted until today that the dress she wears in the picture is yellow.

So inasmuch as you can have a happy ending when you're still in the process of living a life (and our daughter has made us both intensely happy), why do I still feel compelled to tell this story? It all worked out fine, right? We came out older, a little bruised, but stronger and more joyful in the wash. And yet . . .

After our daughter was born, the three of us, my husband and I and baby Z. (my family!) went to L.A. on another magazine writing assignment, but also to visit one of my closest friends from college. When I was pregnant the second time, J. was pregnant with her first, and in the miracle world of girlfriends, our due dates were the exact same day. We had squealed and oohed and ahhed—our babies will be friends! we'll dump them with our husbands and meet up at a spa!—so it amazes me to this day that our friendship survived my second miscarriage. It had been so painful to me to hear her little boy on the other end of the phone, it had been so painful to watch my dear friend enter another phase of life without me. But now everything was different, now we were in L.A., my husband and I were high from having our baby, thrilled to be with old friends. We spent the morning, men and women and children—J. had already had another boy—in their back yard, and then when we couldn't stand it any longer, she and I piled the kids up in car seats and took off for a neighborhood park. We wanted to be alone with each other. It was a beautiful fall day, the sky sky-blue, the sun giving off a nurturing white, hot light. We were lying on a blanket in the grass, gossiping, complaining, exclaiming over our own kids and each other's—all three of them the most marvelous, most beautiful, most whiny, smelly, sweet, intelligent children in the world. J. was breast-feeding her youngest, and my daughter was flipping in the grass, when the older boy went running after his ball. Since my hands were free, I got up and went running after him. I got the ball and gave it to the boy, who called out, "Mommy!" "What is it, sweetie?" J. looked up from the baby in her arms to the boy in the playground and smiled. "The ball," he said, holding it up in victory, and then he bounced it back to her.

And it hit me: I could have had a three-year-old.

Sometimes late at night when our baby is asleep—*if* our baby is asleep—my husband and I will recount everything we went through to have her, how it brought us together and tore us apart, how it almost ruined us, how without that long torturous journey, we would not have had this specific, wonderful child. In a bittersweet way it makes the trip feel worth it. But even though I love my daughter more than life itself, I doubt I will ever forget the babies that I carried that were never born, and the power of that grief still catches me by surprise: in the supermarket, when a toddler knocks a stack of cookie boxes to the floor; in J.'s bathroom, when I noticed the locks on the toilet to keep her kid from tumbling in; when her son called to his mother in the playground.

Here is what it means to be a habitual aborter. You have children—not in the world inhabited by other people but in the private world of your heart—you have children you will never get to mother. They are secret children, like those children you read about, confined to an attic or a closet. No one but you recognizes their existence, you yourself don't even know their form, their genders, the shape of their noses, the color of their eyes, and yet the strength of their souls flutters inside your heart like a caged bird's wings. As a mother, it is your job to get them out into the world, but you have failed them hopelessly, and so they haunt you, inhabiting a hyper-reality that, in the middle of the night, feels truer and more real than any reality you have ever known. They are your children, and you are their mother. Yet you do not stop your life for them. Instead, you go on.

# THE BOYS

SOPHIE CABOT BLACK

,

We call them the Boys, and after three days of travel, they have arrived. Inside a four-foot-high cardboard box marked THIS END UP is a metal tank, filled with nitrogen vapor, surrounding an aluminum cylinder that holds a long handle. At the handle's end are three clamps, each gripping a tiny vial with penned-in numbers, frosted over, barely visible. Inside each of these vials a pearl-colored matter rests, perhaps in dreamland, in some unknowable dimension of frozen time. Our little ship of gentlemen has finally arrived, the overland journey done, another about to begin.

D. dons a pair of safety glasses, work gloves, a bandanna over her nose and mouth, and puts down a glass filled with warm water, presumably holding at ninety-eight degrees, on a nearby table. She carefully breaks the safety valve, twists open the tank, and finds the long holder, at each step yelling, "Okay, what does it say next?" She pulls up the handle, cautiously, as if defusing a bomb, and a blue powder falls out onto the rug. We both scream. The powder does nothing: no smoke, no hole eating away into the brown wool shag. She drops the handle back in the canister. We each tell the other to breathe; she reaches in again. We are trying to make a baby.

Originally, I didn't think I was inclined toward children. Especially infants, invariably surrounded by women who huddle around and speak in high voices. Whenever a friend handed me her new baby, I was afraid I might break it. It's not that I didn't like this microperson—in some deep primordial way, I felt connected to the wriggling thing, especially whenever we stared into each other's eyes. What I didn't like was how babies make adults act: glassy-eyed and goofy. Besides, I thought, I'd evolved into a headstrong woman who had no life for children. (It took a few more years to figure out I was just afraid to go to that depth of caring, the possibility of so much to lose.) Also, after many years of psychotherapy, I still wasn't convinced insanity didn't necessarily run in my family. Yet one late summer morning, without warning and not long after the death of my grandfather, my heart brazened itself, and I began a campaign. Reasons for this are still revealing themselves. All I was aware of then was a vague sensation that I had no one to leave all my stuff to when I die.

But there was one problem: how to get my partner of fifteen years on board. And a second obstacle: my partner is a woman. Somehow, we needed to get a man involved.

At first, D. was nervous and unsure about the idea of me bearing the child instead of her. (I would effectively be "going first" and perhaps, as I was six years younger, be the only biological mother of any subsequent children.) So D. began the process of fertility evaluation, and after a few painful months of bad hormone levels and fertility drugs that wouldn't produce viable eggs, she decided to pass the baton. In time, the other side of that loss was her gratitude that through me she still had a chance at motherhood—one of the great benefits of parenting with another woman.

The idea of needing to work at conceiving a child was not what I'd imagined for myself. And the idea of choosing a donor, indeed even using the word *donor*, has been agonizing. I'd gone through life with the assumption that having children would be something that happened *to* me, by some wonderful accident, and not with the textbook quality of choice (similar to going through the Yellow Pages) of what we were about to undertake. But I was also determined not to repeat what had happened to me: my childhood was filled with misunderstanding and betrayal. And though I wanted something different, I was particularly sad my child's genesis couldn't be more romantic, more spontaneous, as in a one-night stand on a Greek island with a man about to be deported, or in a tent on the side of the Himalayas with someone unlucky enough to fall into a crevasse the next day.

So with the ultimate goal being that our child feel good about him or herself, part of a tribe, whole and safe, we went over the possibilities. First we were determined to use someone we knew. I wanted to be able to look into his eyes, to know he had a soul. In our life were two close male friends who became the subject of intense focus; then over dinners and long car rides we'd widen the search to others we'd just met or those we hadn't seen in years. I originally thought I'd ask three of them to "donate" at the same time, so none of us would ever know who the father was. At art openings, late-night gatherings, even at my mother's birthday party, word got around, and various males offered up their services. We found ourselves scrutinizing features, personalities, pedigrees, the way one might if buying a horse.

But after visits to various legal and child psychology offices in search of advice, we ran into questions we'd never anticipated. Each expert pointed out potential problems using donors we knew and who knew us. The lawyer thought it was too dangerous: always the risk a donor could sue for custody. The therapist's argument was quite different: because of both the innate makeup of a child's ego and the current climate of our culture, the child would ultimately feel responsible for the father's absence. And to answer the question of a missing father with the truth was of utmost importance to us, as we had each grown up with the damage secrets do to families. The therapist's case against using a known donor went something like this: if we could truthfully say to the child, "We don't know who the father is," then the child would not be so quick to ask, "Why isn't he living with us? Doesn't he love me? I must not be good enough since he doesn't want to be with me," etc. To be able to explain to the child, "We wanted you so badly, we went to a doctor, and he found a very special man who helped us have you," minimizes the impact of the absence because it removes the idea that the father knows of the child's existence and yet chooses to be absent.

And so we found ourselves descending into the world of cryobanks. Once we'd made the leap into looking at sperm banks, it became a lot like shopping. Asking around, browsing catalogs, comparing prices. Then it became a little too much like shopping; reading through donor profiles, I'd easily forget I'd also be contributing genes. Certain traits and features in my family have a history of winning out over others, no matter how much my relatives have tried to dilute the next generation. Still we combed through the catalogs, insistent on finding Mr. Right, at the same time talking to the bank's "genetic counselors" about compatibility, attractiveness. The process felt manipulative but absolutely appropriate. Unable to produce a zygote from our two eggs (medical science still hasn't caught up with some of our fantasies), we were determined to find a good gene pool. Minimal amount of alcoholism, no major diseases, acne, or eyeglasses— we even looked for writing samples that sounded suspiciously Republican. Here we were picking the father of our child; why not do this with great care? It was an easy leap from there to the idea that some of us might have done better if our spouses were picked with the same degree of scrutiny, or if our parents had been more conscious when they happened upon each other.

After many nights poring over the profiles, we narrowed it down to three. We looked for those who had characteristics of each of our heritages, facial features, even personalities. We also tried to read between the lines of their handwriting and their answers to questions about favorite color, desire for travel, long-term goals, SAT scores. (There was a disconcerting realization that the age of these donors was almost half ours.)

By now I'd also collected a library of anecdotes and information about the actual process of getting pregnant using donor sperm, and our conclusion was that because of our ages, there was a time constraint, and because of that constraint, we needed to be going to fertility doctors, as they had a procedure that worked best with frozen sperm. That's how we got into this ridiculous enterprise in the summer of 1996. Though we had all the intentions of visiting the doctor's office each month, I was destined to ovulate whenever we'd planned on being away. Seriously away, to rather inaccessible places, where telephones, if they even existed, traveled by microwave, and where

Federal Express is always two days later than they guarantee. So off the cryotank came with us: into the mountains, or an obscure hotel room, or an island off another island off the coast of Maine.

Two of our dearest girlfriends are in the next room watching over the shrine we started building last night. The four of us are at a family ranch in the Rocky Mountains of southern Colorado—not far from the site of the vicious battle over gay and lesbian rights—for a week of wrangling and fertility rituals. They have cleared a place above the fireplace that will eventually hold three empty plastic vials, a used ovulation test kit (complete with its blue striped dipstick), four pastel renderings of a fertility goddess, an old pelvic bone found up at one of the summits (painted this afternoon with various signs), and my medicine bag (consisting of: birch bark, on which is written "Beauty, Brilliance, Bravery, Blood and Bewilderment of Being"; a few magic stones; a photo of me at three months; a scrap of paper with my therapist's handwriting; a pillbox with one strand of D.'s hair—dyed red; a dash of my grandfather's ashes; and three hairs from our Jack Russell terrier). Having reread the instructions, D. screws up her courage and warms the water again while I sit cross-legged on the bed, trying to meditate on the liaison that my egg and this newly thawed, displaced sperm will, Gods and Goddesses willing, be having. I recently read that visualizing the union *before* it happens provides an Opening into the Universe, and so I am trying to do just that. All that bumping around in the dark, each locating the other by smell, then the decapitation of one lucky guy in order for the egg and sperm to merge. Then this newly formed blastocyst starts the long tumbling, down toward the light at the end of the tunnel, to a final leap into the Great Abyss of the Uterus. It seemed to be one of the more complicated miracles my body might ever pull off.

Months of plotting out each cycle, recording early morning temperatures, licking small pieces of glass to look at under a microscope, drinking terrible-tasting infusions—all that preparation for this tiny moment, this hoped-for entanglement with a complete stranger's body fluids. I practice doing a shoulder stand in the middle of the bed while D. has once again attempted to retrieve a vial from the canister. This time she gets it and, grinning, holds it up in the air. Between the safety glasses, the gloves (three sizes too big), and the bandanna, now dropped down to her chin, she is quite terrifying. I am beginning to realize there is no way I'm going to be able to put a romantic spin on this.

It is not as easy as we thought it would be, getting the semen into the syringe. We'd asked around, mostly on Internet message boards, on what the procedure is for home inseminations; the answer came back: we needed to buy a needle-less syringe, of which we promptly bought as many sizes as we could. But now none of their tips will fit into the vials, so D. pours out the specimen into a drinking cup. How remarkable it is, from this pale and pungent quarter-teaspoon of liquid, a child can begin.

Meanwhile, I string the medicine bag around my neck, read a poem I'd written for the occasion, then try jumping up and down several times to bring the uterus closer. Finally, with most of our precious cargo intact, I aim at what I think should be my cervix, plunge, and pray. Up into a headstand I go. After ten minutes I lower myself back onto the bed with a pillow under my butt for the rest of the night. And that's it. The two-week waiting-to-see-if-I'm-pregnant game begins.

One of the problems with letting friends in on what you're trying to do is that they turn up ten days later asking: Did it work? And if they were in some way included during the process, it was even worse, as I now had to deal with their disappointments along with my own. After the first couple of tries, I got better at waiting, and at failure. I tried to busy myself so as not to think about what I had just done. It became a lot like applying for a grant from the National Endowment for the Arts; you'd wait and wait and wait, but as soon as you got rejected, you could reapply. The very day it's obvious you aren't pregnant is the same day you begin the next, possibly successful cycle. Already you are making follicles. Already what you eat, what you're exposed to, what your stress level is like, can affect the outcome. Keeping up that kind of vigilance kept me floating above the crash of not being pregnant.

But by now getting a baby into our lives had become a vocation for me, which meant I was now the woman I was so afraid of becoming, a life ruined by a single obsession. What allowed me even to start this project was believing I knew exactly how much I would let myself get involved, how far I would go. This was my control; I might be spared the indignity of the pain, of a certain kind of failure. I had made a pact not to feel too much but of course, in time, got caught in my own trap. I lived in a constant but conflicted state of surrender and spiritual scrutiny. Into my heart crept all the lives I'd missed out on, all the decisions I hadn't made but instead let happen. Here I was making the ultimate Choice, which could be devastating, as there would be no one left to hinge this responsibility on but myself. All roads leading back to me—and the map was looking quite grown-up and terrifying.

There are times I wish we'd never agreed to try this, yet it was too late to turn back to that innocent place of never having left. Back to where we were waiting for our lives to begin, or at least the next part of a life, the part that would make us parents, older, falling into another slot of experience. Yet whenever it got real bad, I'd remember I didn't want to end up seventy-five years old and not be able to say I'd tried.

And so it was for the rest of the summer. We'd call up Federal Express, they'd ship as close as they could to where we were, and then we'd have to deal with getting the boys past general store owners, neighbors, family members. Each cycle became a variation on the same theme: waiting until dark to sneak the tank into (or out of) the trunk of a rental car, burning the wrappers from ovulation test kits, and burying the vials in a pile of trash. The ritual became easier the second and third time around: a search for extra pillows to prop my hips on, setting up the night table with water and a good book so I wouldn't have to move for an hour or so, and doing a final headstand, at times against a green hotel wall or footboard, or in a bathroom listening to old Joni Mitchell albums. The next morning we'd look up the nearest FedEx dropoff, which was usually in a shopping mall or hotel lobby but at times could require quite a drive into no-man's-land. There, one of us would go in, tight-lipped, in dark glasses, struggling through the glass door with our well-taped tank, while the other kept the motor running. It was never a good part of the country to get political.

Finally, at summer's end, we were in a house on an island in Maine, an easy six hundred strides from my grandparents' house. It had taken our (by now familiar) tank only two days to travel the great American diagonal between the southern coast of California and the northern coast of Maine. Yet it was sitting five miles away in a general store on a nearby island, and we were still at least another forty-eight hours from getting my about-to-ovulate hands on it. After a long and difficult series of phone calls, strategy sessions, and pep talks, we decided to take the ferry to the island to get the tank ourselves. This still meant relying on others to get it to the harbor, where we'd arranged to meet the store manager's son, who would bring the package in his official truck, in time for us to get back on the ferry. When we got to the dock and had only a few minutes to catch the last boat back home, we could find nothing that might resemble his truck. In a panic we ran up the hill to the nearest phone, and his mother reassured us he had to be there, as he'd left almost an hour ago. Back onto the ferry we went in despair. About halfway through our ride home, across what now seemed ominous waters, an older man and his wife came up to us, introduced themselves, and said they'd put a package for us in the back of their truck. With a great sigh of relief, we made our way over to their pick-up, only to find that despite a great warning to the contrary printed on the package, the tank had been loaded in on its side and had been that way for at least half an hour. Barely able to speak, we thanked the couple and put it right-side up between us on the bench, unable even to look at each other.

Off the ferry we walked, one of us on each side of the tank, down the long dock past various onlookers and acquaintances. I could feel their curiosity adding to the weight of our package. Our strange parcel stood out between us like a bad child, with all its persistent and mysterious labels and warnings; at least in Colorado the box had looked like it might hold boots or veterinary supplies. Once again I was trying to sneak a four-foot tank containing the essence of six hundred million California boys around a community that had never been outside of a thirty-mile radius of itself. I started thinking about all the different hands our Boys had passed through, and what all those messengers, perhaps oblivious, wondered. Before it became obvious that FedEx would not even get to our island, let alone our house, I had a dark fantasy they might deliver the tank to my grand-

parents' house instead. It was a scenario that made sense: my grandmother was under twenty-four-hour nursing care, and this particular
package was surely something medical and urgent. So what would I
say after the nurses opened it up? Many nights were spent trying to
see a way around letting this happen or, if it did, coming up with a
perfect story of why we were carrying around a cryotank. One candidate to blame it on was our mare, Annie, who came up with us to
the island every summer. Though she was older and it was unclear
whether she could be a mother, I could always say I had decided to
breed her. Annie had become quite independent, unpredictable, and
the advice from the horse world was that one way to calm a mare
was to get her to produce a foal.

Then there are those family members who stop by on their boats
and like to snoop around our house while I'm out exploring the
island. I became ready to tell them I'd taken up urchin diving and
that our tank was actually a scuba tank. At one point my mother,
who was forewarned about the tank's arrival and its true contents, saw
the package in the living room, momentarily forgot what it was, and
opened it up. I then heard her call, "What the hell is this?" She got
a great laugh after being reminded of what it held.

I had been nervous about telling my mother of my newest project.
She was sixty-eight and still had no grandchildren. It was unclear how
she felt about their absence: whether she would welcome them, or
perhaps instead had steeled herself to the idea that her only descen-
dants would be her three offspring. But we always did things a bit
out of the ordinary. Now my mom was going to be under the same
roof when we inseminated. This was quite a full circle: we were now
in the same waters, just twenty miles away from where I was conceived thirty-eight years before. On the deck of my grandparents' boat,
one bay over from the island on a similarly hot August night, my
mother and father had lain in each other's arms and watched the
shooting stars. They too perhaps felt they were taking part in some
sort of revolution, as they made love just a few inches from her sleeping parents.

But now that I was ready to ovulate, it was a grave possibility our
Boys had thawed out too early. After all the terrain, after the planes,
trains, highways, and ferry they had come by, they ended up in a
fatal position: the tank on its dreaded side. Another full day of phone

calls put me in touch with a woman who carefully explained there was only one way to see if they'd survived. The tank needed to be weighed, with a well-calibrated scale. Yet the prospect of lugging our curious cargo down to the fisherman's co-op to use their lobster scales was absolutely terrifying. I then remembered my grandmother had a bathroom scale I might be able to get to, if only all the inhabitants of her house were out. I was not about to walk in with my large package to face relatives and nurses.

The expert on dry ice shipping had explained that if the tank was still good, it would weigh no less than nineteen pounds. Now all I had to do was wait until they had all gone off together on some errand. Finally I heard the car go by, saw the elderly heads propped up against the back seat, and started for their house. After a struggle to find the key, I got in and, bingo, the tank weighed just nineteen pounds. We were in the clear.

Nervous that I might run into them returning, I snuck back to our house through the woods. The melancholy of summer's end was settling in. The tank was heavy in my arms, and I began to feel like it was keeping me from the rest of my life. All I had to show for the last few months was a notebook of tracked fertility cycles and a deep sense of longing: either to be completely in this new world of parenting, or back where I started, innocence intact. Maybe it was all the same thing, and it was just making me feel older, this trying to have a child. The path ran along a cove, and when I turned the corner to head inland, I ran into our mare, who wanders loose around the island. She was rooting among the oak trees when she saw me. Carefully she let me approach, curious about what I was carrying, but when she caught scent of my package, she stomped, snorted, wheeled, and took off. The last I saw of her was her tail flying its way through the swamp. Perhaps she knew, could sense what I carried, and for a moment my heart went with her.

But as I walked back and came upon the landscapes and gardens that my grandmother, mother, and I had all worked on, a sense of belonging came over me. Even though my grandmother was now too far gone to speak, we continued to bring her over in her wheelchair to sit and watch us weed and plant and to fall asleep in the sun. With her perched on the edge of her chair, and D. and my mother bent over pulling out what had wildly crept out over the old stones, I felt a sense of clarity. We were a veritable constellation, a linkage of mothers and daughters. Somehow my approach to having children wasn't too far off from my predecessors': it had taken a few years for my grandmother to screen suitors for a certain husband, while my mother had turned down Mr. Right (another Boston Brahmin) for Mr. Exotic (a great way to liven up our lineage). I felt a sense of eccentric legacy that needed to be carried on, an inheritance of which I needed to take good care. That night, as D. and I went through the elaborate preparations, as we had done many times before, I thought of my grandmother, just a stone's throw away, and my own mother in the room next door and knew in my heart my own child was not far away.

# MISSING CHILDREN

BOB SHACOCHIS

ne morning last April, groaning with self-reproach but not yet contrite, I woke up in an unfamiliar place, somewhere I had never slept before yet nevertheless under my own roof. I had done this maybe a half dozen times in the two decades my wife and I had been together—abandoned her, crying and curled into herself, in the bed we shared and exiled myself to a spare room or downstairs couch, tugging a stubborn blanket of fury over my head like a temporary shroud.

The image of bedtime estrangement—a potent domestic cliché—evokes fault even in the absence of fault, but the tension between us that had erupted the night before into a matched set of absurd accusations had nothing whatsoever to do with infidelity and everything to do with faith: faith that, despite the odds, we could survive as a couple even as we confronted the defeat not of romance but of the garden of our mutual flesh. For during the past eight years, while America cried crocodile tears over the apparent dissolution of its families, my wife and I had knocked our heads against emotional and physiological brick walls trying to manufacture a family of our own. We had tried our very best to heed Babe Ruth's stalwart advice— "Never let the fear of striking out get in your way"—but if baby making were baseball, our team was now playing its final season, and the last game was all but over.

Early on in our life together, my wife had decided to avoid pregnancy, which is not the same as the desire to remain childless, although that's how it had seemed to me at the time, back at the beginning of the 1980s, when I was in my early thirties and first raised the subject of children with the woman I lived with and loved. More than wanting the freedom to anchor herself in a career, she simply didn't wish to be pregnant, she told me, ever; pregnancy was synonymous with trauma, perhaps even self-destruction. And although I was alarmed by her rhetorical absolutism, I was also willing to tell myself that this was not her final word on procreation, that the subject could be deferred without disadvantage and then favorably resolved —that, like all things, it would be held accountable to its own season.

Still, my literary and biological clocks had apparently been set to the same mean time, synchronized to similar imperatives, and it made full sense to me that my first breaks as a writer, when I began faintly scratching the fact of my existence on the palisades of the external world, coincided with the wistful clarification of my desire for offspring—on one of many levels, the impulse to secure readers, to pitch a rock into the generational pool and contemplate the concentric rings that ripple through a self when one's blood-past has made a concerted effort to speak to the future. This was a gift I myself had not inherited (only the dimmest record of my peasant ancestors survived), and for reasons of self-admiration, I envied my future progeny, whom I hoped I might one day engage, through my writing if nothing else, on terms so intimate that the existential distance between parent and child would compress to mere logistics, and never would I be mistaken for a stranger but recognized as a fellow traveler.

Although children arrive on earth adorned with metaphorical ribbons of immortality, a life with a child is, finally, only a life of days actually lived. Shakespeare's third sonnet, which warns "Die single, and thine image dies with thee," is quaint and sentimental, vulnerable to the vicious paradox of time and the technological eternities, illusory and fleeting, that proliferate across the surface of contemporary life. Beyond the increasingly bad moral premise of the biblical command to go forth and multiply, the rationales for having children felt rather metaphysically arbitrary to me, weighted with self-love and often preempted by accident; but there were lines in the sonnet that struck me with the force of crippling hunger, lines that made me imagine one day seeing the face of my wife in the face of my son or daughter—"Thou art thy mother's glass, and she in thee/Calls back the lovely April of her prime." If my words were meant to reproduce myself, my corporeal seed had a loftier, more lovesick goal: to reproduce my wife. And although I understood this was, in its most gentle form, the ideal scenario of love and most represented my preference, it was, I had to concede, only one of many variations on the theme of parenthood.

For if love itself were a destiny, like geography or genetics, once a child washed ashore in your life, was it really so important where that child came from, did it matter how it arrived? The shape of her eyes, the color of his skin? Maybe, I told myself, yet maybe not. Which is to say, however much I wanted a child, I didn't feel bound to any specifics or obligated to motivations that reared inward, back to the barn of DNA. Nor did I believe that having children was what it meant to grow up, or that having children was an innately self-magnifying event for an adult rather than, as is sometimes the case, pathetically self-subverting. We weren't, to our knowledge, fundamentally lonely, needy, or incomplete people, my wife and I; we could discern no gap in our collective psyche that needed to be repaired by a child. Yet if procreation was not the zenith of an individual's existence, it was still an immense and astonishing opportunity. Why ignore a vital clause in the divine contract, not necessarily between men and women but between humanity and life? Why show up at the celebration empty-handed, with nothing to give back to that from which you have taken?

If, for the moment, my wife resisted the appeal of kids underfoot, fine, because as the years passed, our life was whole without them. So when, at her prompting, we stopped using contraceptives, it seemed to me we had tacitly decided to wait and see what happened, and this rearrangement seemed a workable balance between what chance found and determination might deliver. I told myself that, regardless of what either of us intended, someday an alarm clock would ring, wake my wife from her reluctance, rouse me from my dreamy ambivalence, and we would consciously, conclusively, propel ourselves into the future and mate. And it did, in fact, happen . . . the way sadness happens, the way it takes up permanent residence in your life. One heartbreak and then another, and then that's it: something precious has receded, beyond reach, forever.

Sooner or later, I suspected, the focus would sharpen, and so it did on Christmas Eve, 1988, in a cabin in the Uinta Mountains of Utah. My wife and I found ourselves trapped in a blizzard with Tyrone, our aging Irish setter, our surrogate son. He was dying, and as I watched his labored breathing, I hated myself for removing him from the old-dog comforts of Florida to expose him to this terrible blast of cold. Finally my wife insisted we buck up, drink a bottle of wine, try to enjoy the meal I had cooked on this damaged but still sacrosanct occasion, and then afterward the Christmas treat she had been anticipating all day: we'd repair to bed and listen to our friend Ron Carlson on National Public Radio, reading his beguiling short story "The H Street Sledding Record."

But as the moment approached, the radio's reception tore away into tatters of static, and my wife howled. It was Ron himself who had lent us the cabin; there was a copy of his collection, *The News of the World*, there. My wife announced she would read the story herself, out loud. Shivering on a couch across the room, she began. The story is about a young couple in Salt Lake City who each Christmas Eve go sledding with their daughter. It's a law, I think, not of life but of humanity, that you create your own myths, find things to believe in, things smaller than God but larger than a credit card, in order to inhabit a loving universe, and this fictional family's annual attempt at the H Street sledding record—the moment the daughter wedges herself between her mother and father atop the sled and they accelerate into the snowy darkness—becomes the defining rite of their union. My wife kept her composure until the last two paragraphs, when her voice began to waver: "Now the snow spirals around us softly. I put my arms around my family and lift my feet onto the steering bar."

I watched dismayed as my wife locked up in agony on the final lines, the book slipping from her hands. "I want my own daughter," she said, her voice barely audible. She lifted her head, her lower lip trembling, and looked at me. "I want my own daughter," she cried adamantly, as if suddenly understanding that she had been opposed in this desire and it was time to fight back against whatever it was within her fate that had designed this prohibition. "God! God *damnit*, where is my little girl?" I leaped up from the bed to rock her in my arms while she exhausted herself into sleep. She was thirty-five years old. I was thirty-seven. This was the Christmas when my wife and I realized there was indeed a missing person in our life together, and this was the moment we began the enormously difficult quest to track and rescue that person, that child, from the wilderness of our shared imagination.

That Christmas also marked the end of our biological innocence, our sense of ourselves as autonomous beings patterned by the mystery of creation rather than, after technology's sublime seduction, mere organic systems as readily manipulated as the electrical impulses inside a machine. And although this is a story that has counted and recounted its years, its blood cycles, begging an ending that never arrives, becoming a small, private tale of weariness and despair, but equally of tenacity and hope, it is also, and primarily, a travelogue about a journey we took into the kingdom of science and beyond. I couldn't tell you what this other place was called, the world beyond the envelope of empirical remedy, but its cities are named Dream and Myth, Angel and Supplication, and its central crossroads are named Anything You Want and Delusion.


A few weeks after we returned from Utah, we lost Tyrone, our alter ego: the purest, simplest, and most viscerally consistent reflection of our joy in togetherness. Tyrone had been with us since the early days of our relationship. We, a childless couple, were not and had never been two, always three. I didn't expect our lives would ever be the same. For weeks I sat mourning in a chair, stupefied by the awful, intolerable emptiness of the house, and yet I thought I didn't want another dog; maybe now was the time to seize complete freedom, take advantage of our lack of responsibility for another life, however much I savored the clarity and mechanisms of such responsibility. My wife coaxed me back to my senses. It was time, she finally said, to go on.

We got a new pup, very much like obtaining a new chamber for one's heart, and now implicit in my wife's domestic building code was a clause acknowledging that our relationship had been re-zoned for kids. "You're sure?" I was compelled to ask. We had been together thirteen years, and after our first year, when she had told me she never wanted to be pregnant and told me why, I told myself to be patient and never pressed the issue. She is a remarkable woman, beautiful and strong, an intelligent and mature woman who, as a junior in high school in the late 1960s, was out of it enough to get unwittingly pregnant. This happened before *Roe v. Wade*, and her parents, as you might imagine, reacted in a manner that could not have been mistaken as sympathetic. In order to have a legal abortion, she had to be declared mentally unfit by not one but two psychiatrists, and so her folks dragged her off to the shrinks, then dumped her alone at Columbia Hospital for Women in Washington, D.C. My dear girl. No one thought to tell her what was about to happen, that the fetus was too far advanced for traditional intervention and instead would require a saline-solution abortion, actually a method for inducing labor, and its result would not necessarily be immediate. The ob-gyn doctors pumped my wife, who was once this frightened girl, full of salt water, and then housed her away in a room for three days, waiting for her body to evict the child, which it did on the fourth day, her womb evacuating its voluminous contents onto the tile floor. She was sixteen years old and five months' pregnant and alone. I never knew this girl, but I knew and loved the woman she had become, and if what had happened to the girl was something that the woman could not overcome, I understood, however helpless I felt in that understanding.

Now I needed reaffirmation of her own certainty, her willingness to push off from shore into the unknown and its surprising challenges, especially now that she was enrolled in law school, and yeah, she answered, she was sure. For the next two years we did what, conventionally, you do: we threw away the condoms and fucked. Beyond the customary rewards of lovemaking, nothing happened, although there were subtle changes in our conjugal pattern, a density that clustered around significant days of the month. I developed a keener sense of my wife's bodily rhythms, the tempo between ovulation and menses, and now I awoke to the *peep* of her digital thermometer as she tracked the rise and fall in her temperature that would signal the ovaries' release of eggs into the fallopian tubes. Without urgency, we went about our lives, conscious of our agenda but not (yet) neurotically enthralled by the process. We had set up shop, we were open for business, we had a modest goal, one customer was all it would take to measure success in our enterprise, we were frustrated but not alarmed, yet in the back of our minds, increasing in frequency, was an unsettling echo: *Nothing's happening.*


For baby boomers approaching middle age, the narrative of baby making has been ironically reversed, and frolicsome screwing no longer can be relied upon. The goddess Technologia is not now the protector but the enhancer—the madam, the pimp—here in the brothel of reproductive science, with its endless promises of redemption.

We had been living in Florida only a few years; my wife needed a trustworthy gynecologist. Female friends recommended a specialist, the best in town—let's call him Dr. Cautious—and, after an examination, which revealed no obvious cause for her inability to get knocked up, my wife became his patient. I soon fell victim to the diagnostic chronology and became suspect number one, ordered to sample the male version of the small but memorable humiliations commonplace to women in the literal maintenance of their inner lives. What I mean is, I had to provide semen for analysis—ejaculate into a jar, a dubious, shabby pleasure. How absurd the moment: the cold glass cunt, the quick indifferent hand, the presentation to a technician of this pathetic colloid specimen.

Several days later, we received the results. On the face of it, the news was somewhat of a relief. The analysis suggested that I might be the bump in our reproductive road, a condition easily repaired: no hot baths, boxer shorts, and to compensate for my smoking, large doses of vitamins B and C. After two weeks of this regimen, it was clear my semen was adequate, and we were instructed to have sexual intercourse, after which my wife had to throw on her clothes and rush to the gynecologist's office for an appalling postcoital examination meant to determine if her body, reacting to my sperm, was issuing the wrong chemical signals, treating the pearly troops like hostile invaders. But no, nothing was amiss, we were all friends here in the birth canal. Dr. Cautious was cautiously optimistic. My wife and I allowed ourselves a half dozen months of mindless normalcy, bed-wise, before we were forced again to admit the obvious, only this time the obvious echoed with unsuspected depth and darker meaning. As two halves of a projected whole, we were failing to come together, turned back from our greatest ambition as a couple. We were failing to connect, not with eternity but with the present, the here and now, and the danger in that was a sense of self-eradication.

While Dr. Cautious stoically advised patience, my wife, tentatively at first, tried to convince him that what she felt instinctively was true—that she was walking around with a rare disease, nonsymptomatic endometriosis—and although she won this battle, she lost the war. Who would not agree that one level of hell is exclusively reserved for the insurance companies, medicine's border guards, who cast a beastly eye upon all would-be immigrants. Finally Dr. Cautious acquiesced to exploratory surgery, but our health insurance company responded with Las Vegas rules: if surgery identified a problem, they'd pay; if surgery was inconclusive, the $10,000 cost would have to come somehow from our own empty pockets. Lacking hard evidence that anything was wrong, the gamble seemed foolhardy indeed, and it took a full year, another year of futility, to switch our policy to a more magnanimous HMO.

Exploratory laparoscopy confirmed my wife's worst suspicion: the most severe class of endometriosis had gummed up her reproductive tract, and fibroid tumors as well as scarring condemned her to permanent infertility without corrective surgery. Good news, sort of; the procedure had a high success rate, but the preparation for it was a hormonal nightmare: my wife was made to endure two months of chemically induced menopause designed to shrink the marble-size growths and thus facilitate their removal. The operation was, in fine postmodern fashion, videotaped, so that later my wife and I could review it at home, watch in macabre fascination her uterus being scorched by a laser. "Look," came Dr. Cautious's laconic voice-over, "there's your gall bladder."

Five months later, my wife was pronounced fit, and a month after that she waved in front of me a little plastic stick from a home pregnancy test. Pregnant. I cheered, of course, I felt a surge of joy, yet no true sensation of accomplishment, knowing full well we would have to hold our breath as we crossed the immeasurable distance between a blue line on a stick and the deliverance of a child. A month later my wife returned home euphoric after her first sonogram, waving the indecipherable image of our embryonic union—a fingernail-size fish-baby. I couldn't relate to the linear storm of squiggles, which seemed of secondary importance to the sea change in my wife's demeanor. She had never felt better, she claimed, she had never felt this good in all her life. I soon found her on the phone, talking excitedly with her friends, her sisters, her mother, and I told her perhaps she should wait until the end of the first trimester to spread the happy news, but she couldn't contain her jubilation, she wanted to share the hard-won moment with those who loved her, and if the unthinkable happened, then, she thought naively, she would share the pain of that moment too.

The following month, December, I was on assignment in northeastern India, waiting for the sun to rise over southwestern China and burst forth among the peaks of the Himalayan range that dominated the near horizon, a mammoth uplift of the earth's crust culminating in the five summits of the world's third-highest, and most sacred, mountain—Kangchenjunga. As I climbed out of my jeep, something amazing happened. A shooting star blazed down, burning *below* Kangchenjunga's 28,099-foot summit, streaking down perhaps another mile before it extinguished. I was dumbstruck for a moment, and then I blurted out to my companions, "That was about my child." In the days ahead I would recount the story of the shooting star, and my listeners would congratulate me on such a lucky omen. Within a few weeks I would receive their letters at home in Florida, prayers that all was well with the child, that my firstborn would be a son, but by then I knew that the very hour I had seen the star flame across

the face of Kangchenjunga, halfway around the earth, the fetus had
died and my wife was in the midst of a miscarriage.


Twelve months of rueful insularity passed, the condolences of our
friends and relatives met by my wife's self-imposed silence. Faith returned us to the bedroom and failure returned us to another Christmas, another cascade of tears. I was caught by surprise and sat down
next to my suddenly bawling wife on the sofa. "Honey, what's wrong?"
I asked, embracing her. "The baby died a year ago today," she wailed.
I didn't quite understand and stupidly asked, "What baby?" The truth
was, I had never permitted myself to imagine the child that had inhabited her womb for a scant three months, a most ephemeral bond
between us, tissue-thin, and prematurely ruptured. I had stored away
my acceptance until I saw her belly inflate, until the day she placed
my hand on its roundness to feel the first kick. Of course I knew the
fetus had existed, but other than the enigmatic experience on the
mountaintop in India, I had not connected with that existence, and
for me this shadow-child remained shapeless, faceless, and nameless,
forever lost in the cosmic mail, something that had profoundly in-
spired us but had come no closer to our lives than a falling star.

But for my wife it was different: she had acknowledged this baby's
presence in her breasts, her toes, her skin; and when its thimble of
life had spilled—not a miscarriage technically but a death that would
have to be cleaned away in the hospital—she had known that too,
before any doctor's confirmation.

There were cognitive and psychological issues I came to realize
were not mine and never would be, given my gender and its biological limitations. In the ongoing rehearsals for parenthood I was conception's silent partner, a passive investor, spermatologically speaking,
whereas my wife was the line producer, subject to the paralyzing
responsibilities of opening night. Awash in melancholy, I watched the
burden of doubt crease her face. She felt under siege by the possibility
that her continuing infertility would defeat our relationship: Was she
dispensable? Would I awake one morning as merciless as Henry VIII?
Such questions seemed anachronistic and landed like punches on
my heart, yet it was true that it became more and more difficult to
conceal my dissatisfaction with the progress of the campaign. Dr.

Cautious ordered more tests, but to me his stewardship seemed defined by infuriating hesitation. Let's find out where we're going and get there, I lobbied my wife. All problems ought to have solutions.

As the year went by, I was often on the road, one of us parachuting in on the other the days she ovulated. The schedule grew tedious, but there was a certain harried romance to it all. In six months we made love in Florida, London, New York, Missouri, and twice in Washington, D.C. My wife had finished law school and landed herself a demanding job as a staff attorney in the Florida State Senate drafting First Amendment legislation, her area of expertise, but she made no secret of her loneliness, falling asleep twenty-five out of every thirty days sandwiched between our two new dogs but otherwise deserted, and my guilt whispered to me: *give her a child to keep her company.*

Instead of abandoning hope, we amended it, developing contingency plans. We began to speak about adoption matter-of-factly, with an explicit though not fully parsed understanding that we would stay the biological course, run with the trickle of our luck until the trickle ran dry. Adoption was and always had been our safety net, and we in fact considered it a second act, a sequel; once we got rolling, we were going to fill up the house. Whenever I headed overseas, before she kissed me goodbye, my wife would say in a fanciful voice, "Bring me home a baby," and I knew she meant it. First, though, we were going to expend all biological options like a twelve-step recovery program: one day at a time.

That summer I went to Haiti to cover the U.S. military intervention, traveling between the island and Florida for the next eighteen months. Dr. Cautious injected dye into my wife's womb, discovering a blockage of scar tissue in one fallopian tube and clear sailing in the other. I was made to jerk off into more bottles, then more tests, more pale assurances. My wife was beginning to feel like a tawdry lab experiment, and I frankly was getting fed up, not with her but with Dr. Cautious.

One night I returned from Haiti and found my wife in bed, her face swollen from weeping. She didn't often cry, and never for sentimental reasons. It was her habit to put on a brave face, to cloak her tribulations behind false cheer. Once or twice a year her suffering would overflow the cup of its solitude, and this was one of those times.

Someone close to us had died in an accident, another was terminally ill, and her sister, she had just learned, had breast cancer. "I've been lucky," she told me bitterly, the tears streaming down her face. "There's tragedy in every life, but I've been spared. My tragedy is to have no children. I waited too long for everything."

Never had I heard my wife venture so near to self-pity, either before or since. Our struggle wasn't making either of us strong, only resigned, our hearts slowed by sadness. Her words frightened me, and their wretched poignancy galvanized me into action. Our advance to the next level was long overdue, and I insisted on accompanying her to a consultation with Dr. Cautious. Was I pushing this beyond her capacity and desire? No, she said, this is what she wanted too. But no matter how much a couple discusses such things, the right and the wrong of a decision are never easily determined or entirely resolved. At the gynecologist's office, I listened to him murmur the platitudes of his profession—"just keep trying, hope for the best"— and I felt my pulse rise in reaction to the complacency of this well-intentioned but uninvested man. "This is no good, and I want it to stop," I said. I was now forty-three years old, my wife was forty-two, and time was the luxury of other, younger couples. "What do you want to do?" he asked, and we left with a referral to the fertility clinic at the University of Florida.

On the morning of our appointment in the summer of 1995, we drove to the Park Avenue Women's Center in Gainesville, Florida, where we sat in a waiting room filled with madonnas and infants, inhaling the postnatal smells—diapers and talcum and milky vomit —of our imagined destiny. We were fetched to an interview room and introduced to Ginny, a compassionate nurse who would serve as our guardian and guide into the enchanted forest of in vitro fertilization. The questions were common sense, the literature lucid and comprehensive—ovulation induction, egg retrieval, fertilization, embryo transfer, egg donation, and cryopreservation of "surplus embryos."

Ginny explained success rates: IVF—25.3 percent; egg donor IVF —43 percent. A roll of the dice, we were told, but also a "realistic option for many infertile couples who might otherwise never become pregnant." A doctor came in to scan our medical histories, cluck over our age, and close the deal. "I recommend we proceed aggressively," he said, and despite my wife's apprehension, I seconded the motion. Ginny returned to discuss the finances: in the next eight months, in $5,000 increments, we would empty our savings account, take out a bank loan, and borrow against my future earnings.

After we were both tested for AIDS, my wife underwent a pelvic exam. I was directed to the bathroom, given old copies of *Playboy*— erotic white noise—and told to masturbate. This fatuous, unwanted pleasure was my one sacrifice on the altar of fertility, a free ride compared with where my wife now stood poised, a seasoned veteran of repeated bodily invasions, on the feudal threshold of new tortures. We reunited in an examination room, where Ginny began uncapping syringes and lining up innocuous vials of saline solution. Once we started down this path, I would be called upon to give my wife a monthlong sequence of daily injections in the ass, with a needle the length of my middle finger, and now Ginny was going to teach me how to do it. She demonstrated how to mix the hormones, fill the syringe, tap it free of air bubbles, jab it to the hilt into an orange. There was a pamphlet Ginny showed me, with a line drawing of a woman's backside, identifying the half-dollar-size area on each buttock that could safely receive the needle without injuring the sciatic nerve.

"Okay," said Ginny, "let's have your wife lie down and pull up her skirt." I felt a flush of vertigo. "You're kidding," I protested, but of course she wasn't: this was my only opportunity to get it right with the proper supervision, and as I leaned over my wife's butt with the gleaming needle, I told Ginny I didn't want to do this. "Just plunge it straight in like a dart," Ginny coaxed, and so I did, horrified as I watched my wife grimace, her hands contract, and her knuckles whiten, and as soon as I removed the needle from her flesh, I lay down atop her, aggrieved, kissing her cheek and apologizing. Teamwork, I thought, had never been so ruthless. Ginny had been a paragon of empathy, though, and I thanked her. "You have the perfect job," I said ignorantly, "bringing so much joy into people's lives." She brightened for a moment, but then her eyes turned doleful, her mouth grim. "Yes," she said, "but when it doesn't work, it can be devastating."

We soon would be well educated in the exact nature and magnitude of that devastation. Mid-August I was back in Haiti, and my wife began self-injecting Lupron, a drug that produced hot flashes and insomnia, into her abdominal wall to suppress and then synchronize egg development in her ovaries. A few weeks later I was home in time to begin turning her backside into a pincushion, shooting doses of Pergonal and Metrodin, to begin stimulating egg development, into her buttocks morning and night. Neither of us was brave about the hateful needles, and the tension between us rose; under the stress of hurting her, I'd yell, she'd weep, and for a month the process itself made us adversaries. We both lived in dread of the injections. Frequent blood tests, which turned her arms black-and-blue, and ultrasound exams, in which she was painfully prodded by a wand inserted into her cervix, multiplied the hellishness of her torment.

Finally, when her ovarian follicles had achieved the optimal size, I shot her up with a hormone to trigger ovulation, and we drove to Shands Hospital in Gainesville to be "harvested." For the second time in our lives, I impregnated my wife, although this time fertilization occurred in a petri dish, at the hands of Jack the white-coated embryologist, who, like a reincarnation of a nineteenth-century Fabergé artisan, further manipulated the cluster of cells in a new technique called "assisted hatching" and painstakingly abraded the shell of each embryo with an acid solution in order that it better adhere to the uterine lining. Two days later four embryos were placed inside a Teflon catheter and transferred into my wife's womb. We drove home. By the time she dragged herself to the clinic for a pregnancy test, the results were moot, because two days earlier, in a gush of tears and blood, whatever children would ever unite our separate DNA structures, marry the essence of our flesh, and blend our natures into the next generation of us had vanished back into the unknowable starry night of nothingness. We were permitted two more attempts by the wizards of reproduction, both aborted early in the game when it was clear that my wife's body would not respond to the drugs.

It seems it's always meant to be December, and I am always meant to be away, when the news that fractures the foundation of our lives arrives. I called her from Haiti and listened quietly to her ragged, fatigue-ridden voice. Ginny had phoned that afternoon: my wife's ovarian reserve was depleted, her infertility was irreversible, she was biologically incapable of procreation and permanently exiled from the purest form of motherhood, though not from motherhood itself.

I came back home to watch my wife, shattered and bereft, decorate the Christmas tree, to rise early in the morning, day after day, to bake cookies for the holidays—*to bake and bake and bake and bake*. What was she going to say, what words would she use to describe her anguish, to tell me what was going on in her mind, to explain what happens to the heart when a woman's reproductive time runs the course of its season? And what more could I do than promise her, with a lover's force of conviction, that another Christmas would not pass without a child in the house?

Time in season, mine; time out of season, hers. How do you reconcile this severance, the split that occurs in a couple's imagination when what ends for the female continues on for the male? For a man, history's answer, unlike technology's, had been brutally simple: choose between the barren woman and your unborn children. But science had rolled the dilemma between its magician's fingers and come up with another option.

The April argument that sent me trudging to the guest room dispersed much, if not all, of the pressure that had built between us as we ventured further on the thin ice of possibility, loaded down with the weight of our decision to proceed with our fourth in vitro fertilization attempt. I had been afraid that my wife was balking at this, her final commitment in her role as immaculate guinea pig, afraid I had somehow coopted her into agreeing to try something she didn't want to do—accept the oocyte of another woman into her womb. It was the most delicate of issues, and I thought I had given my wife plenty of room to arrive at her own decision. Six months earlier she had said she would consider egg donorship only when it was clear that all other options had been foreclosed. If she said no, that would be okay; we would redirect our dwindling money, time, and energy toward adoption. What she said she expressed rather bluntly—"At least we'll know half of what we get, right?"—and whatever her doubts, she still wanted to seize this last chance to carry a child. But this would be it; for my wife the process had escalated toward the time when she would hand herself back to nature and be at peace, beyond reproach, beyond the secular optimism of machines and the artifice of miracles.

It was stress, not the strategy itself, that caused our freefall into that April night's hostility—a silly detail, the timing of a phone call to Ginny—but by the next day the conflict was forgotten, and the following month the last xeroxed calendar—OVULATION INDUCTION/ ASSISTED HATCHING—taped to the refrigerator came down, a calendar similar to its three predecessors, each an anxious countdown through the spectrum of faith and the torment of science to the imagined felicities of maternity, and each climaxing with the death of hope. It was hope, more than anything else, that my wife most feared these days.

The next morning we were in Gainesville, in an operating room at the university's hospital. High-intensity lights, state-of-the-art computer-age electronics. Everyone was in green surgical scrubs except for my wife, who was draped in a flimsy institutional gown, prone on the table. Her feet were placed flat, and her legs were bent at the knees, a drape spread from one kneecap to the other, making an open-ended tent between her thighs. Her expression was upbeat, but in the far, courageous recesses of her eyes, under the surface of her resilient smile, I could see the look of someone persecuted over and over again with no possibility of escape.

The three faces of the stork—the doctor, Ginny the nurse coordinator, the embryologist—hovered over the table, gaily inspecting what my wife held in her hand: objects, icons, fertility fetishes—things she kept in a yogurt container. Her desperate cocktail of beliefs. There was a walnut-size clay sculpture of a Paleolithic Venus—the prototypical earth mother—sent by her ill sister in San Francisco. In a doll-size leather pouch, a saint's medal, perhaps the Virgin Mary with child, carried throughout World War II by the father of a friend who herself had two IVF daughters. In a spice bottle, several grams of holy dirt, said to produce miracles of healing, that my wife had scooped up from the floor of the mission chapel in Chimayo, New Mexico. On a chain around her neck she wore an evil eye I brought her from Turkey, her schoolgirl confirmation cross, a prelapsarian mosquito embedded in amber, and a small ring of happiness jade, a gift from a friend in China. Here on the frontier of neoprimitivism and the techno-voodoo of the new millennium, I couldn't resist a wisecrack. "Hey, she's even got a chicken's head from last night's sacrifice," I joked.

"You don't notice them pooh-poohing any of it," protested my wife.

"Why not?" said the embryologist. "You don't really think we have all the answers, do you? Who knows how all of this really happens?"

Collectively, we were all trying to ignore how bizarre this was—so weird it made me spin, the moments when I contemplated what we were doing. In my own hand I held a questionnaire filled out by the anonymous twenty-three-year-old woman with whom, two days previously, I had had test-tube sex. There was a cover page, a profile of the donor—short, "attractive," in Ginny's eyes, of German descent, a college graduate, a family history of heart problems—and on it, a statement of motivation that both intrigued and baffled me: "She wants to do something nice." Something *nice*? The language of altruism struck me as girlish and archaic. The night before I had dreamed about this young woman I will never meet; we sat in a room together and talked, although I couldn't remember what we said. At breakfast before coming to the hospital, I told my wife about the dream. "What did she look like, what color was her hair?" she asked (Ginny had told us the donor's hair was dark blonde). "Not really dark blonde," I said to my wife. "It had red undertones." Now, as I flipped through the questionnaire, my wife placed her finger on the page, pointing to a box stating the woman's hair color: strawberry blonde.

This is the part my wife prefers that I not write about—not the quirky, clutching mysticism but the enormously complicated choice of egg donorship, which neither of us had ever suspected would elicit such a callous response from our closest friends. *Why would you want to do that?!* they challenged my wife on the telephone. Almost invariably these were women with their own children, women whose souls had never been lacerated by the psychic catastrophe of infertility, women who would never know the toll of our quest to have what for them was so easily given, women who would never blink at the mention of a sperm bank. Their swift, unthinking judgment brought out the devil in me: in my fantasies I took away their children, then proposed a deal—they could have them back, altered yet recognizable; their children would more or less look and act as they always had, yet they would no longer possess their maternal genes. It would be as though I had given them the opportunity to bear their own stepchildren in their wombs. That, or never see them again. What do you suppose they would choose?

The doctor pushed a button; above my wife's head, a television monitor descended from the ceiling, and there, on the screen, in translucent cabbage-green monochromatic simplicity, were the magnified kids, in truth no larger than the molecules of ink in the very tip of my pen, poised to write the word *gestation*, the word *family*. Three perfect human embryos in colloidal suspension: one five-cell cluster and two four-cell motes that, within the next few minutes, would be implanted into my wife. I studied the images with a mixture of awe and alienation. These were fairies, I suppose, angels dancing on the head of the embryologist's pin. More idea than substance, spirits videotaped on the cusp of potentiality, not quite of this world, clinging to the slightest speck of flesh in transition from nonexistence to being.

On the OR boom box, Jimmy Durante was singing "Make Someone Happy." The doctor had his head between my wife's legs. The embryologist approached with a stainless-steel cylinder in his hands, something that resembled a cake-frosting applicator. The doctor fed the tube's catheter past my wife's cervix, the embryologist unscrewed a cap at the top of the cylinder, and gravity nudged the embryos home. "We don't want to see you coming back out of there," Jack told the fairies, "for nine more months."


A Saturday afternoon, ten days later, the beginning of Memorial Day weekend, May 25. We were nervous wrecks, my wife and I. She had spent the morning sweeping the patio, then making mango sorbet and baking almond cookies for a dinner party we would host that night. A few moments earlier I had asked her how she was feeling, and she said, "Weird," but there was no way to gauge the significance of this, and she went upstairs to lie down. In two more days— Monday—she would go to the hospital for a pregnancy test, if she could hold out that long. In the newspaper that morning I had read that on this day, sixty-one years ago, the great Babe Ruth hit the final home run of his career. That's something, I told myself, feeling a pang of encouragement.

Writers are perpetually giving birth to the vastly extended family of their characters. Sometimes, at night in the bathtub, I say their names, testing their appeal, the weight and music of the life-creating sounds: Kyra, Catherine, Jerusha, Jack, Sam—Sammy? Who are these people? I wonder to myself, trying to visualize their every detail. Sometimes they fall out of the cradle of my mind into a quasi-immortal existence on the page. The other night, though, I said their names and knew differently. Kyra, Catherine, Jerusha, Jack, Sam—Sammy? These are the children who will not come to me, to us, our ever wayward children.

Because it was a holiday, not business as usual at the chain of clinics and hospitals she depended on, my wife had meticulously prearranged the logistics of that Monday, Memorial Day, to avoid a breakdown in the lines of communication. After my wife's morning blood test, the clinic in our hometown would call in the results to the answering machine at the Park Avenue Women's Center in Gainesville; the on-call (but off-site) nurse who was substituting for Ginny would telephone the machine, listen to the recording, and then contact us with the news before noon. That's not how it went, however, because instead of phoning Gainesville as we had planned, the clinic that performed the blood test sent a fax to an empty office, and by noon, when we hadn't heard anything, my wife called the clinic, where the technician confirmed that the results had been "sent" to the women's center hours ago but refused to tell her anything else. She screamed in frustration and fear.

"Go run some errands," I said, shoving her out the door. "And by the time you get back, they'll have called."

But no one called, and when she returned, I watched my wife flip out, flinging the packages she carried into a window, knocking things off countertops, hitting back at me as I tried to subdue her, refusing any attempt at consolation, until finally her uncontainable hysteria imploded and she stumbled vacantly up the stairs to bed. I spent the remainder of that afternoon on the phone; finally I connected with an on-duty IVF doctor at Shands Hospital, and after he had phoned me back with the results of my wife's blood test, I opened a bottle of wine, took a glass from the cupboard, climbed the stairs, and have never felt so dead as when I stood by our bedside and watched my wife face me and saw, *still*, the quick, upturned hope that was there, shining through the pain, as she turned to hear what I would say.

Sometimes I have to hold my wife harder than I ever dreamed or wanted, and repeat—as I have throughout the worst moments of the years behind us—a faith-borne cruelty, telling her yet again that this story has a happy ending.

# IN VITRO

AGNES ROSSI

,

W hen I first began to suspect that there might be a problem, I went straight to the library. There were eight or nine books on infertility. My palms were sweating as I opened one and flipped through the first chapter, which explained the principles of human reproduction. How familiar and reassuring the diagrams were, the penis and testicles in profile, the vagina, uterus, fallopian tubes, and ovaries head on. The text and the pictures made getting pregnant seem simple, just a matter of sperm meeting egg. So why wasn't it happening for me?

Chapters two and three were full of suggestions, simple things I could do to increase my chances of becoming pregnant. Reading about boxer shorts, basal body temperatures, fertile mucus, ovulation predictor kits, and optimum times for intercourse, I felt hopeful. This was the kind of information I was after, do-it-yourself-in-the-privacy-of-your-own-home tips. I'd buy a thermometer and an ovulation predictor kit immediately. I'd tell my husband to put away his jockey underwear because it might be killing his sperm. I'd learn to recognize fertile mucus when I saw it. I could hardly wait to get started.

My gung-ho attitude faltered when I got to chapter four, "Assisted Reproductive Technologies." It won't come to this, I thought, leaning back in my chair, wanting to put some distance between myself and the straightforward and terrifying description of in vitro fertilization, a procedure by which eggs are surgically removed from a woman's ovaries and placed in a petri dish with her husband's sperm. If fertilization occurs, the resulting embryos are then injected into the woman's uterus in the hope that a pregnancy will result. It all seemed too high tech, too dependent on strangers with advanced degrees, and much too desperate.

I bought one ovulation predictor kit after another, kept incredibly detailed records of my menstrual cycle (FM for fertile mucus), and lay with a pillow under my rear end after sex so that gravity might help the sperm find their way. A couple of times I even stood on my head.

Six months went by. A year. Nothing.

I made my first appointment with a fertility specialist, believing that I'd avail myself of what medical science had to offer up to but not including in vitro. Babies were supposed to be the result of love-making. The substitution of aluminum probes and fluorescent lighting and lab attendants chatting about their weekends for copulation, flesh into flesh, grunting and groaning, had to be bad, had to cast a shadow, set a tone. I wanted my baby to begin life in the dark and bloody interior of my body, not in a cold and sterile Pyrex dish. I cultivated various images to explain my distaste to myself. Conceiving a baby in a laboratory would be like being married via satellite or speaking your dying words into a cell phone. In vitro was clearly the intrusion of technology into a realm where it plainly didn't belong.

The fertility doctor examined me, drew blood, sent Dan for a sperm test. "Everything checks out so far," she said at our second appointment. She suspected that my fallopian tubes were blocked, so she sent me for a hysterosalpingogram. Dye was injected into my uterus and should have come out in the vicinity of my ovaries. It didn't. Scar tissue, the result of an infection I may not have even noticed or a long-ago IUD or God knew what, was keeping sperm and egg apart. My doctor proposed a laparoscopy. She'd make three small incisions below my belly button and try to open my tubes with

a laser. "There are no guarantees," she said. "It works for some people. What I'd like to do is put you on the waiting list for our in vitro
fertilization program. It'll take you at least a year to get in, and by
then, with any luck, you'll have gotten pregnant naturally."

The laparoscopy was exactly the sort of treatment I'd hoped to get,
Band-Aid surgery, no big deal. The doctor would fix my plumbing,
and I'd take it from there. I went along with being put on the waiting
list for in vitro, believing, really believing, that I wouldn't need it
when the time came. A year is a long time, I thought. Twelve cycles.
Twelve chances to get pregnant the right way.

Resorting to in vitro seemed an admission of failure. I didn't want
to believe that I was handicapped to the extent that I needed drugs,
doctors, an operating room, and a laboratory to do what I should have
been able to do simply by having sex with Dan in our bed.

Our language needs a word for the feminine equivalent of ma-
chismo. *Feminisa*, or something. Just as the ultimate symbol of ma-
chismo is the erect penis, the essence of feminisa is the ability to
create a living, breathing human being in the space between one's
hipbones. I wanted to be able to do that, wanted to add getting pregnant naturally to my list of accomplishments in life.

Coming to in the recovery room after the laparoscopy, I was freezing
cold. A nurse's aide said, "I see that you are shivering. I will get you
a blanket." It seemed the kindest thing anybody had ever said to me.
He took a cotton blanket out of a warmer and covered me. After a
while he helped me into a wheelchair and took me to a room where
outpatients were monitored until they got the okay to go home.

I felt optimistic sitting there. The laparoscopy was done, and now
I'd be able to get pregnant. I drank the juice and ate the crackers a
nurse gave me as if doing so would increase my chances. I was being
a good patient, snapping back, taking the laparoscopy in stride. Then
my doctor came into the room and knelt down beside me. The scarring was bad, she said, much worse than she'd thought it was going
to be. She'd managed to open both tubes, but the chances of their
staying open long enough for me to get pregnant were slim. "I've
already explained this to your husband, so you don't have to," she
said softly.

I remember looking out the window of the cab on the way home and thinking, It didn't work, it didn't work, it didn't work. My husband read an early draft of this essay and was surprised to learn that the doctor had been so frank with me. He says I acted that night as if I thought the laparoscopy had gone pretty well. It's something like hearing how you've behaved when you've had too much to drink. I was definitely in an altered state just after the laparoscopy. I was running scared. I couldn't even begin to acknowledge the intensity of my disappointment. Lurking within it, lying in wait, was the possibility that I might never get pregnant and have a baby. Never ever.

Over the coming weeks, a little at a time, I let the disappointment come. Rather, I lost the battle to keep it at bay. The pain was at once piercing and diffuse. It involved every part of me. "What's so hard about it?" a friend asked. She wasn't being dismissive, she genuinely wanted to know, so I tried to explain. I talked about feeling defective, about the sadness I felt knowing I might live and die without ever feeling my baby's skin against my own, about finding out that something—someone—you'd always assumed would be a big part of your life and the best part, wasn't going to be at all. I heard myself going on and on and knew that I wasn't even beginning to get at the truth of my experience. I could not articulate all of what I was feeling. I might have done a better job—no clearer, maybe, but truer—if my friend had asked, "Where does it hurt?" In the back of my throat, I'd have said, right behind my eyes, between my legs, in the joints of my fingers, in my memory and my imagination and my dreams.

The sorrow I felt when I confronted the possibility of never having a baby forced me to acknowledge how desperately I wanted one. There's great vulnerability in desperation. How much safer you are if there isn't anything you want too badly. And how much cooler. Cool is, I suppose, the absence of desperation, of urgent desire, of neediness. I had wanted to believe that I was somehow different from all the women who were undergoing one high-tech procedure after another in pursuit of pregnancy. I'd hoped that I was more highly evolved, less sentimental, less traditional. I wasn't. I wanted a baby as badly as anybody did. When I finally understood this about myself, I was deeply grateful that while I'd been figuring it out, my name had been slowly making its way to the top of the waiting list at Cornell.

In August we got the call. The wait was over. At the first appointment, Dan and I sat in a small room with four other couples while a pretty nurse told us what to expect. In front of us a couple in their early forties, tall, raincoated, accomplished-looking, held hands. To our left sat an Arab woman, her husband, and either her mother or her mother-in-law. "I will give the shots," the husband said proudly. Then the pretty nurse showed us the long needle. "We can arrange a nurse to come to our home?" asked the husband.

I went to the pharmacy and bought the drugs and the needles, a medium-size paper bag full. I put it on the kitchen counter and waited to get the word from Cornell to start the injections. The weather turned hot, high nineties every day. I called the pharmacist, and he said to put the drugs in the refrigerator. I felt virtuous for having thought to call.

Two days later there was a message on our answering machine. Start tonight. So many cc's of Metrodin, so many of Pergonal. Come in tomorrow morning for your first ultrasound. Dan gave me the shot. He wanted to be gentle, but that made him slow. Over the coming weeks he would perfect a quick jab.

Six o'clock the following morning, we left our apartment in Brooklyn to make it to Cornell by seven. I'm an early riser, so I didn't mind being up. In fact, it was exciting in the way of big days, like when you're leaving for the airport on your way to Europe. The number-two train was about half full. Most of the other passengers looked like shift workers, going in or returning home. A woman in a white uniform nodded off beside me. This is an ordinary Tuesday morning for you, I thought. You're on your way to work. I'm on my way to get pregnant.

It was eerie going into a public place, a medical building, so early. There was nobody at the desk in the lobby, which made us wonder if we were really supposed to be there at seven. When we stepped off the elevator on the third floor, though, we found ourselves looking into a crowded waiting room, three or four receptionists behind a long desk, a woman with a clipboard calling names. It was a world unto itself, the world of in vitro, and it was up and running.

Dan put my name on the list at the desk, and then we found seats together on one of the many couches. Waiting for my name to be called, I began to do something I would do, off and on, for the duration. I looked at the other women and tried to figure how their chances of getting pregnant compared with mine. Age is an important factor. The younger you are, the more likely it is that your in vitro will be successful. I felt jealous of the women who were obviously younger than I was and smug toward those who looked older. I knew that I shouldn't be doing what I was doing—after all, here were women who'd gone through their own versions of what I had, nobody gets to that waiting room without her share of heartache—but I couldn't help it. Sitting in a room full of people who all dearly want the same thing you do evokes a particular sort of anxiety, the kind that comes when you know there's not enough of whatever it is you all want so badly to go around. Cornell has a success rate of about 40 percent. I counted out ten women, including myself. Four of us will get pregnant, I thought. Which four?

A name very much like mine was called, same initials and a two-syllable Italian last name, the very one, in fact, that I'd given to the narrator of a novella I'd written a few years before. The woman stood, and I saw that she looked like me, short, solid, brown hair and eyes. I felt an immediate kinship with her. When my name was called a few seconds later, she turned and smiled at me, one Italian girl to another.

My blood was drawn, and I was taken to a small room for a vaginal ultrasound, a procedure that's a lot like sex, like intercourse anyway. A handsome young doctor tore open a familiar plastic packet and unrolled a Trojan rubber over a penis-shaped probe. The lights were dimmed. The doctor squeezed some lubricant from a tube, inserted the probe into my vagina, and wiggled it around. "Looks good," he said. "Looks really good. See you in three days, okay?"

While I put my clothes back on, I thought that I'd just come as close as I probably ever would to dating a doctor.

Dan and I went back every couple of days and then every day as we got closer to the retrieval, the procedure by which the eggs I produced would be "harvested" so they could be mixed with Dan's sperm. I continued to see the woman with the name like mine. We didn't talk beyond saying good morning, but we smiled a lot, and warmly, each comforted, I thought, by the other's presence.

Finally, after a dozen ultrasounds and several dozen shots in the ass, it was time to retrieve my eggs. Dan and I stood in a hallway with five other couples, my Italian friend and her husband among them. While I was in the operating room under general anesthesia, Dan had to go into a room stocked with dirty magazines and videos and masturbate. Both procedures went off without a hitch. In the recovery room, the handsome young doctor who'd done my first ultrasound smiled and said he'd retrieved sixteen eggs. "Sixteen really good-looking eggs." I was relieved and proud. I'd done well, or my ovaries had anyway. Still groggy, I became aware of a commotion at the other end of the room. The woman whose name was like mine was crying loudly while a nurse stood by her bed saying, "All right, all right now." Something had gone wrong with my friend's retrieval. With her sobs ringing in my ears, I began to doubt the memory of the doctor telling me he'd retrieved sixteen eggs. Had I dreamed that, or had it really happened? The harder I tried to remember the sound of the doctor's voice and the exact words he'd used, the cloudier the memory got. I sat up, looked around, and saw him, the young doctor, half a room away. I waved him over and asked if he really had told me he'd retrieved sixteen eggs. He didn't seem at all surprised by my question. "Everything went beautifully," he said. "You should try to relax."

I was taken to a private room on the maternity floor, an old room. Waiting for Dan to turn up, I thought of the thousands of new mothers who must have occupied that room over the years. Were they happy, I wondered, or were they exhausted and sore and hormonal? Dan came in smiling, having just talked to the doctor. We kissed, rested forehead to forehead a moment, and then he told me that he'd run into my friend's husband on the elevator. None of her eggs had survived harvesting. They'd broken apart, gone to pieces. I remembered the sound of her sobbing and wanted to feel badly for her— Dan clearly did—but what I felt at that moment was a kind of retrospective dread. I didn't know that eggs sometimes shatter. God, what if mine had?

Dan took me home, and we waited to find out how many of his sperm had found their way to my sixteen good eggs. Eleven, it turned out. We had eleven tiny embryos in a petri dish in a laboratory on First Avenue. My sister came over, and we all went out to dinner to celebrate. In the elevator of the subway station in Brooklyn Heights, I told her how happy it made me just to think of my embryos, their cells busily dividing. She smiled her widest smile, glad, I could tell, that I finally had some good news in the baby department.

Two days later Dan and I went back to the hospital to have four of the embryos put into my uterus. I was lying in the operating room, fully conscious, with my hips elevated, when a technician came in carrying a large syringe. "Four beautiful embryos for Ms. Rossi," she said, and I started to cry because I was finally in the same room with the possibility of a baby. I was closer than I'd ever been before. He or she was right there in that clear liquid. Before I was wheeled out, the technician gave me a Polaroid of the four embryos, greatly magnified. Three of them looked especially healthy, the borders of their cells vivid, the cells themselves as round and regular as they could be.

I bought a needlepoint the following day, hoping that having something to do with my hands would make the wait to find out if I was pregnant easier. It didn't. The two weeks were torturous. Every twinge was a menstrual cramp. Every wave of irritability, and there were dozens, PMS. I was incapable of waiting for the doctor-administered pregnancy test, bought an EPT, and did it first thing Saturday morning. I couldn't bear to put the plastic wand down and walk away from it because if I did, I'd have to pick it back up when the time came and get the news all at once. If I wasn't pregnant, I wanted to find out slowly, one second at a time. I sat on the couch with the test wand in my hand and groused to Dan. I'm sure it's going to be negative. I know I'm about to get my period. Fuck. And then a faint blue line appeared. "Do you see it?" I said. "It's there, isn't it? You see it too, don't you?"

I was pregnant. With the help of half a dozen doctors, bless them, and their computers, cameras, operating rooms, and laboratories, I was finally pregnant.

Very pregnant, it turned out.

Alina, Grace, and Mary Rossi-Conaway were born strong and healthy eight months later. Triplets. I spend much of my time now on the floor, literally, down on the carpet tending our three baby girls. They were about eight months old, I think, the day my head cleared for several long seconds and I knew, I really understood, that I had what I wanted so badly. I had babies. I wrapped my fingers around Gracie's good sturdy calf and squeezed so I could feel the reality of her, the bone and the baby fat.

Given the reluctance I had felt to attempt in vitro fertilization, does the fact that my daughters were conceived as a result of it have any effect on my feelings for them? No. It's as simple as that. The reservations I had about in vitro were abstractions, arguments I formulated in response to another set of abstractions, notions I had about the way a woman should go about becoming a mother. What *being* a mother has taught me is how paltry abstractions are, how utterly beside the point, compared with the heft and meatiness of the concrete. My passionate attachment to my girls is the result of my taking care of them, feeding and soothing and spending some very long days and nights with them. The particulars of their conception are merely a medical fact, no more resonant to me than, say, their blood types. I do sometimes wonder what Mary, Grace, and Alina will make of their beginnings when they're old enough to understand them. Will it matter to them that they spent a couple of nights swimming around in a petri dish? Will they, perhaps, attribute some portion of whatever degree of alienation they feel from their father and me when they're fifteen to the manner in which they were conceived? If they do, they'll be wrong. But they won't know that until and unless they have babies of their own, naturally, artificially, any way at all.

# A SMALL MEMORIAL

## PETER CAREY

,

*To the Children the Author Tried to Forget*

L ately when I think of my children, I have begun to remember not just the four-year-old who is rattling on my doorknob as I write, or the eight-year-old whom I will take to a swimming lesson this afternoon, but those other children I have spent a long time trying to forget.

These are children from my first marriage, children now a long time dead.

In 1961, when I was eighteen years old, I sat in the waiting room of an illegal abortionist in Melbourne, Australia. Beside me sat an attractive, easygoing woman who would later be my wife but was at that moment my first girlfriend. Let us call her H.

There were many others waiting with us, but H. and I felt alone and frightened. We knew we were at an abortionist's, but it never occurred to us that all those other men and women (standing by the door, reading the *Sporting Globe*, the *Woman's Weekly*) were also conspiring to terminate pregnancies. They looked married, respectable, not illegal at all. One woman, who had swollen legs and varicose veins, sat with a paper bag on her lap, knitting a green sweater. It was hard to associate any of these people with sex or the back seat of a car at the Star Drive-in Theatre—with any of the things that had brought us to this point where one of us might be injured, the pair of us arrested.

Years later, when we were both in our early fifties and were married to other people, H. and I met for breakfast at the Melbourne Hilton, and she brought, as I had asked her to, photographs from our early days together. And it is because of these photographs, spread out before me now as I write, that it is so easy for me to recall H.'s open, fresh face, her handsome bones, her tanned skin, her curly, short hair. She wore a shirtdress that we incorrectly called a "muumuu"—a light, striped summer dress that is somehow mixed up in my mind with the events that got us "in trouble." I wore a yellow terry-cloth shirt and black-and-white checked cotton trousers.

A year before, I had been at a boys' boarding school. Now I was free, smoking cigarettes, having sex. I was an enthusiast, a compulsive talker, a would-be cartoonist. I had an Ornette Coleman record called *Change of the Century*, which I played for H. when I first met her— the track called "Una Muy Bonita." We may not have kissed that time, but still I'd like to think so, with Ornette Coleman playing in Melbourne, Australia, in 1961.

In Melbourne in 1961, the bars closed at six o'clock at night. The White Australia Policy was still in force. You could be arrested for having an abortion or reading James Joyce's *Ulysses*.

H.'s brother had an M.G. TD and a heavy Ronson cigarette lighter that bore a family resemblance to a Cadillac. He and his friends lay around the living room in the industrial suburb of Dandenong, light-ing their farts with their Ronsons. They lay on their backs and drew their knees up to their chests. They stretched the fabric of their trou-sers tight across their butts. The farts burned with a sudden blue flame. H.'s brother had a pair of cook's Daks; I can see them now with the blue flame shooting out of them. I thought lighting the farts was infantile, but I knew the trousers were very cool. I bought a pair myself within a month of meeting him. (Thirty-four years later, you can still see kitchen workers in New York City sitting on the pavement smoking, wearing trousers exactly like the ones I wore all through that spring, when I was busy falling in love, trying to be a poet, faking my experimental results for the force of gravity, busily on my way to flunking out of a science degree.) And I was still wearing them four months later, when I set out to procure an abortion, dropping the coins into the pay phone to call a doctor (whose name and address I must now alter). It was eight o'clock at night, and concrete trucks were rumbling past. I was about to ask this doctor to break the law, and I was both amazed at myself and terrified.

"Freddie," I said when the doctor answered. "It's Peter Carey." He knew who I was, of course. He was a doctor in the beachside town where our family vacationed. His father had been my father's friend. He was Dr. Colman, they both were, the father and the son, but they had been known more usually as Dr. Freddie and Young Dr. Freddie. Now that the father was dead, the son had assumed his father's title: Dr. Freddie. He was an educated man, young Freddie, and liked to say "varsity" rather than "university," which seemed to my ears most cosmopolitan. He was Catholic and lived in the same house as his receptionist, although I did not appreciate the nuances at the time. "Hello, Peter," he said when he took my call.

"Freddie," I said, "I think my girlfriend might be pregnant."

"Okay," he said. "What makes you think that?"

"Her period is late."

"How late?"

"Two months," I said, "and I was wondering: Is there anything you can do?"

There was a longish silence.

"I didn't know who else to talk to," I said. "I'm sorry, Freddie."

"I think the best thing is, you should come and see me."

"Tomorrow?"

"That's the trick."

"Should I bring my girlfriend?"

"Not necessary, old bean."

"Thanks, Freddie."

"And, Peter, don't call me Freddie. You can call me Dr. Colman." When I hung up, I was no longer preoccupied by H.'s pregnancy but by this last, mortifying rebuke. I felt fourteen fucking years old.

———

Next day, I drove south toward the town of Portsea, not to Portsea itself but to a small town nearby. I sat in Dr. Colman's waiting room, with the farmers and the retired men with white Panama hats and the young mothers from the Housing Commission developments, where the streets had names like Amethyst and Sapphire. My family had been coming here for so many summers, so many Easters, Christmases, and weekends, that people I didn't know, total strangers, could tell me about the time when I was two years old and cut my foot on broken glass.

The contents of Dr. Colman's office were as familiar to me as my own living room: the eccentric gas fire; the broken oar from a surf lifesaving boat; the ashtray made from an artillery shell; the photograph of old Dr. Freddie standing on the beach in a black overall bathing suit; the cracked leather examination couch where I had had the papilloma burned from my toe in extremely painful circumstances.

When I was finally admitted to the surgery, young Freddie sat behind his desk in his Harris-tweed sports jacket, smoking a Craven A cigarette. It was clear from the moment I walked in that he had decided what to do. He pulled a small pad of paper toward him and began writing on it.

"This is what we use as a test," he said, tearing the sheet of paper off and sliding it across the desk to me. "Just a little test."

"Okay," I said. "Thanks. This is really nice of you."

"Maybe she's not pregnant at all. So this is a test. Do you understand?" he asked me sternly, looking over the top of his glasses.

"I think she really is, you know. She's two months late."

"It's just a way of making sure she's not pregnant," he said.

"But if she is . . ." I insisted.

"It'll give her a period," he said at last. He was a Catholic. Perhaps he did not like to think about what he was doing.

"Okay. Do I take it to the chemist's?"

"Yes, but not here. Take it to the city, that's a good bloke."

"Thank you," I said. "Thank you so much, Dr. Colman. Is it okay if you don't tell my parents?"

He shook my hand. "Just take it to the city, that's a good chap."

———

I had a 1949 Armstrong Siddeley with leather upholstery, a sunshine roof, and a preselective gearbox of seemingly futuristic design. Six months later, this elegant old English car would fall apart and nearly kill me. It would slice off the top of my scalp and splash melodramatic blood all over my undergraduate poetry. But on this spring morning in 1961, it seemed to work just fine, and I drove it back to the city, my foot flat to the boards. I took the back road, with my arm out the window. The sky was a huge cobalt blue. I imagined our troubles were over.

What then happened in that Melbourne chemist's shop I later made into an amusing scene in a novel, but at the time it was not amusing at all. The pharmacist looked at the piece of paper and said that it was not a prescription, because it did not have the doctor's name on it. He showed it to me. What he said was true. My friendly family doctor had suffered an attack of cowardice too complicated for me to imagine even now. He had written the name of a drug on a plain sheet of paper but had neither signed it nor identified himself.

The pharmacist asked me if I knew what the drug was for. He asked this very loudly.

I was an eighteen-year-old who looked so young that I often could not get served at Jimmy Watson's Wine Bar. I stood there in the chemist's shop with my skinny arms straight by my sides, feeling the blood rising in my cheeks.

"Do you know what this does?"

I hesitated. "Yes," I said.

"I could call the police," the pharmacist said. There were other people in the shop—grownups, respectable people, who turned to stare at me. I fled the shop, and I can still remember the feeling of panic, of wrong, of impending disaster as I rushed to hide myself deep inside the city crowds.


A few years later, abortion became a very public issue. There were police raids, judicial inquiries, pictures in the paper. The names and addresses of abortionists then became very public knowledge. But in 1961 the names and addresses were much more difficult to obtain: a friend gave us a phone number scribbled on a torn scrap of paper.

H. phoned the number from a public call box. A voice answered with a simple "Yes?"

H. nervously explained her "situation," and we were told where to go and when, and to bring fifty pounds in cash. This was a huge amount of money in 1961. No one we knew had fifty pounds.

Finally, however, we found a benefactor—one of my zoology professors. Professor T. was a kindly man. He asked us to his home, and his wife cooked us dinner. Just the same, we were not surprised that he had taken legal counsel before making us the loan.

When we had those ten deep-blue five-pound notes, when we had found the waiting room, when H. had submitted to examination, the news was still not good.

"She's three months pregnant," the strawberry-blond receptionist said. She said this to me, not to H. "We can't do anything without her parents' consent."

"We've got the fifty pounds," I said. "We brought it with us."

"Go away," she said. "Come back with her mother or her father."


This was 1961, but not yet the sixties. If the Pill had arrived, we had not noticed it. It was before Haight-Ashbury, before Woodstock. It was, in effect, the fifties, and teenagers were expected to keep their clothes on when in each other's company. To tell the woman, whom I will call Mrs. Z., that her daughter and I had had sex was just unthinkable. To say that she was pregnant was to imagine a disgrace too shattering even to contemplate.

But of course we did. We did it as we had done the other things, as we had borrowed the fifty pounds, rung the doorbell at the abortionist's. We did it on a quiet suburban afternoon in Dandenong, in a comfortable, untidy house that I had come to think of as my second home.

We sat in the kitchen and drank tea.

Then one of us said *it*. Which one? I don't know. One of us opened our mouth and made the words come out.

H.'s mother was sometimes given to picturesque upset, but she took our news calmly—far more calmly than anyone could have anticipated.

If we had been a little older, a little less frightened, we would not have been so surprised: in the suburban world we lived in, this was a woman famous for her eccentricities. As a teenager, she had attempted to flee an isolated bush town carrying nothing but an unloaded revolver. She had mailed her wedding invitations with the wrong date on them, on purpose. She did not like housework—dishwashing, dusting—and she had been known to leave unfolded sheets lying in the laundry for months on end. She did not make the bed. She kept a five-foot-high stack of newspapers in the kitchen, waiting until she would have time to read them. This was before feminism, and there was no one to tell her that this behavior was okay. She did not care.

This was not, I now see, a woman who was going to persuade her eldest daughter to begin life as a mother at the age of twenty.

Thus she quickly became our co-conspirator, and when it was time to go back to that single-story Victorian terrace house in G—— Road, she came with us. While the abortionist's receptionist counted the fifty pounds, Mrs. Z. stood by our side. When H. went in for her operation, Mrs. Z. sat with me in the park.

And there, on a park bench, in the sunshine, my future mother-in-law and I talked. Doubtless I was being insensitive, but when she said, "This doesn't happen from doing it just one time," I decided not to hear the question she was really asking me. I remember being relieved that we were so companionable and easy with each other.

While we sat on a park bench, H. lost her baby. I met her afterward in the waiting room. She was strangely unchanged and yet also changed absolutely. She was pale and shaky, lost in her own pain. We drove back along the Prince's Highway, down through the industrial suburbs with incongruous names like Noble Park, to Dandenong, where poor H. went to bed with a hot-water bottle. I don't remember what lie we told her father. He was a good and decent man. I still stand, guilty and embarrassed, in his imaginary presence.


I don't think H. and I ever talked about that baby, and yet I don't think, given the choice all over again, that we would have done any of it differently. She must have grieved for the child, but she never said so, and I was young and callow and it would not have occurred to me that she might.

Our hearts were not broken, and we went on to our new young marriage and our new young lives. H. was twenty-three, and I was twenty-one. We traveled the world—Asia, the Middle East, Europe, London.

We came back to Australia, to three-quarters of an acre and a little house. We planted hundreds of trees—eucalyptus, acacias, melaleucas. We were ready to begin our family.

I had a job in an advertising agency and wrote short stories at night. H. was working at the Red Cross. We were now twenty-seven and twenty-nine. We did not speak about the lost baby. That had been so long ago.

H. quickly became pregnant. I remember her slowly swelling belly, the nights by the log fire, the feeling of domesticity, the certainty of how my life, our life, would continue.

This was 1970, and the world was changing. We were active in the Vietnam Moratorium Committee and knew that our phone was tapped. We were socialists. Our bookshelves were stuffed with Frantz Fanon and Regis Debray, but also Beckett, Faulkner, and Ursula Le Guin. We played *Blonde on Blonde* so loudly that it rattled the windows, and yet our own expectations of life were anchored in the fifties. Neither of us expected that H. would have a career. She had been a gifted philosophy student but had dropped out of university to become a photographer's assistant. And while she was a talented photographer, she was never particularly ambitious. She could take things or leave them. She could lie in the sun. She liked to pursue abstract philosophical puzzles. In her forties, long after we split up, she began to study cartography, and when I think of her doing it, I imagine her pursuing her studies with fascination and wonder rather than with ambition. H. had a placidity and an intelligence that I, with all my nervous energy and extravagant dreams, found enviable, sexy.

She did not feel ambivalent about abandoning a career to have children. It was our plan, and as her belly grew, our plan became more and more real. There were no birth classes, no pre-birth education of any type, but there was our baby: we lay in bed and felt it kick.

H. says it was summer, but in my memory it was autumn. The frosts had not arrived, but it was still cold enough to light the fire. It was around midnight, the ashes in the fire were gray, and the house had lost its heat, when H. shook me awake.

I can still see that bedroom: its unadorned convict brick walls, its long jute curtain. I turned on the light—a single naked bulb that stuck out from its black Bakelite fitting on the wall.

"My waters broke," H. said.

"The waters can't have broken. You're only five months. That doesn't happen until the baby's being born."

"Well, everything's wet."

It was. In harsh, unsentimental light, I could see that the sheets were sodden, but I would not believe that what had happened could happen. "Maybe you peed."

"It's not pee. My waters broke."

We phoned the doctor, and he said he would meet us at the hospital, some twenty minutes away.

The thing is this: We did not know what was happening. We had not the least damn idea. We locked the house and bumped down the steep clay track and drove out along gravel roads into the suburban night.

I could direct you to the hospital now: Lower Plenty Road, Heidelberg Road—but I forget the suburb's name. It was a small, suburban red-brick hospital near a railway line, but I don't know what it was called.

And there, in a single hospital room, my wife went into labor. She had not been in labor before. Was this labor induced? I have no idea. At the time, I knew less. Did we know we were losing our child? Yes, we did. No, we didn't. We knew because we were told, but we did not believe it because of the pain, its endless pulsing contractions, because of the birth taking place. I held H.'s hand but did not know how else to help her. And when, finally, I was sent away, I left gratefully and stayed in a neon-lit corridor that still keeps pushing its way into my fiction.

But then the baby was born, dead. Did I see her? No, and yet I sometimes imagine that I did. It is mixed up with the next time— and there was a next time, although on that night we did not know there would be one.

Let me tell the next time now, too. Let it stand for both times, because in truth the two have become the same in my memory.

We had accepted that there was "something wrong" with the first baby, that it was "right" to lose it, but we did not know that more babies would die before this story would be over—that it would be years before H. and I would meet in the Melbourne Hilton and show each other, along with photographs of our youthful selves, baby photographs—babies from our new marriages.

When we were still married, we did not know that the fifty pounds the strawberry-blond woman counted so carefully had also procured an "incompetent cervix," which was why the next pregnancy repeated itself like a sequence from *Last Year at Marienbad*. It unwound its long, sickening strand of story in the same bedroom, with the same convict brick walls, the same bare light bulb that still had no shade to soften what it showed.

Like all nightmares, the repetition was not exact. This time there were twins, and when the labor was over, they were alive. The nurse emerged from a door and asked me if I wanted to see them. I was again in that damned corridor.

I was afraid.

I walked through a door, and there they were—a boy and a girl, with perfect little hands and faces. They were tiny, and delicate, but there was nothing wrong with them. They had familiar family features which I would later recognize in my sons. I stood and watched our beautiful babies in the oxygen tent and could not believe that they would die.

To the nurse, I said, "Will they be all right?"

"Oh, no," she said. "Oh, no."

How long did they live, my babies?

I swear I do not know. How could I have been so ignorant? I think only that I fled the pain, that *we* fled the pain, the knowledge, chose not to remember. I could not bear to know what it was we had lost. I sat with H. in her hospital room.

"Did you see them?"

"Yes."

We wept together; we wept for our loss. Obviously, I was not heartless. And yet, when I tell you the next part of the story, I fear that I will appear so.

It is eleven o'clock in the morning, and I am sitting in a funeral home with Mrs. Z. We sit on one side of a desk, the funeral director on the other. He is a man of fifty, with a gray sweater underneath his suit. I am a writer of unappetizing short stories, with a pasty face and long hair that needs a wash.

He sits, this man, and asks me how I want the twins buried.

I sit beside Mrs. Z. I can barely speak.

I am not religious, and I cannot bear the religious smell of the funeral home, the flowers, the unctuous voices, the false comfort. Dead is dead. To put a name on plaques, to say prayers—all this is lies, bullshit in the face of the nothingness of death. And in believing this I am at one with my wife, who, even as we meet with the funeral-parlor man, is taking the first of the pills that will dry up the painful milk that has come to feed the dead babies we are discussing.

Slowly we go through the options. We agree on cremation. We agree that the ashes will be put in a wall. I do not ask where the wall is or what it looks like, but I imagine it to be made of damp red bricks with doors like a set of mailboxes. It is an enduring image— one I will be able to see clearly long after I have forgotten the funeral director's face.

"And what names?"

"No names," I say.

"Are you sure?" my mother-in-law asks.

"I don't believe in God," I say.

It is not the point, of course. She knows it is not the point, but she sees the fierceness and fragility of my grief.

"Later," she says gently. "Later—don't you think you might be sorry?"

Surely she is thinking of her daughter, of what she would feel herself.

"Are you sure you won't be sorry?"


It's later now.

Looking back on Australia in 1961, I feel I grew up in a dark and ignorant time: a racist immigration policy, great works of English literature banned, abortions performed furtively, illegally, not always well. When I look back on how our story went, H.'s and mine, I don't really see that it could have gone any differently.

I wish only that we had honored those children with a plaque, a name. I will always wish that, forever.

# ORACLES

RITA GABIS

,

I found the small skull of a red fox in the woods today, where a high, diffuse sun had melted away snow from the deer path. I almost stepped on it, a delicate curvature of bone directly in front of my feet. A strange, weathered jewel hugged to the ground by the downdrift of autumn's old shimmerings; rough-edged pine cones, black ash, striped oak, and sugar maple leaves.

*I cannot easily dismiss the subject of fallen leaves,* Thoreau warned, hinting at mystery. Ground pine rises out of the old overlay. Shakespeare's stagehands collected the pollen of the low evergreen, fleck by invisible fleck, and used it as a stage prop, set it afire for its lightning flash.

The fox skull startles me the way the bright whip of a storm across the sky does. I dig it free, hold it in one hand, the secret of its death, birth. The empty eye sockets stare ahead at the thick of winter, backward in the direction of last summer's heat when these woods were tick rich, wombed in the shadow of the canopy. I want a child, and don't know if I will be able to conceive a child. I rub a clumsy, gloved finger down the slope of the cranium, touch the faded gleam of the teeth still stubborn in the jaw.

*Conceive* comes from the Latin *concipere*, "to take in." I slip the skull in my pocket, walk out of the woods with fox memory, the wind creak of white pine, dead maple, young oak. Walk the path of the fox pup's only summer, soft crush of a paw on softer trillium, the catlike stalking dance of play and hunger, learned from the mother, a solitary hunter.

*Red fox leaped in me,* wrote Meridel Le Sueur. She might have been talking about the way longing accrues and deepens, becomes part of the force of a life, a craving hammered out of the bones of things, of winter, frozen groundwater, the sudden naked appearance of spring. The way one woman watches another scoop up a restless child in a practiced, easy gesture and feels, for a moment, the young body molded against her own.

Two years ago in late summer, when my husband came in from the barn, I sat down with him by an open window, the crazy twists and extensions of the mulberry tree just outside alive with the wings of berry-drunk birds. *Let's talk about having a baby,* I said. *Why this month, this season,* he asked, rubbing a smear of oil on the back of one hand across the denim of his jeans. *We're getting older,* I answered. *It's a good time to start a family.*

It was August of a drought year. Redgrass whitened in the slow hours of sun. Watered at dawn, leaves of tomato, squash, and broccoli wilted by eleven in the morning. Dogs panted the minute they left the shade by the side door. Heat intensified, magnified, as if we were burning under a thick glass held close to the eye of summer.

In the back field brown crickets skittered and danced, the staccato of their wing scrapings a strange poetry of dust and light. *One ought also to be guarded about the rising of the stars,* wrote Hippocrates, *especially the dogstar.* We were not guarded, my husband and I. On the night of my thirty-sixth birthday, we made love without using any contraception. Dry lightning shattered the country dark, slamming against asphalt roads. A brief, violent rain slanted down the electrified air. I imagined the semen inside me, the grooves and passageways of my body. I had been used to thinking of things in manageable numbers; two people lying side by side in the storm flare, two fields behind the house, one bright slip of a thin, cloud-covered moon. Trying to make a child, the world suddenly grew larger; twenty million sperm driven, mindless, packed tight with encoded messages only the future deciphers. Two hundred crickets in the field, a thousand bleached blades of redgrass. The rain ended. In the sky, summer constellations came alive, a wild grid of brightness that seemed to be resting momentarily above the sloping roof of the house before whirling off to a new destination.

In the morning there were chores to be done; ten-gallon buckets of spring water to haul up two flights of stone steps to the garden, a thick split branch of the mulberry to bring down with a chain saw. At work my husband caulked oakum into the seam of an old whaling boat, his hands and clothes picking up the smoky scent of it. My day was a mix of remembering and forgetting the choreography of the last night's desire. I already felt pregnant, tender.


My husband and I are the live-in caretakers of a large, saltbox homestead that was once a working New England farm, now owned by the mostly elderly members of a local historical society. (*The hysterical society*, one member said to me poker-faced.) Our duties are loosely defined, we are presences, witnesses of the way time spins its silks across the flare of a thorny quince bush, antique lilacs, a ridge of trash roses, a stream winking out of a mudbank.

One afternoon in the garden when the temperature topped out at a hundred, I thought I heard a child calling me by name, and stood up from a weed crop in the large enclosure, a makeshift fence of turkey wire. Sweaty and a little faint from the sun, I heard it again, a girl's voice, apparition, dream, wish, I don't know. Paper wasps buzzed in the scarlet bean flowers. Above me a few white strips of cirrus clouds drifted. I looked around at familiar shapes—a dead ash tree, a weathered ladder propped against a stone wall, bindweed and poison ivy tendriled around the gray slats.

In the stream out of my sightline, minnows gulped down dragonfly eggs. Beyond the cirrus clouds, invisible stars shed mass, molted. Brilliant-backed beetles, glued to each other in fat marigolds, lumbered in clumsy union. The voice I heard or imagined opened up a space in me, the force of its emptiness made me weak at the knees. Maybe it was sunstroke, a neighbor's child calling, hidden from view. In the hot air, I felt for a moment the singular spiral of my own life. I could dip in the stream and let go a clutch of eggs, shed thirty-five years and leave them, molted away, right there, among speckled beans in the green clasp of their long pods, cabbage moths, sugary tomatoes hanging in a crowded galaxy from their stems.

At puberty my ovaries stored close to a half million eggs, or oocytes. Half of a million, enough to line the entire muddy edge of the stream, glittering. Enough to people a small city. I never thought of this as a girl. I was trying to figure out sex, its slickness and dangers and de-lights. Of the wealth of eggs in my body, only five hundred or so would mature, ovulate out of the little micro-anatomy of their folli-cles. How many did I have left? A hundred? Thirty, fifty, twenty? My gynecologist, a prim woman in her late fifties, assured me I had plenty of time. I was still egg rich.

When the last stroke of heat lightning zigzagged over August, and we turned the page of the calendar over to September, my period came. I thought of the egg that got away with a shrug and a slight twinge. A small event in a cycle of gains and losses, Vega moving into the night sky with its powerful light, tree crickets measuring the dip in temperature with their waning rhythm, the endometrium shed-ding to make room for another chance.

One of my favorite creation stories is indigenous, a Native Amer-ican tale of a big monster who eats all of Coyote's friends—geese, bears, elk, deermice. To get them back, Coyote asks the monster if he can crawl inside his stomach and visit with all his old companions. Once inside, Coyote slits the monster's stomach open with a knife, freeing his friends and killing the monster. Quartered, pieces of the monster are thrown toward each corner of the earth, and a tribe springs up where the pieces land. Finally Coyote washes the blood from his hands and shakes them. Where the drops fall, the Nez Percé are born. I love this story for its casualness—a hunk of monster, a drop of watery blood, a new life-form.

*See how different the leaves of the cabbage are, and how extremely alike the flowers*, wrote Darwin. Maybe we're all stitched together with the same pair of Devil's Darning Needles. True fall came on, and I felt a trickster's presence in my life, sore breasts that added up to nothing, a craving for salt, a period that came six days late. In a class I taught in a local college, a student stopped me in the hallway, a wide-faced, lovely young woman from Turkey. *I'm pregnant*, she said, beaming, and I hugged her, imagining the fetus curled in the curve of her body.

In the back field the red-orange streaks of paintbrush faded, the ground delivered the old jaw of a raccoon, the lustrous feather of a jay blew across a bright arch a birch made between the field and the emptiness of sky. I was happy, with the kind of diffuse joy that attends the making of almost anything one cares about, a poem, a kinship with a new friend or lover, a story, a dent in an old sadness. The decision to have a child gathered my husband and me into the common weather of life while history unspooled and stripped itself down around us. Bark curled off the birch trees. In a trunk in the dry, high-beamed attic, I found a bolt of old cloth and unraveled it, a ghost garment another woman might have held up to the light, shaping it by eye around the contours of her days and nights.

Anxiety was a loose thread through my happiness then. You can make a plan for the future, someone told me once, but you never know what the future plans for you. The birthsmell of the fontanel, midnight cry of a teething infant were not mine yet. Unable to control whatever was waiting across the threshold of the unknown, I was drawn in by the Homestead's past and relics, their stories and secrets already given away to time.

Flipping through an old diary in the Homestead library, I read about a dye-shed that burned down on the property. In the southwest corner of the field, where sugar maples and spruce overlook the streambed, I dragged a stick in the dust, squared off the shape of the vanished building, made room for it in my imagination, the way I was making a place for a child in the landscape of my life.

I went to a local quarry I'd heard might be the source for the Homestead's granite walls. The owner was away on a job, but his petite wife shook my hand in their sideyard, encouraged me to walk on my own through a ragged orchard to the quarry. A plastic tricycle

lay on its side near her basket of laundry. Her small boy turned one
of the black wheels with the intensity of someone discovering the
earth's rotation.


For one person, a particular refrain of a song is a reservoir of memory,
for another a late-model car, a prom dress swathed in tissue paper,
the rough canvas of a lover's jacket. In a midwestern orchard I lay
down with the first boy I loved when I was fifteen.

It was dark, the year already on the cusp of winter, the thick sweetness of rotting windfalls permeated everything—the cold grass, weight
of his chest against mine. I wanted to feel the soft, ruined apples
crushed under my back, wanted to strip off his cotton shirt and jacket,
feel skin and heart and bones, the stars and drift of night above the
scrawl of low limbs.

And ten years later in a field of Northern Spies in Massachusetts,
in the drunken heat of late spring, among the flowerings and wooden
bee boxes, I sat crying in the confusion of my life—a time I never
believed I would look back on with a peculiar sweetness. *Comfort me
with apples, for I am sick of love*, so goes the Song of Solomon. I wept
then, and I was comforted.

Heading for the quarry, I passed leaf-rust and unpruned branches.
At the bottom of a treelined hill, granite was heaped and scattered
around a cool body of water, shallow and clear near the edge, black-
brown at the center. I tried to lift a stone wedge, the pink and crystal
striated through it rubbing off on my hands. Stone tells us how old
the earth is. I flashed on the small boy in the yard turning the black
wheel, the shape of his head under close-cropped hair evidence of
life already lived; his mother's girlhood, his father's boyhood among
water and rock. I'd never thought of the body as a record before.

The slabs surrounded by sumac and willow, birch and ash, seemed
to be artifacts, remains of a fallen temple gathered up again piecemeal
by those of us who no longer know the names of the old gods. Back
home that evening, sitting on a granite step under a hunter's moon,
I touched a tiny sliver of rock I took from the quarry to my lips. I
prayed for a moment to one of the nameless gods and then felt foolish
with my need for oracles, explanations of past events, whispers about
the future, *will I, won't I, this month, next month*.

Friends reassured me with stories that started to collect around me like Thoreau's fallen leaves. Someone someone knew who tried for two years to get pregnant finally smoked a joint one night, and voilà—two weeks later the blue line appeared on the home pregnancy test. I began keeping basal body temperature charts, but only haphazardly. They looked like seismographs of hope, my own geography. I saw my gynecologist again, and she ran some preliminary blood tests that came up normal. Your ovaries are the size of walnuts, she said, just as they should be.

I studied my growing collection of books full of statistics and details. A man and a woman have a 20 percent chance each month of conceiving. Eighty percent of people are successful within one year. Ninety percent within two years. I got stuck on that 20 percent a month. One fertilized egg out of five takes, matures, results in a pregnancy.

I thought of the five hundred oocytes again. The percentages seemed foreign to me, not unlike the old equations in a ciphering book from the early 1800s I pulled from a file, its brown binding soft and ragged, the tinted pages wearing their own pattern of the years beneath an impossibly elegant script, a hand only a calligrapher would write in these days. *If 12 men can build a wall in twenty days, how many men can do the same in 8?* And on the next page—*the earth is about 95,173,000 miles from the sun and a cannonball at its finest discharge flies out at a mile in 8 seconds. How long would a cannonball be at that rate in flying from here to the sun?* (24 years, 33 minutes, 20 seconds.)

When a strong gust riffled the temperature charts from a bedroom tabletop to the wideplanked floor, I crouched down over the incomplete graphs, thought of the equations I was creating out of lovemaking. If my husband and I made love two days in a row, in the morning because light stimulates ovulation. And if we did this the minute my temperature dipped, but before the release of the egg raised it. And if I imagined a field inside me, or the flat silver of a wave, the water colder now that summer was gone, I would conceive. Magical thinking gave way to practicality. Someday, I mused, recording the numbers off a digital thermometer as a way of timing conception would be as outdated as calculating a cannonball's journey to the sun.

November blackened leaves with hard frost. The month for the ax, Aldo Leopold called it. Memory honed itself against the cold, took its place beside the mysteries of the Homestead. *Why now*, my husband had asked in summer. *Is it too late*, a voice inside me started echoing back. I looked over my shoulder at the past, trying to imagine where a child would have fit into my life when I was twenty-five, thirty. Like the index of old diaries and land records in the library, I cataloged the last few years of my life, a history skewed and clarified by my distance from old roads, riprap and faultlines.

One winter day I watched blizzard light thicken by the old window in my workroom (soon to become a space for nightfeedings, newborn's dreams). Snow that started falling in November was still falling. The wingspan of a cardinal fanned red outside at the feeder, and just then the phone rang, my grandmother Rachel, one hundred and three years old, a shrill octave in her voice.

*They've stolen all my jewelry*, she said. *They've taken it all, hidden it. Help me.*

*Who is stealing from you?* (Not old filigreed rings, but memory, the suppleness of skin, eyes skimmed free of their cataract whiteness.)

From the island cottage where she lived alone off the coast of New England, she whispered frightened answers into the receiver of the telephone.

The next day, we spoke again and she was calmer. *We're trying to have a baby*, I blurted out. And what I was imagining was her in me, a vision not unlike the fanciful Aristotelian notion of procreation. A woman moves through life with tiny, perfectly formed humans inside her, cocooned, waiting for the impulse to unravel, travel out of the crowded uterus.

In the Old Testament Rachel rails in frustration to Jacob, *Give me children, or I shall die.* My grandmother bore two sons and a daughter, but I could never picture her holding an infant, singing lullabies. She grabbed at life, hammered it, worked it, sand into loam, loam into sour ground, shingles, latches, a small house eventually, away from the alleys and swell of a city.

Divorced and then diminished in the eyes of her family, she cultivated a passion for music and painting, marched her daughter to the doors of the Curtis Institute, stuck a flute in the hand of one son. A young Leonard Bernstein flew his hands up and down the keyboard of the upright in her walk-up apartment all hours of the day and night. His racket got her evicted, and when I envision her as a mother, it is that sight that comes to me. The fine profile, thick shock of black hair, moving down the smoky twilight of a neighborhood street, three teenage children in tow, a piano, trail of music, a troupe of fledgling composers and artists in the quick step of their youth.

*We're trying to have a baby.*

*What? A baby?* The crisp inflection was back, the fear gone.


In the bone-crack cold that evening, I touch the round slope of my husband's arm, tell him I want to have a child before my grandmother dies, before the million swift divisions of her days are gone.

*We should get tests done, see if something's wrong.*

My husband rolls over from his side to his back, blinks up at the high ceiling, and I wonder which of his twenty-three chromosomes hold the thick chuff of his hands, the slight shy stoop in his tall frame, the black fleck in the gold edge of the iris of his left eye. He's a boatbuilder, steambends planks into curved shapes. I pray to stones, scrub weather off inarticulate bone with a toothbrush soaked in bleach and water. He has a different kind of faith, believes in fixing things, redrawing the lines of our life, framing again whatever has to be framed to make the boat float, to make a baby.

*If something's wrong, we'll fix it.* His words pay out slowly, and then he is asleep.

Waking him later that night with my touch, the shudder of our bodies together one erotic seam, I felt time quickening.

The next morning I arranged, through my gynecologist, for my husband's semenalysis. A few weeks later a urologist called me with the results, his voice booming out through the phone line. *You're definitely in the pregnancy ballpark, no problem on this end, if nothing happens in a few more months we'll run some more tests.* But I was already one step ahead of him. I phoned my doctor again and asked her about sperm antibodies, an autoimmune reaction that can occur in a man or woman and prevent sperm from fertilizing eggs.

*It sounds awfully complicated dear,* she countered.

As the receiver clicked into place, and another fraction of a minute went by, I decided to find a specialist.


Hippocrates, more generalist than specialist, mapped out his diagnostic procedures with admirable certainty: *If a woman do not conceive, and wish to ascertain whether she can conceive, having wrapped her up in blankets, fumigate below, and if it appear that the scent passes through the body to the nostrils and mouth, know that of herself she is not unfruitful.*

The tests I'd read about, hysterosalpingogram, endometrial biopsy, seemed oddly similar in makeup and diagnostic reliability.

I circled a name in the phone book under "infertility," set up an appointment. Sat, ankles crossed, hands in my lap, a few weeks later, in a cluttered, woodpaneled office and studied the framed diploma from Guadalajara Medical School next to a certificate from the American Fertility Society. The doctor shuffled papers on his desk, peered at me as if trying to make me out in the haze of smoke from fumigation.

I waved my half-created temperature charts, feeling schoolgirlish.

*The trick is,* he squinted over the graph lines, *to get you ovulating, if that's where the trouble lies.*

We nodded our heads at the same time, in firm agreement, and then, in an effort to console or understand, he looked down at my hands, fingers laced across my pelvic bone.

*Many couples find this process difficult, the energy it takes. Some even divorce in the midst of this kind of thing.* He patted the graph paper for emphasis, smiled, glint of his eyes narrowing under dark eyebrows. I left the office holding appointment cards scribbled with dates for tests, past the large corkboard crammed with snapshots of newborns and toddlers, the complimentary copies of *Parents* magazine stacked under an arrow that had "Take This Home" scrawled over it.

Outside the doctor's office, a sprawl of naked forsythia hinted at spring around the next bend, waiting to shear away the density of winter.

Yeats wrote, *In the beginning of important things, in the beginning of the day, in the beginning of any work—there is a moment when we*

*understand more perfectly than we understand again until all is fin-
ished.* But how is it, I wondered, as the quick filmstrip of a life clicks
by, those moments come to us and are kissed by time. Moment the
first word of a love poem is scratched on a page, still empty of end-
rhyme, moment my grandmother first sighed in the fetal sleep of her
dying.

A school of sperm travels through the epididymis, the girl I was
ties her shoes, days spindle splashed with indigo, and we're stained
by what claims us and frees us.

The ground by the forsythia was soft, the warming air a tripwire
for summer. I closed my eyes, saw wasps cooling their wings in split
stone. Opened my eyes to the thin stripe of my shadow. The spring
equinox was four weeks away, the round-bellied brightness of the
world waited.

There would be many more seasons of waiting for the outcome of
tests and treatment; three cycles of insemination, two cycles of in
vitro fertilization. The waiting would change the way I mark time.
Weeks would be fenced in by a protocol of daily injections, the day
of a pregnancy test, the moment I noticed the spotting of an early
miscarriage. Finally my husband and I would hunger to return to a
life no longer defined by a calendar of hope and loss. We decided to
adopt a child.

Shortly after we made that decision, I dreamed of a fox, maybe
the one whose skull the snowmelt surprised me with. In my dream
the fox was alive. We were in a clearing, and it didn't notice me until
I was close enough to touch the rust-colored fur, unmatted, each shaft
of hair like a filament of light. I wanted to run my hand down the
narrow slope of the animal's spine. Knowing that the fox would sniff
me out and slip away didn't diminish that desire, or my delight in
the slight body that side-stepped my own, moved into the thicket, and
was gone.

# BRINGING HOME BABY

TAMA JANOWITZ

‚

## Days 1–2

We are in Beijing, en route to adopt our baby. Our group consists of eight couples and two single women, along with our leader, a woman named Xiong Yan, who will serve as tour guide for two days in Beijing before we fly down to Hefei to collect the babies and where Xiong Yan will do our final adoption paperwork.

Even though I had been anxious, even desperate, to get our baby when I was back in New York, for some reason I calmed down the minute we arrived in China. The other couples are all frantic to get to the kids, most of whom are around nine months old and whom we have seen only in photos. Now, after more than eight months of excruciating waiting and paperwork, now that we have landed, I suddenly begin to wonder—what's the rush?

The endless adoption process has been like a scavenger hunt: The FBI, for example, needed fingerprints to prove we weren't on their most-wanted list. Birth certificates with original signatures had to be acquired, then sent to city departments, taken to state departments, federal departments, then to the Chinese consulate. Medical exams were required, along with tax returns and letters of recommendation. Our heads even had to be probed and analyzed by therapists.

During that time, it seemed we would *never* get our baby. After all, she was getting older by the minute, and in the only picture we had, taken when she was two months old, she already had a surly expression—a positive attribute, by my standards.

I might have adopted years ago, even before I met my husband, but I had never been entirely certain that I had maternal tendencies toward babies. I knew I had maternal tendencies toward dogs. And since I always knew any child of mine would have doggish qualities, I wasn't too concerned. I was a novelist and worked at home, so I had plenty of time on my hands. Since I could never write for more than a few hours a day, when I was finished all I had left to do was to stare at the ceiling, wondering why I had picked novel writing as a career. Fourteen years ago, I came to Manhattan in search of other human beings and found myself, only a short time later, on the cover of *New York* magazine in a meat locker with a lot of animal carcasses, the author of a hit novel. Now, I felt, I was on to even bigger adventures.

I knew Tim would make a wonderful father, but I rarely picked up friends' children, since whenever I did, they usually burst into tears. Also, I never could believe that anyone would let us adopt— for one thing, we lived in a small one-bedroom apartment. Two adults, three dogs, and both of us fanatical collectors of books (Tim is a curator). There was scarcely any room left. But the adoption agency assured us that two rooms were an improvement over a crib in a crowded orphanage, and that once we were driven out of our minds, we would double our efforts to find another place to live. Soon we would be a family—or whatever they call it at the end of the twentieth century. So I was thrilled that, once I was in Beijing, my anxiety and apprehensions had disappeared. We were taken to see the Great Wall and the Forbidden City. In Tienanmen Square a woman got run over by a taxi—not someone in our group, though.

I loved everything about the place—the sights and the shopping (cashmere sweaters were $100, and they came in the richest, lushest hues I had ever seen; huge cashmere shawls for $150; and dresses of fantastically patterned silk for $30). The antiques market had beautiful old Chinese elm chests lined with camphor ($50), and brilliant vermilion lacquer and leather trunks ($40). And the restaurants! We ate in our hotel, which was a modern skyscraper—our last night alone as a couple—and I couldn't get over the menu, which was the most fabulous menu I had ever seen. Under the category "Danty of Sea Food" was listed: Fried Fish Maw with Stuff and Green Cucumber; Sautéed Cuttlefish with American Celery; and Sea Blubber with Cucumber Shreds. Under "Vetable," I found Braised Hedgehog Hydnun and Fried Whole Scorpion.

"Let's stay away from the Dry-Braised Dick Strip in Brawn Sauce," Tim said.

"Okay," I said. "But why don't we try the Fried Whole Scorpion? It's only ten cents, and it can't possibly really be a scorpion—it's under the Vetable heading."

The waitress seemed astonished that we wanted Fried Whole Scorpion. "Maybe scorpion's out of season?" I said.

"Only one?" She shook her head. "Only one?" she repeated.

"Okay," said Tim, to placate her. "Two."

A few minutes later two fried, whole black scorpions—claws outstretched, tails curled—arrived at our table, each dramatically positioned on a rice cracker.

"Do you think people usually order a whole platterful?" I said. Tim was looking at the scorpions appreciatively. "Well, here goes," I said, shutting my eyes and putting the scorpion in my mouth. Under normal circumstances, I probably wouldn't have done this. It might have been my last attempt at extricating myself from a situation— getting our baby—which, as the hour grew closer, I was beginning, far too late, to question.

The scorpion was crispy but did not have a distinctive scorpion flavor nor any instantaneous venomous effects. I really did want a baby, as long as it was quiet and gurgled to itself in a crib. Anybody I ever knew who had a baby always said, almost continuously, "You should have a baby. It's the most fantastic thing that can happen to you." I could never figure out why they kept saying this when the look in their eyes was that of a survivor of an airplane crash, but I figured it was something I would understand later.

## Day 3

Everyone is impatient on the flight to Hefei. One father-to-be says he feels like we are Elvis fans, waiting for a glimpse of Him.

I am beginning to get to know our group a little bit. Everyone is in their mid-thirties to mid-forties—a physiologist, a pediatrician, a photographer, an editor, an insurance agent, an education researcher, a marine engineer. One or two of our group have grown children from a previous marriage. Two couples already have four-year-olds waiting for a new sister. In China, it's the girls who are abandoned. Chinese couples are allowed only one child, and girls just don't have much cultural status. In addition, it's the boys who look after the parents in their old age: In other words, no son, no pension plan. In the future, China will be like New York City, only in reverse: Men will outnumber women one hundred to one. When a single Chinese woman walks into a party, she will be as desirable as a movie-star-handsome billionaire bisexual bachelor is in Manhattan.

Under normal circumstances, the people in our group wouldn't have much in common, but the fact that we are all joined together in this adventure makes me feel like a timid opera buff who has signed up for a packaged Perillo tour to La Scala.

At the hotel in Hefei—another modern skyscraper—we all disappear to our rooms, still laughing, smiling. The next time we see one another, we will all be with our smiling, adorable, happy little babies. I only wish I had brought other clothing. All the women seem to be dressed as Mothers, in long floral-print dresses or crisp linen outfits. A glimpse in the mirror as we all get off the elevator reveals a sophisticated crowd of parents-to-be and one hippie type with hair like black scrambled eggs, wearing a T-shirt Tim found in Beijing that reads CDLVIH-KLEIN, with smaller letters beneath that explain it is UHDERWEQR. (The Chinese love T-shirts printed with English words. They don't seem to care that they are almost always misspelled and that they make very little sense.)

Two o'clock, 2:15, 2:30. Tim and I pace back and forth, as if our wife were in labor next door in the delivery room. I keep running to the bathroom to brush my teeth. If the baby detects even a whiff of stale breath, it could put a damper on our relationship for years to come. Finally, around 3:30, the call comes: *She* is on her way.

After months of arguing, we have decided to name her Willow. I had wanted to call her Thomasina, or Letizia. Tim was thinking more in terms of Hortense or Hattie. It no longer matters. Maybe the name Willow is a safeguard: After all, the background information and photograph we received several months ago indicated that—for her age —she was extremely short and fat. With a name like Willow, this will have to change. The doorbell rings: Xiong Yan and a baby-nurse from the orphanage arrive with Willow.

Willow is very cute, dripping with sweat (the Chinese believe in keeping their babies bundled up even in the heat), with giant ears. When the nurse hands her to me, she smiles, even though she and the other babies have been riding for six hours in an unair-conditioned bus from the orphanage. "This is the first baby I've ever held who didn't burst into tears," I say, smiling.

"She doesn't cry," says the nurse in Mandarin. Xiong Yan translates. "She likes to play."

"She's just been fed," Xiong Yan adds. "When you give her food, make sure it's boiling hot—that's what they're accustomed to. She should be fed at six a.m., nine, twelve, three, six, and then she goes to sleep and gets fed again at eleven at night. Keep her warm—never let her stomach be uncovered."

Then, handing us a box of rice cereal and a bag of formula that we are to combine in specific amounts at the next feeding, Xiong Yan and Willow's nurse leave.

Immediately, the smiling happy baby in my arms bursts into tears. The nurse was right, Willow doesn't cry, as long as she is played with—every single second. This baby doesn't want to cuddle; she wants to be bounced, rocked, swooped around the room, then turned upside down to stare grimly while adults flap their arms and hop around the room like parrots. Because Willow has been confined to a crib for the past nine months—ever since she was abandoned in a park at two days old—she has no muscle tone, so all the swooping, jostling, and jiggling has to be by the person holding her. The minute that person stops tossing her around, she screams.

Despite her physical weakness, she has an abnormal amount of energy. I'm wondering, hyperactive? Her head has been shaved— another Chinese custom, to assure thicker, more luxuriant growth— and she definitely has sideburns. It really may be that Baby Elvis, complete with all the troubles of his past life, has been reincarnated. I wonder if they selected her for us after they saw the picture of Tim and me that we had to send with our application.

She cries nonstop, and since I have read somewhere that babies cry only for a reason, Tim and I decide to change her diaper. We put her on the floor and try to get her out of her clothes. Though she is weak, she is able to fight like a wounded fox in a leghold trap. Even with the two of us working hard, the task is next to impossible.

My face is bright red; sweat is pouring off Tim, dripping onto the sweating baby. We look at each other. "Is it too late for her to catch the bus back to the orphanage?" I ask.

This diaper changing takes around an hour. When Willow is back in her clothes with a diaper haphazardly strangling her midriff, the sobbing diminishes somewhat, which makes us realize it is time for her bottle. Trying to get the lumps out of the gruel with the lukewarm water in a thermos provided by the hotel takes almost another hour. By then, I can tell, she is really angry and bored—obviously this was not what she expected.

The hotel has provided our room with a purple metal cage, a crib with bars that are spaced just far enough apart to trap a baby's head. Willow doesn't like the crib. Being in the crib makes her very upset. If she was angry before, now she is furious. The toys we brought from the United States are lousy; any fool would have known. But finally, after several hours of strenuous entertainment—songs, the hora, arm wrestling—and another feeding, we are able to get her to sleep. By now it's quite late, though how much time has passed it's hard to say. I was ready for bed hours ago.

Unfortunately, though she's already snoring, I can't sleep. What if we have unwittingly killed her, and each snore is her last gasp? A kid who survives being left in a park, only to be murdered by two witless foreigners. If she lives, though, I don't know what we are going to do: It will be eighteen years before she's ready for college. I suppose we can send her to summer camp and boarding school in the meantime.

At least I know she's not dead when she decides—at three a.m.— to take a second look at some of the toys. She discovers that if she pounds a button, the tinny electronic version of "It's a Small World," a song I have always loathed, will play over and over.

### *D a y*  4

Dawn. First there is the feeding, the bathing, the changing, the attempt at cheering her up while the other adult member of our family unit tries to shower and put on some clothes and vice versa. At no time must she be ignored. The kid has no inner resources—can't read, write letters, put on nail polish—and seems to have nowhere to go.

It is now eight—it has taken us only three hours to get ready for breakfast.

In the lobby, large groups are patrolling the halls, and I see that —although they are speaking Norwegian or Swedish, or have Canadian accents—every single one of them is lugging a sobbing Chinese baby. No wonder the place was so noisy last night. What I thought was simply bad singing coming from the karaoke bar downstairs was a hellish chorus of babies.

A woman approaches Willow in her stroller. Willow looks up at her and coos appreciatively, as if she is about to be rescued from what is obviously a mistaken placement. "Oh, what a cute baby!" the woman says. "I was supposed to get mine yesterday, but she's not going to be delivered until today. It's like torture, waiting for her!"

"You could take this one," I offer.

Our group has already gathered in the dining hall for breakfast. Tots in their strollers are lined up in a ring around the table. "How's everything going?" I ask weakly, expecting a response similar to one I would have given.

Instead, and in unison, they shout, "Great!"

### *D a y*  5

The horror. The horror.

### *D a y*  6

By now the other parents also appear to have aged ten years. They're so worn down that at last they, too, are willing to admit everything is not perfect. Two babies cry constantly and even if they can be stopped will start again the moment anyone looks at them. One baby is on a hunger strike. Two babies have been given the wrong ratio of rice cereal to formula and are severely constipated.

I have definitely bonded with the group, if not the baby. There is nothing like discussing techniques for relieving constipation over breakfast to make one feel close. But then at every meal we have the most fascinating conversations on topics ranging from diaper rash and diarrhea to baby dandruff.

## Day 7

How could I have been such an idiot? It was Tim who had his doubts and apprehensions about adopting, but it's he who has bonded immediately with Willow. No wonder she looks at him so adoringly. He is a natural: strong enough to throw her around, adept at changing diapers, and he laughs with honest delight when she viciously inserts one sharp-clawed finger as far up his right nostril as possible.

When she tries to pull out my hair by the roots, I can't help but believe her intent is malicious. My arms are too weak to toss her into the air. For this, it is obvious, she will never forgive me. And I will never forgive myself for believing all those girlfriends who kept telling me, "You should have a baby! It's so great!" I see now that it was their method of revenge. I must remember to encourage others to do this marvelous thing—adopting a hyperactive, sweating lunatic unable to change her own diaper.

The Chinese paperwork is complete; our next stop is a week in Guangzhou (formerly Canton) to complete the American immigration process. After that, we fly back to the United States, where, I suppose, the real nightmare begins and where Willow will soon begin demanding Barbie dolls, Nintendo, and pure-white Arabian mares, start taking drugs, contract sexually transmitted diseases, insist on attending the fanciest, most expensive private schools, and sob uncontrollably when she doesn't get into the college of her choice.

*Postscript: Four Weeks Later*

Despite what my journal predicted, we have been extremely lucky. Our baby is so easygoing; she's laughing, laughing, laughing all the time. Sometimes she laughs so much, staring at her beautiful little rosebudlike face in the mirror, that I, too, begin to cackle uncontrollably.

Honestly, no matter how many times anyone insists I wrote those earlier entries in my diary, I truly can never believe them. It must have just been the jet lag. Or something. Willow is so sweet! Just the other day our pediatrician told me not to worry—hopefully by college age she won't need a bottle and will be on to the harder stuff. Having a baby is the most fantastic, wonderful thing a person can do. And Willow is so cute! So smart! I'm thinking. Maybe in the fall I'll look into adopting one from India. Yes, I can see her already: perhaps a bit older than Willow, one of those gypsy/street-urchin/waif types, with dark skin, gold bangles at her slim wrists and ankles, and thick, wild hair. I wonder just how long it will take to convince Tim . . .

# DEATH BEFORE LIFE

## KEVIN CANTY

,

Sometimes I think of the worst thing. That October, with my wife five months pregnant, the words were ugly and familiar: brain damage, birth defect, deformity, miscarriage. I would carry the bad thing around with me, like a stone in my mouth. It was reassuring: If I could imagine it, then it wouldn't happen. A charm or incantation for a lucky life.

This happened in the desert, in the fall, a beautiful day with clear skies and sun and shadows on the mountains. An ordinary day in the middle of our lives. Lucy was to pick up our two-year-old boy on her way home from work, and I'd get the groceries on my bicycle, et cetera. I can imagine the evening that did not take place: news on the radio, dinner cooking, a glass of wine for me but none for Lucy, who was taking care of herself. We were over the risky part of the pregnancy, the first few months, and were already picking out names, setting clothes aside, planning where the crib would go. It's a pleasant kind of game, like dolls or dress-up.

But Lucy wasn't home when I got there, and wasn't home a half hour later.

I called her at work, and a voice I didn't recognize said she'd gone for the day. I waited another half an hour and called our day-care person, and she hadn't seen Lucy either. Our son was with her; he was fine. There was this gathering fear. Car crash, passed out on the sidewalk, something with the pregnancy. I ran through the litany of terrors so that none of them would come true. I couldn't sit still. I paced around the living room, making up explanations: She went shopping, or out for coffee—decaf, of course, or maybe just a glass of water. She was getting her exercise, watching her diet, taking care. I'm trying to tell you that we didn't do anything wrong.

Finally a voice I did know called me from her work and said that there was a problem and Lucy was at the hospital, no other details asked or given. I left the house unlocked and drove to the hospital as quickly as I could, which was slowly: five o'clock and the streets were jammed. This is one of the two parts I remember best, though I don't understand why. It was a lovely afternoon, and I had the window down and the sunlight was warm on my arms, and I had this feeling that I was riding something big. Inside I was blanked out, except for the fear. There were no specifics. There was something big, something coming to carry me along, but I didn't know what. I knew I wasn't going to stay blank. Car crash, passed out on the sidewalk, something with the baby.

At the hospital, they directed me to Labor and Delivery.

Lucy was lying on a metal bed behind a curtain in the intake room and she was alive and awake, and the weight lifted off me for a second, only a second. She wasn't even crying, although she started as soon as I touched her hand with mine, like she'd been waiting for me. A little doctor was standing next to her bed. When I saw his face, I knew it was the baby.

"I'm sorry," the doctor said. "Your child is dead."

In a moment of confusion, I thought he meant my son, who was just fine; and then I saw that he meant the pregnancy. The words came as a physical shock, like a broken bone or a bad cut, although part of my mind had known this already. I wanted to slap his face, this stranger who had hurt me, who had hurt my wife. This doctor was not one of the medical gods. He was gray and old and carrying too many things in his shirt pocket: pens, spare glasses, a pad of paper. In a brief moment of hope, I saw that he didn't know what he was talking about, incompetent, it was all a mistake.

"There is no heartbeat," the little doctor said. "We took an ultrasound and we saw the heart and it was not moving, just so you know. I'm afraid that we're completely positive."

I looked into Lucy's face, and I don't know what I was expecting. I thought she would be transformed into something else, someone else. The other part of the daydream of terrible things: Tragedy would turn us into pillars of fire, into beautiful, terrible beings, into angels, a thing that poetry taught me. But it was only her regular face, except that she was so pale. And it felt strange, the way that everything stayed the same. The clocks on the wall told the same time as before; the cars drove by on the street.

"What do we do now?" I asked.

"We have to wait," the little doctor said. "Your wife's body has been trying to expel the pregnancy. It's like labor, and we've given her the same drugs that we would to accelerate labor. I think that if we give it time, she should be able to do the rest on her own. Otherwise, we'll see." He looked at me, looked at my wife. "I'm very sorry," he said, and left us alone behind the curtain.

Then it was just the two of us.

"What happened?" I asked her, but she couldn't talk yet, and I held her hand while she wept. Women were moaning and crying and cursing all around us, but we couldn't see them. It was a busy afternoon in Labor and Delivery, and all the rooms were taken. New patients were stuck in the intake room, to wait out their labor until a room opened up or their time came. Most of them were Mexican or Mexican-American, and their curses came in Spanish. All around us were women giving birth while we waited for the remains of the pregnancy to leave Lucy's body. We were not going to have this baby, and Lucy was weeping. I couldn't find the right thing to feel. It was like swimming in some dirty soup of feelings, anger and sorrow. A resentment, directed at no one, that I was being made to go through this. A feeling that this was going to hurt Lucy to the heart and there was no way I could protect her. And then the mothers all around us, talking soft Spanish between contractions.

And always the anger: Fuck you, fuck this, get us out of here.

She was in the library at work, and she started bleeding. A friend drove her to the hospital. She didn't understand why nobody called me right away. As she told me the details, Lucy seemed like she was ashamed of herself, like this was all her fault. I realized that we were both amateurs, that neither one of us knew anything about how to feel. We waited and waited in the room full of cursing women. The nurses, and once in a while the little doctor, would poke their heads in through the curtains and check on us. Sometimes they would apologize for making us wait in that room; in fact, it was like some kind of bitter joke, and we all felt it. Finally, after a couple of hours, Lucy had a series of contractions and the pregnancy was over.

I was there, I saw it: the little gray body of the baby girl lying out on the bloody towels. This is the other thing I remember and will always remember. She had the shape of a baby but she was tiny, six or eight inches long. She looked so close to life, and it was hard to think that she would never make it. The umbilical cord was twisted tight, like a rubber band tightened to make a motor for a model airplane. This twisting had cut off the blood to the baby girl and killed her. It was an odd thing, a fluke. The little doctor, who was almost ready to retire, had seen this only two or three times in his career. It didn't matter whether it was likely or unlikely or even impossible. The child was dead, and within a minute she was gone, carried off to some other part of the hospital. We never saw her again, and we were never able to find out what happened to her.

I know this is a secret. I'm telling you this because I don't want it to stay a secret. We didn't want to talk about it, and so we did a lot of our suffering in private; but afterward we heard about the miscarriages in our families, in our friends'. It sounds like a small thing, a mistake, a misdemeanor, but it doesn't feel like a small thing.

There was more, and none of it was good: a night in the hospital for Lucy, flowers and television and trying not to think about it. I had to try to explain this death to my son, how the sister we had been telling him about was not coming after all. There was this sense of embarrassment, calling people on the phone. Also this sense that I was not performing well, that I was supposed to be feeling something other than what I was feeling. I don't know what. I wanted to say: I don't know what I'm doing, I don't know what I'm doing, I don't know what I'm doing.

Maybe this is the reason that nobody will talk about a miscarriage: because there is nothing to say. We wanted the baby; we didn't do anything wrong; it was not our fault but the baby died anyway. The bones are simple. The hard part is shaping yourself around these hard facts.

I was grateful for the television for the first time in my life. It was a way of being alive and not being alive, passing the time without thinking. Of course, I can't forget that now; I know that when I'm watching TV, I'm taking myself out of life, and this seems idiotic. But in the weeks after the hospital, it was a comfort.

Then after a while, longer than you think, it's over. There were Saturdays to spend with our son; there was Christmas and then the summer. We had another baby girl, in the same hospital. There's something brutal about the way that time erases the feeling, but it is efficient, so that now the baby girl is only a memory, a painful memory but safely in the past. There was this baby doll that we had given our son, I guess in some attempt at gender equality. It didn't work. He hated it; he left it to sit outside in the sun and the rain while he played with his dump trucks, and the skin of the baby doll turned from pink to gray. And the size and the gray skin of the doll reminded me of the baby girl on the bloody towel, and I put it away where I wouldn't have to look at it.

Lately, though, it has surfaced again. Our daughter, two years old, likes to play with dolls. This morning I saw her playing with the little gray doll on the wood floor of our house, in the spring sunlight, and for that moment at least I felt lucky.

# THE LAKE OF SUFFERING

PHILLIP LOPATE

A bout a week after my baby daughter Lily was born, she began to throw up. Usually a gentle gush of whitish stuff would flow down her chin, and a minute later she would seem peaceful, no worse than before. Sometimes, however, the vomiting was harsher. Since my wife Cheryl was breast-feeding Lily, she wondered whether something was wrong with her technique (the angle of tilt, the pillow arrangement) or with the consistency of her milk.

We had been told that all babies "spit up." Part of our problem was that, Lily being our first child, we did not know how to distinguish between normal postnatal events and symptoms that should indeed alarm us. For instance, we rushed Lily to our amiable neighborhood pediatrician, Dr. Brenda, because blood seemed to be collecting in the umbilical area. It turned out this was a natural result of the umbilical plug falling out. Or when Lily got the hiccups (another benign occurrence), Cheryl frantically bade me read all the "hiccups" entries in the child-care manuals on our nightstand, to see what we could do to stop it. (Nothing.) As the entries did not alter when left unattended, I didn't see why I had to read every word aloud each time Lily started hiccupping, but it was indicative of how everything that first week made us nervous.

We had amassed a shelf full of baby books in the time between the start of Cheryl's pregnancy and Lily's delivery. My intellectualized response to any unknown situation is to buy a book; and since Cheryl designs books for a living, she also finds security in them. So we immersed ourselves in Dr. Spock, Penelope Leach, and the authors of the *What to Expect* series, among others.

I could write a whole essay about these infant-care books as a peculiar literary subcategory, the antithesis of the horror genre. Suffice to say that a butterscotch sauce of reassurance covers them all: they address new parents as a set of middle-class worrywarts, counseling you that your fears are natural, even your ambivalences are natural (Leach goes so far as to empathize with the husband who resents ceding oral monopoly of his wife's breast), but that underneath, you have nothing to worry about. Chronic illness, spinal taps, oncology, and death are not in their indexes. They are addressed to *well*-baby care. As soon as the reality sank in that we had a sick baby on our hands, I closed these volumes, never to consult them again.

But I am getting ahead of myself. Before plunging into the story of that first cruel year in the hospital, I want to pause and consider why we had so wanted a child.

During my first marriage, we were in our twenties, young and poor and ambitious to become writers and in no hurry to take on parental responsibilities. Our fertility seemed more a curse than a blessing, necessitating as it did two abortions. By the second abortion, the marriage was already tottering. I left it to embark on twenty-one years of bachelorhood. Whatever my political support for abortion, I began to regret the two chances for fathering I had personally let slip, and to feel, at times keenly, the absence of those children who might have been mine. This feeling was accentuated by ten years of working with elementary school kids, teaching them writing. I had stumbled into the profession as a way to support my own writing habit. Not expecting to be good with kids, to my great surprise I was, and I wrote up the experiences in my book, *Being with Children*, which led to my being considered (and regarding myself) as something of a child-expert.

When parents came by after school, I would sometimes go on about how much fun I'd had with their kids during the day, and they would invariably say, "Yeah, that's because you don't have to take care of them after three o'clock." I wasn't sure this was fair; their remarks became a challenge I was eager to accept. I certainly liked being around children and keeping up with their improvisatory moves. Why wouldn't I respond fairly well to my own?

By my mid-thirties, I was sold on having a child. The problem was, I first had to find a *wife*. By no means had I worked through the neurotic patterns of mistrust, cruelty, and abandonment that my mother and father had passed down to me as masculine-feminine relations. So I continued to stumble from one woman to the next until, at forty-seven, I met Cheryl. She was creative, attractive, humane, and last but not least, thirty-five. Two of Cheryl's painter friends—dynamic, accomplished, and lonely women in their late forties—noted wryly how typical it was that an eligible single man their age would marry someone twelve years younger. I understood their point, but I couldn't help it, I wanted a wife of childbearing age. That was important.

Everything else seemed to be in place. I had established myself as a writer, had a teaching post, and felt a certain largesse, a willingness to take on this new *work* (O sacred word) of bringing up baby. I fantasized loving my child unconditionally, as I had never been able to love before. To be honest, I was also secretly a bit bored with my professional life: I could no longer be motivated by fear of failure, as in younger years; I had written eight books, taught for twenty-five years, and anticipated more of the same. I wanted something else, some new adventure to engross me—a child.

Cheryl was at first resistant to the idea. She had yet to make it as a painter, and her income-producing work, graphic design, seemed to be taking her further away from her artistic dreams. She feared, legitimately, that much of the burden of child-rearing would fall on her, and that she would get lost in the process. Moreover, she wanted us to spend our first years of married life as a couple, by ourselves. A reasonable request, I thought. I could wait. Not indefinitely, but . . . "What if I *never* want to have children?" she asked. "Would you still love me? Stay married?" I swallowed hard, said yes, and meant it. In the back of my mind, though, I gambled that she would come around eventually.

Which she did. Three years into the marriage, she told me she was ready. She wanted to get pregnant in time for my fiftieth birthday party, giving me what she knew I wanted most in the world. As soon as Cheryl made up her mind, her eagerness to conceive began to outstrip my own. She kept saying, "If only I hadn't held out, if only we had started sooner!" It took us nine months to conceive—not long as these things go, but long enough to plunge us into high anxiety. Two months after I turned fifty, we received the happy news that Cheryl was pregnant, and on September 16, 1994, she gave birth to Lily.

That first week home with our baby, the shock of eighteen hours of contractions and an episiotomy fresh in our minds, we had no chance to catch our breaths before jumping onto the roller coaster. I am well aware that every new parent feels overwhelmed. How much of the initial hysteria would have occurred anyway, in optimum conditions? This is another form of the question that haunts us: What would the experience of parenting have been like if Lily had had nothing wrong with her?

Actually, by the end of the first week, Cheryl seemed a confident and placid mother. Then Lily started throwing up her milk. We took her to Dr. Brenda to be weighed, and found she had lost over a pound since birth. "Failure to thrive," those creepy, self-accusative words, were spoken for the first time, but only as a distant possibility. Brenda thought it might be gastroesophageal reflux; into alternative medicines, she recommended trying chamomile tea, which an Andean tribe fed their babies to calm their stomachs. She also had us supplement breast-feeding with formula twice a day, and Pedialyte (a Gatorade for infants that refurbishes electrolytes), to prevent dehydration.

So I began feeding a bottle to Lily. Cheryl was very critical of my efforts: "I can't believe how tensely you're holding her," she would say, or "Talk to her—no, not in that dead voice!" All these orders only made me more flustered. Underneath Cheryl's criticisms was a panic that unless we fed Lily letter-perfectly, she would throw up. (As we later learned, she was regurgitating not because of something so correctable as the bottle angle, but because her system couldn't process protein correctly.)

One Saturday, toward the end of the second week, I offered to watch the baby while Cheryl made herself breakfast. After giving Lily a feeding, I held her upright for about forty minutes, as I had been instructed, then let her sleep on the bed, supported by pillows. Lily was napping peacefully, when suddenly she woke up and began choking. Turned bright red. I lifted her in my arms to get her upright, but she arched her head rigidly away—choking, spewing, gasping for breath. It was the most frightening thing I'd ever seen. She's going to die, I thought, right in front of me, and I can't do anything. I was also terrified that this was a seizure and began thinking epilepsy, brain damage. "Cheryl," I began yelling. I tried to support her head but was amazed at the strength of her arching. Cheryl ran up the stairs and shouted, "You can't let her head go back, that's the worst thing in the world, she'll choke on her own vomit." I tried to explain that I'd been supporting her head to the best of my ability, but she cut me off, screaming, "Fuck you! You're killing my baby!" For a moment I was prepared to believe I had caused the whole thing, and shrank back, letting Cheryl take over. But the attack had seemed to possess a dynamic all its own; I knew deep down it wasn't my doing. (Later, the doctors confirmed that this head-arching is a familiar reflex in certain infants; nothing you can do but let it run its course.)

In retrospect, that red choking baby reminded me of something—the creature from *Alien*. I wonder how much horror imagery comes from our terror of the crying newborn. The theory that Mary Shelley wrote *Frankenstein* after losing her baby now makes sense to me.

I called Dr. Brenda, but she was away all weekend. In desperation I phoned Dr. Lou Monti, a pediatrician connected to Mt. Sinai, where Lily had been delivered. He suggested Lily be taken off the breast and given nothing but Pedialyte, and if she couldn't hold that down, bring her into the hospital for observation. Lily threw up the Pedialyte; we drove to Mt. Sinai, turning her over—with relief, I confess—to the high-tech medical establishment. Dr. Brenda, with her holistic, soothing chamomile methods, was off the case.

The initial diagnosis at Mt. Sinai was that Lily had a severe milk-soy allergy. Though it is rare for a baby to be allergic to her mother's milk, perhaps Lily was; or perhaps a little of the milk-based formula (it only takes a drop) had led to the stripping of her intestinal villi, the hairy coating that helps transfer nutrients. But I believed Lily's physiological problem, her "disease," was in place before she took in any formula, since she was already throwing up regularly. And while she *may* have had a milk-soy allergy as well, the fact that her problems with digestion persisted long after she was taken off milk-soy products leads me to suspect a deeper cause.

It is not easy for an unscientific layman like myself to explain the nature of Lily's problem—especially one so baffling to her doctors. In her first year of life, a good deal of effort was spent in eliminating possible diseases: pyloric stenosis, cystic fibrosis, lymphatic dysfunction, or some autoimmune disorder. The closest they ever came to a diagnosis was "protein-losing enteropathy," a vague way of saying that she has a problem with the transfer of amino acids. This causes some of the protein she takes in to "spill" into her bloodstream, instead of being absorbed by her cells as food. The albumen blood test measures the degree of protein absorption in the body. We began to live and die by two numbers: Lily's weight and her albumen level.

As soon as Lily was admitted to the hospital, Cheryl made a heroic and, I think, correct decision, that one of us would stay with the baby at all times. This meant, as it turned out, that Cheryl spent a year in the hospital, putting her own life on hold, sleeping (or trying to, in the interruptive nocturne of clinics) on a cot next to Lily's crib. Some nights I or my mother-in-law would spell her. But for the most part Cheryl wanted to be there, to oversee that the erratic night staff did not make a mistake with one of Lily's meds or her food pumps. Just as important was the guarantee that Lily would receive as much stimulation as possible, keeping her mentally sharp. We had seen some ward babies, left to the hit-and-run care of nurses and attendants, who would stare listlessly up at the ceiling for hours or keep wailing until someone had a moment to look in on them. Cheryl's vigilance paid off; but it also took a toll. Sleep deprivation and constant worry made her depressed, angry; she lost weight and felt bruised all over.

If the arrival of children routinely places a couple under pressure, nothing can put more stress on a marriage than having a sick child. In our case, each of us had a different way of handling stress. Cheryl's heroism took the form of mastering all the physical procedures involved with Lily's care, so that she could assist. Indeed, she became so adept that nurses would often let her do their jobs. But she got furious with anything that looked like bungling: she would throw interns out of the room if they took too long finding a vein to draw blood from Lily, or forbid anyone (even surgeons) from approaching the crib without washing their hands first. She was a tiger protecting her cub.

My way of facing the crisis was to stay calm, pleasant, stoic, even-tempered, and hopeful. I also tried to be a "supportive" husband, though whenever Cheryl's anxiety rounded into an attack on me, I regrettably withdrew some of this support. Mostly I struggled just to hang in.

Before this experience I'd suffered my share of traumas, betrayals, unhappy love affairs, deaths. But in a sense I'd led a charmed life, in that I always felt strong enough for the circumstances that presented themselves. In fact, I had often felt stronger than my circumstances, fantasizing a reserve tank of energy and courage that I might tap into if, suddenly, I found myself in a situation like war. Faced with the experience of Lily's illness, I quickly went through my reserve tank. I was discovering the irregular nature of courage: two days of pluck, two of bitching and breakdown. Besides, heroism seemed beside the point; patience was needed. A different virtue, more demanding, in the face of exhaustion. Now we were In It. I understood what it meant now to suffer, *really* suffer, night and day: to be in up to our necks in the lake of suffering.

I was commuting in a triangle between Hofstra (my teaching job) on Long Island, Mt. Sinai Hospital on the Upper East Side of Manhattan, and our home in Brooklyn, where I crashed and fed the cats. Often I would drive to Mt. Sinai directly from work, taking the Long Island Expressway to the Midtown Tunnel, then up the FDR Drive to 96th Street, relinquishing any residue of work-joy the closer I approached the hospital.

The neighborhood around Mt. Sinai, how well I came to know it. Those sad takeout places, those bleak sandwich shops, bars, and restaurants, the five-story brick tenements along Madison Avenue, the borderline air. It seemed fitting that Mt. Sinai existed in a no-man's-land between the posh, elegant apartment buildings below 96th Street and the East Harlem projects that started above 100th Street, because as soon as I entered the hospital complex, I had the feeling that I was nowhere, crawling past the soda machines in the underground tunnel that connects one wing to the other, along with other marked creatures. A whole planet of illness, a leper colony. I would take the elevator up to the fourth floor, making room for gurneys, and prepare to hold my breath for five, six, eight hours. The hospital felt like a spaceship. No up or down. White. Weightless.

After you had spent a time-crawling morning and afternoon in the hospital, etherized with small talk, inedible meals on trays, and diaper changes, the doctor would arrive around four, on his rounds, and everyone would snap to attention: the day would acquire a shape, good or bad, depending on the words he dropped or his tone of voice.

Fifty years ago, a baby with Lily's problems would most likely have died. Then came the invention of catheter technology: a device surgically attached to a main artery, which transmitted a steady stream of nutriments to the bloodstream, bypassing the stomach entirely. The catheter was a godsend; but it had a tendency to become infected at the entry site after a few months, which meant it would have to be removed and another artery found. (The body has a limited number of arteries for this purpose.) Catheters also require cumbersome tubes and a stationary pump, making a baby patient less mobile, more awkward to hold.

Terrifying as the catheter was, we also disliked the less surgically invasive nasogastric tube, which went down Lily's nose. Not only did it mar the perfection of her face and give her skin rashes, but it required a nasty insertion procedure: you had to stick a tube down her nostril and keep pushing until it came to rest in her stomach, all the while with her flailing, screaming and twisting her head to avoid that unpleasant gagging sensation. She soon figured out how to yank the tube out of her nose: flick a fingernail under the surgical tape and rip it loose, triumphantly. Then we would have to hold her down, ignoring her wails, and reinsert it.

The hospital universe preoccupied us. Though I still loved the outside world, it began to recede in reality, partly as a consequence of our isolation: no one on the outside knew what we were going through, and we couldn't explain it to them. I would get home some nights and find messages on the answering machine from friends and relatives: "Tell us what's happening, we can't stand the suspense." They wanted to hear that everything was okay. It wasn't. Some people still didn't know about Lily's illness and would leave messages saying, "Congratulations! You must be on cloud nine!" I would try to get through these calls as speedily as possible. As the gregarious one, it was my job to stay "in touch" with the world. But after several conversations, relaying the same information, I felt awful.

I began to suspect people's motives (idle curiosity? *Schadenfreude?*). Sometimes the little things they said seemed so insensitive: a friend bragging how much her child was eating, another forever mentioning news items about medical breakthroughs in a different field, or telling some anecdote about a second cousin who was born with stomach problems and now played tackle for his high school football team. Yet I knew that if they didn't call, I would also have felt slighted. I came to realize that there was literally nothing anyone on the outside could say or do that would be right. The only person I could talk to without feeling wounded was my friend Max, who had a little girl with problems even more serious than Lily's. I remember when his baby was born in a coma, with disabilities resultant from a botched delivery; I thought his situation unimaginably pitiable. Now we shared the same vocabulary: catheters, cyclotrons. Max was my reality check. He told me that when it first happened, he refused to talk on the phone and hated everyone. Now he just hated most people.

It irritated me that friends and relatives, unable to grasp the nature of Lily's problem, wanted me to go over and over the details; and when it didn't get solved right away, they told me to change doctors, though we had the best. "The problem is a larger social one," Dr. Leleiko, Lily's chief physician, told me. "In America, babies are not supposed to be sick. If they're sick, people expect one of two outcomes: one, the baby dies; two, it gets all better. Americans don't know how to deal with chronic illness."

Of course, Lily was not just a medical problem but an increasingly defined little person whom you couldn't help but fall in love with— a charmer, who "lured people in," as one doctor put it. First (I say this as an unbiased father), she was the most startlingly beautiful baby, with porcelain skin, flashing dark eyes, long eyelashes, masses of brown hair, cupid lips. "Like a doll," everyone said. And her mother dressed her in refined costumes, accentuating her old-fashioned, Victorian-doll look. Second, she had remarkable interpersonal skills: from the moment her eyes could focus, she would fix you with an interested gaze, follow you around the room, react with pleasure or laughter if any opportunity offered, allow herself to be held and hugged by visitors, and generally flatter them with her attention. It is conceivable that babies like Lily, who undergo early the pain of needles, splints, CT scans, and spinal taps, may develop survival skills that enable them to mature faster in order to attract the love of adults. Lily was the pet, the darling of the ward: sometimes she would be brought up to the nursing station, catheter pump and all, and hang out amid doctors and nurses having conferences, ordering up meds and takeout food, answering the phones. Her three male physicians competed for her love. The best attendants on the floor—Aloma and Averill from the West Indies, and Chilean Norma—were all devoted to Lily: bathed her, changed her, sang to her, helped her stand, encouraged her to take her first steps around the crib. One hospital study, I was told, confirmed that babies perceived as "cute" receive more care than those seen as homely. Lily's beauty and winning ways seemed at times a Lamarckian compensation.

In March, Lily looked healthier, and there was much talk about going home in a few weeks. Then the lab test came back, showing her albumen level down to 3.1. No one knew the reason for this setback: maybe they were pushing her too fast, maybe it was a lab error.

I remember vividly one night around that time when, to cheer us up, one of our favorite nurses, Suzanne, came in with two gifts: pearl earrings for Cheryl, and a tape of Disney's *The Lion King*, which had just gone on sale that day. Suzanne wheeled the floor's VCR and TV into our room so that Cheryl, Lily, and I could all watch the movie in bed. (This was a powerful fantasy of Cheryl's: that we would all be at home someday, lying comfortably on a bed together.)

*The Lion King* opens with scenes of rejoicing over a newborn, which hit us with special poignancy. I dozed through the middle: I was so tired those days, I would nod out as soon as you put me in front of a TV. Lily and Cheryl napped too. When it was over, Lily seemed restless, so Cheryl decided to feed her. I prepared the bottle. Lily was crying and agitated as the bottle approached. I thought: Something's wrong, let's not do this. But we went ahead anyway, because we felt it important to keep up the habit of oral feeding. Cheryl brought the bottle to Lily's lips, and Lily puked up everything, all over her mother's blouse. For mesmerizing spectacle, there was still nothing like Lily throwing up. "Get some cloth diapers, a wet washcloth, do something!" yelled Cheryl. I had frozen in the spectator role, while castigating myself: Why didn't I speak up? Warn her not to feed Lily? Well, Cheryl was the one in charge, I didn't feel I had the authority. But why were we always looking for someone to blame for Lily's throw-ups, as though they were only a matter of human error?

Shortly after the *Lion King* episode, we agreed to Dr. Leleiko's recommendation that we suspend oral feedings. Leleiko had wanted to regulate strictly the quantities Lily was receiving and did not like these random extra feeds; he also feared that they might exacerbate Lily's tendency to vomit, since liquid was being introduced from the bottle at a faster rate than drips through the tube. Cheryl had been resisting his advice, afraid that, if we suspended bottle feedings, it might be difficult to get Lily to take food through her mouth later (which in fact happened). This time we acceded. Maybe it was the wrong decision.

Seven months into this ordeal, we wanted desperately to get Lily out of the hospital: that became our main focus. Aside from our own burnout, she kept getting set back by flus. In a children's hospital, you pick up every infectious ailment. Fortunately she was doing well at the moment, her albumen level had risen, all the way up to 4. We had battled with the insurance companies and even gotten them to agree to give us night nursing. (Since Lily was still on a catheter at the time, she would require constant supervision during her nocturnal feeds.) Finally we got the word: we could go home. The nursing staff threw us a going-away party, we drank champagne, packed up the room, and said goodbye to Mt. Sinai.

I was surprised that Cheryl did not seem happier. Here a major character difference asserted itself, which may have something to do with gender, or the different roles of father and mother. As soon as I ascertained that Lily was not in mortal danger, I breathed a huge sigh of relief, whereas Cheryl continued to be anxious and distraught because no one could give her a clear answer as to what was wrong with Lily. Feeding a child is so basic a part of a mother's functioning that she could not sit still and wait for some far-off solution. "Will this child ever eat normally?" she kept demanding. She fretted if Lily's stools were becoming looser, or if her skin looked blotchy. At the time I thought her alarmist; but I must admit now that Cheryl's pessimism made her more quickly observant of the dangers Lily faced. It was Cheryl who, two weeks after we came home, voiced what I had been thinking but dared not say: that Lily was starting to look puffy. "I'll bet her albumen's gone way down," Cheryl predicted. "Oh, not necessarily," I said. "It could be just a cold."

A month later we were back on the ward. All the symptoms had returned, one by one. Her albumen had plummeted to 2.4, which only confirmed the external signs: throwing up, diarrhea, swelling in the face and fingers, distended stomach, lethargy. I was living a recurring nightmare. The first day back in the hospital, I felt a powerful desire to write the whole story of Lily's illness; the words were marching through my head, and writing seemed the only way of expressing the emotions inside me. The next day I felt devastated, had no desire to write, wanted to lie in a fetal position and be fed intravenously myself.

Cheryl took it better, was stronger at that moment, perhaps because she *was* a pessimist. I had directed all my energy to getting out of the hospital: we had made it, I was happy, I felt we had put the whole sorry story behind us. And then to go back in made me insane. I didn't know what to live for anymore. A healthy Lily, of course. But how? And what was the matter with her in the first place?

Cheryl admitted the next day that she was trying to fight down a major depression. She had just enough energy to attend to Lily and the medical arena but not to the outside world. Even comments in the street about normal babies would scald. She had stopped returning friends' phone calls. Other people couldn't give her what she wanted, so she had no interest in them.

"What do you want from them?" I asked.

"An answer. To make the problem go away. To unplug it. I know it's irrational, but I have so much anger against the world. And so much guilt, for bringing a sick child into it."

"Why guilt? What do you have to be guilty for?"

"You're not a mother, you wouldn't understand. I feel guilty, that's all. As for distraction, people telling me I should get out more, jog around the park, see a movie—it's a joke! I'm not interested."

More setbacks, other recoveries. A little over a year after she was born, Lily came home, seemingly for good. (The "seemingly" is a fingers-crossed gesture.) She had gotten so much attention that when we finally took her home, she tested on track for her age, no intellectual or physical lags to speak of—which we were told is rare for a baby institutionalized her first year. Since then she has shown even more remarkable mental powers: speaking early, forming complex sentences and jokes, flashing a large vocabulary. At three years old, she is quite the chatterbox, quite the beautiful young ballerina. She also has the sweetest personality and is unusually perceptive and considerate. She has not been on the catheter for over a year. But—she still throws up more than she should, which tells us her constitution remains fragile, and she is still fed via n.g. tube. (Eventually, we changed the entry site of the n.g. tube from her nose to her stomach. This was better, because it was hidden from strangers' sight and Lily herself could forget about its existence, meaning we no longer had to watch her every second so she wouldn't tear it out.) She now gets forty-five-minute feedings five times a day and can run free the rest of the time.

She still, alas, doesn't show much interest in taking food orally, perhaps because she missed the earlier milestones and is afraid of gagging, though there is nothing anatomically wrong to prevent swallowing. We could always cut off her feed and see if hunger prompted her to learn more quickly, but that would be a risky gamble, especially as she is small for her age. The doctors, meanwhile, are sanguine that she will eat and that her malabsorption problem will resolve itself in time.

As for fatherhood, if anything it is a lovelier, richer, more compelling experience than I could have imagined. As I'd hoped, but more so, I love Lily to distraction. She is, as the saying goes, "the love of my life." That she made me enter the Kingdom of Anxiety, which is the lot of all parents, seems a small price to pay for the plenitude of her being.

Some might say that my pride in wanting a child to "complete" me, and my smug expectation of a perfectly healthy one, brought down the wrath of God as a lesson in humility. The problem is that I am no more humble than when I started out, and I am too humble to think myself important enough for God to bother punishing for the sin of pride. I have my doubts that the sufferings I've undergone constitute a valuable lesson, or have made me a better person; and certainly the sufferings Lily has undergone seem to me entirely, enragingly undeserved. What kind of God would put a child through such physical pain to chastise the conceit of her father? However, since I don't believe in God, it is childish to berate the non-Deity. The point is that the divine Lily is alive, and for that I am very grateful.

# THE GHOST MOTHER

### MARLY SWICK

,

The first night the girl is in the house, I don't sleep at all. In the morning she sleeps late, still tired from the flight, I assume, even though we are two hours ahead of her time. Clifford tippy-toes around the bedroom and bathroom as he shaves and dresses for a 10 a.m. meeting at Paramount. His exaggerated effort not to disturb her—probably sound asleep in the guest room down the hall—irritates me. I want to say "Knock it off. She's only a knocked-up teenager, not some visiting dignitary." But I know how awful that will sound. When he swoops over for his good-luck kiss, I pretend to have fallen back asleep.

As soon as I hear his car back out of the driveway, I haul myself out of bed, down the hall past her closed door, and into the bright sunny kitchen. Another cloudless day in Southern California. The girl is from Wahoo, Nebraska. Too perfect.

Our best friends, Buddy and Eleanor, fellow Hollywood hacks, went berserk when we told them and accused Clifford of making it up. "We've got dibs on it," Clifford had said sternly. "After all, it's *our* life."

When the girl contacted us in response to our ad in the local newspaper, she said she had always wanted to live in California. She wanted to know if we had a swimming pool. She wanted to know if we were involved in "show business," as she called it, rather quaintly. She seemed pleased when we answered yes on both counts but still said she needed a week to think it over. She said she was also considering couples in Tampa and Santa Rosa. That night we FedExed her Polaroids of our kidney-shaped pool with the sun sparkling on the blue, blue water, along with a picture of the two of us in what would be the baby's room, and two videocassettes—an episode of *The Waltons* I'd worked on and an ill-fated TV pilot about a farm family in Iowa Clifford had written. We figured we'd cover all the bases: the glamour of Hollywood coupled with the wholesomeness of the heartland. The whole time she was making up her mind, I held my breath. I dreamed about her. She had long wheaty hair and teeth as strong and even as a row of corn kernels. Halfway through the week she called once to ask if it would be okay if she brought her cat. I hesitated for a moment—Clifford is allergic to cats—and then said sure, fine, we'd be honored to have her cat. The next night she called and said she had reached her decision: We were the ones.

Pouring myself a second cup of coffee, I frown at the clock on the stove. Ten thirty-five. Twelve thirty-five Nebraska time. Clifford and I have always been early risers, high-energy overachievers. Now, instead of the sleepless nights everyone warns you about, I picture us standing over the crib of a sluggish, complacent baby, tapping our fingers, waiting impatiently for it to wake up. I don't know what's suddenly come over me. I don't know where all these nasty, negative thoughts are coming from. Like any good liberal, I have always championed the nurture side of the nature-versus-nurture debate, but the moment the girl stepped off the plane, I found myself harshly scrutinizing her for possible undesirable genes: stringy hair, bitten-down nails, bad grammar. In the car during the ride home from LAX, I sat silent as a judge while Clifford made amiable conversation with the girl. From time to time, he would look over at me and smile encouragingly, probably thinking I was struck dumb with shyness or choked up with emotion, while the girl exclaimed over all the Mercedeses and Jaguars and the palm trees and the balmy temperature. She said it had been five below with the windchill factor in Nebraska that morning. She stuck her head out the window like a dog. Clifford chuckled, seemingly enchanted, even though his eyes were already starting to water and itch in reaction to the cat, which she had immediately released from its carrier. Doped up as it was on tranquilizers, the cat managed a feeble hiss as I reached back to pet it. I sighed and popped an aspirin, without water—a trick I had learned while sitting bumper-to-bumper in freeway traffic jams.

Everything about her annoyed me. After three years of fertility specialists—tests, drugs, inseminations, in vitro—it had come down to this: some gum-chewing, wide-eyed teenager in fake pink Reeboks. A domestic import from Norman Rockwell country. *Midwestward ho!* is the cry of all of us prospective baby buyers from the coasts. You go to Hong Kong for silk, Italy for leather, Switzerland for watches, and the prairie for private adoptions. All this talk about crack babies and fetal alcohol syndrome has us running scared. Buying a baby brings out all your most embarrassing retro instincts, straight out of Laura Ingalls Wilder and *The Mary Tyler Moore Show.*

"Where's the beach?" the girl had asked—frowning suspiciously, as if the entire state of California had perpetrated a huge media hoax—and even though we were only a couple of blocks from our house, Clifford had indulgently swung the car around and headed off in the opposite direction, toward the Pacific Coast Highway. We drove a couple of miles up the coast and then pulled off into one of the deserted parking lots. It was dark already, but you could see the white ruffle of surf and hear the waves swooshing and thudding. The girl got out of the car and kicked off her shoes. As she scuffled across the sand toward the water, Clifford reached over and put his arm around me. "It's going to be fine," he said, squeezing my hand for emphasis. "She's not going to change her mind."

I nodded but didn't squeeze back. For the past month, ever since she had chosen us over the couples in Tampa and Santa Rosa, I had been scared to death she would change her mind. I sighed and pulled my hand away. "But what if I change *my* mind?"

He laughed, as if I had made a joke. "All sales are final. No refunds or exchanges."

I forced a little laugh even though it wasn't so funny. We had paid ten thousand dollars to a private adoption broker. Less than a Honda Civic, Clifford had pointed out philosophically. When we told Buddy and Eleanor, Buddy said, why not pay fifteen and get ourselves a Buick? Who wanted an economy baby?

As the girl waded in the surf, the cat in the back seat suddenly seemed to sense her absence and sprang to life, scratching and yowling at the upholstery. At the sound of the cat, Clifford started to sneeze in violent little arpeggios. I got out of the car and hollered for the girl, waving my arms until she finally looked up. She sprinted back up the beach. She was wearing a baggy, drop-waist dress—the kind that all the young girls were wearing—and you couldn't really tell for certain that she was pregnant unless you already knew. The baby wasn't due for another ten weeks. That was part of the deal. She wanted a place to stay. She didn't want to stick around Wahoo once she really started to show. And we were only too eager to oblige. We wanted, we said, to be involved. We wanted everyone to get to know and like each other.

The instant she climbed back into the car, the cat calmed down.

"Your cat was upset," I said.

"Poor baby," she crooned, scratching behind her ears. The cat purred mechanically, as if she had flicked some switch. "I've had Bobbie since I was six years old," she said. "Her full name is Bobbie Sox." The cat was jet black except for its paws, which looked like they had been dunked in a can of paint.

"You got any Kleenex?" Clifford asked me.

I rummaged in my purse and handed him a wad of tissues. He blew his nose and wiped his red, runny eyes as we pulled back out onto the highway.

"Look, there's the ocean!" the girl said, holding the cat up to the window and pointing. The cat sniffed the ocean breeze indifferently. "Wow, I really love it here." She sighed in starry-eyed contentment and settled back in her seat.

"Good!" Clifford handed me his soggy Kleenex to dispose of and beamed at her in the rearview mirror.

"Do you have a cold?" she asked. "Want me to roll up the window?"

"No, no," he shook his head. "I'm fine. Just a touch of hay fever."

The girl leaned forward and gave Clifford a spontaneous hug, then looked at me uncertainly, like a dog waiting for you to reach out your hand and pet it. "This must be hard for you," she said.

I was surprised, caught off guard, embarrassed. "Harder on you," I mumbled. Which was true enough, although somehow I didn't really believe it. The only thing in my whole life I had ever failed at was getting pregnant, and here was this semiliterate pom-pom girl who had succeeded without even trying.

Down the hall, at last, I hear the water pipes groaning to life in the bathroom. Ten fifty-five. From the clock, my glance shifts downward to her purse, slumped there on the kitchen counter. A gaudy striped woven bag that looks like a deflated beach ball. The shower blasts on, and the shower curtain screeches shut. The purse draws me like a magnet. The zipper is half-open, and I can't help myself. I don't know what I expect to find, but what I find is just what you would expect to find in a teenage girl's purse: lipstick, mascara, Dentyne, a couple of movie ticket stubs, an old hairbrush with a rat's nest of cornsilk hair entwined in the stubby bristles, a couple of packets of honey-roasted peanuts from the airplane—one of which has split open. At the bottom of the purse, loose sticky peanuts are glommed onto shreds of Kleenex and a couple of stray bobby pins and tobacco flakes. When I see the tobacco flakes, I have to restrain myself from marching down the hall and demanding to know whether she has been smoking during the pregnancy. The adoption broker assured us repeatedly that the girl did not do drugs, drink, or smoke. If he was wrong about the smoking, who knew what else he was wrong about?

As the shower continues to run, I pull a fat shabby pink wallet out of the bag and study her driver's license. Giselle Marie Nelson. *Height* 5'5", *Weight* 115, *Eyes* blue, *Hair* blond. *Birth date* 7/5/74. It is not a flattering picture. The camera has caught her with her eyes half-closed and a self-conscious twitch of a smile. It looks as if her hair is growing out of a bad perm, half-straight and half-frizzy, like the fur of some mythical hybrid beast. I flip to a picture of her family, a posed studio portrait. Straight out of central casting. The parents, Giselle, two younger brothers, and a dog. All blond, even the dog. In the bathroom down the hall I hear the shower clunk off, and I flip quickly through the other cloudy plastic windows, thinking maybe there will be a picture of the boy, the father, but all I find are some grandparents and a couple of girlfriends' class photos. The girlfriends are also blond, blue-eyed, and pert-nosed; they could all be sisters. Disappointed and vaguely relieved, I slide the wallet back into the purse.

An instant later the girl appears in the doorway clad in an oversize hot-pink T-shirt and rubber thongs. "Hi," she says. "I thought I'd lie out by the pool. I mean if that's okay." Her long wet hair drips down the front of her T-shirt, her inflated breasts. She twists a strand nervously, then reaches into her purse for the hairbrush.

"Great." I nod and smile. "How about some breakfast?"

She shakes her head. I wince as she yanks the cheap wire bristles through her hair. Something brushes against my ankles. The cat mews once experimentally and then again more peremptorily. "Looks like someone wants breakfast," I say brightly. Glad for something to do, I walk over and open the cupboard, where I have stocked up on a variety of gourmet cat food. "I didn't know what she likes"—I start pulling cans out—"Chicken, liver, seafood"—as the cat continues to kvetch at my feet.

The girl seems stunned and befuddled by the selection. "Usually she just eats dry food."

"I'll pick up some dry food later," I say, vaguely miffed, "but for now, how about seafood?" I open the can briskly and scoop its smelly contents into a bowl. The cat lunges for the bowl before it even touches down.

"Now. How about you? Are you sure you don't want something to eat? You must be starved. We've got eggs, cereal, English muffins." I laugh. "You've heard about Jewish mothers?"

The girl looks at the cat greedily smacking away at its bowl. "Maybe an English muffin," she says meekly. "But I can fix it myself."

"It's your first morning." I pull out a chair and gesture for her to take a seat. "Just relax."

As I cut and toast a muffin, she says, "I've never known any Jewish people before. At first I was sort of worried about the baby not celebrating Christmas and all, but then my friend Leslie, who used to live on Long Island, said you get presents for eight days and that seems okay. I mean, it might even be better, spacing it out and all like that." She pulls a wad of hair out of the brush bristles and shoves it into her purse, then falls abruptly silent, as if afraid she might have said something to offend me.

I smile to show that I am completely unoffended. The cat, having licked the bowl clean, starts acting weird, pacing and circling the kitchen. "Does she need to go out?" I set the toasted muffin on the table along with a jar of marmalade.

"She's an indoor cat. She's been declawed." The girl spreads a thick layer of marmalade on the muffin and takes a huge bite. "Do you have a kitty litter box?"

I shake my head. Great, I think, a smelly cat box. But I smile stoically and say, "No problem. I'll just zip out to the store and get something." Happy for an excuse to get off by myself for a few minutes, I grab my car keys off the counter. "Do you want anything while I'm out?"

The girl is holding the cat on her lap, nuzzling her face in its fur like a little girl with a stuffed animal. It occurs to me how alone and scared she must feel. I pause on my way out the door and attempt a reassuring motherly smile. "How about a matinee later?"

She shrugs and nods. "Sure, if you want to."

"Good. Back in a flash. There's beach towels in the linen closet."

I head out to the carport and then think of something else. When I duck my head back into the kitchen, she is down on her hands and knees with a wad of paper towels, cleaning up a mess the cat has made the minute my back was turned. When she sees me, she jumps guiltily.

"I'm sorry. She never does this," she says. "It's just that she doesn't have her box."

"No problem. It's my fault. I should have thought of it myself." I sniff the air and walk over and take a charred English muffin out of the toaster oven.

"I'm sorry," she says again. She looks about ready to burst into tears as I toss the muffin into the trash. "Don't be silly. There's plenty." I hand her the pack of muffins. "I just wanted to tell you there's suntan lotion in the medicine chest. Be sure to use something strong. You don't want to get burned your first day out."

My little bit of motherly advice seems to relax her some. "You

think maybe you could pick up some Canfield's diet chocolate soda?"
she asks timidly as I'm heading out the door for the second time.

"Sure," I say. "Anything else?"

She shakes her head, then says, "Well, maybe some potato chips.
Pringles, you know, the kind in the can. I'm sort of addicted to them."

I fish a little notepad out of my purse and dutifully jot this down,
inwardly moaning at such trashy prenatal nutrition. The phone rings.
I don't bother to pick it up. It's only Eleanor wanting to know how
it's going so far with "The Incubator," as she has taken to referring
to the girl. I cringe and blush, but the girl, intent upon buttering her
second muffin, seems oblivious. To cover my embarrassment, I adopt
a businesslike tone and ask the girl if she knows how to work the
answering machine. She shakes her head, her mouth full of muffin.
"Just let it ring for now," I sigh. "I'll show you later."

On the way back out to the carport, I sneak a glance in at her
through the window. She is eating ravenously, as if she has not eaten
for days, and talking to the cat in between mouthfuls. I can't quite
make out the words, but it sounds like some sort of pep talk. When
I get back from the store, the girl is floating on the raft in the pool
and the cat is sunning itself next to a bowl of fruit on the dining
room table. I chase the cat onto the floor and lead her to the utility
room to acquaint her with her new kitty litter box. She blinks up at
me unimpressed. It is a hot day, high eighties, and I imagine the girl
must be thirsty. I watch her through the window as I pour some
Canfield's diet chocolate soda into a glass of ice. The stuff looks
revolting and I had to go to three stores to find it, but when I take a
sip, I have to admit it's not bad. The girl has on a tropical print bikini
and is lying on her back, trailing her hands in the water. My gaze
lingers on her naked belly, hovering above the water like a pale moon.
As my eyes trace the smooth warm curve of it, I grip the icy glass so
tight, it almost slips out of my hand. How weird life is, I think as I
trot outside: some sixteen-year-old girl in Nebraska gets carried away
in the back seat of some boy's car after some prom or other, and now
here she is, floating in my back yard, our baby floating inside of her.
If our newspaper ad had appeared a couple of months earlier or later,
it would be some other girl, some other baby. Somehow this thought
depresses me. I prefer to think of this as fate, destiny, a thread in

some grand design. According to some celestial, all-wise and knowing weaver, *this* baby was meant for Clifford and me.

"Hi," I say, then realize she's wearing a Walkman and can't hear me. I shudder to think what sort of musical education the fetus is receiving. Kneeling down, I make waves in the water until she raises her head and sees me. "Want a drink?" I hold up the glass. "Canfield's."

She paddles herself over toward the edge of the pool, and I hand her the glass. "Thanks," she says. "It's so great here I can't believe it. I feel like a movie star."

"Your nose looks pink. Did you use the sunscreen?"

She nods.

"Well, I think maybe you should put some more on. The sun's very strong here."

"Okay." She shrugs and drains the dregs of her soda. She hands me her glass, and I hand her the Bain de Soleil 15 in lieu of the Hawaiian cocoa butter she must have brought with her.

"You want any lunch?" I glance at my watch. "It's twelve thirty. I can make you a sandwich."

She shakes her head. "I'm fine."

"Tuna? Ham and cheese?" I bend down and check the thermometer attached to the aluminum ladder. "Or I could make a salad."

"Okay. Tuna sounds good. Thanks. But I don't want to be any trouble."

"It's no trouble. I'm hungry too," I assure her, although I generally skip lunch.

"You're going to be a good mother," she jokes as I walk back toward the house. For some reason the joke irritates me. Although I am glad to see that she has some sort of sense of humor. Of irony, even. Clifford and I would hate to have a baby with no sense of humor.

The instant I open the can of tuna, the cat materializes at my feet. Through the window I can see the girl turn over onto her stomach, a painstakingly clumsy maneuver, and I bet she hasn't put any sunscreen on her back. As I mince the onion, I glance irritably at my watch. I should be at the computer, working on the revised treatment I'd promised Al Denker at NBC by the end of the month. And the afternoon was shot, too, since I'd promised to take her to a matinee.

Still, it was her first day here, two thousand miles from home, and I couldn't very well just ignore her. It was just typical somehow that Clifford was all booked up for the day so that taking care of the girl was my responsibility. Long ago, when I had first decided to have a baby, I had come to terms with the fact that no matter how noble Clifford's intentions, I had better be prepared to take on the bulk of the grunt work. But that was the baby, not the baby's mother, which was a different matter altogether.

The cat was whining pitifully. I set the tuna can on the floor by its water dish to shut it up and then got the mayonnaise and pickles out of the refrigerator. As I scooped out the last of the Hellmann's, I recalled Eleanor joking that I had better stock up on Miracle Whip —everyone, she claimed, was addicted to Miracle Whip in the Midwest. The girl's eyes were closed. She looked blissfully peaceful floating out there. Her long hair shone like silver in the bright sun. I had to admit she was a pretty girl. And seemed to be polite and considerate. There was nothing about her, really, to account for the sudden wave of hostility—so intense I'd actually felt nauseated—that seemed to hit me the moment I saw her walk off the plane. I had recognized her at once, from the picture she'd sent us; she looked just like how I'd imagined she would look, no surprises there. The only surprise was my reaction.

For weeks, I had been waiting impatiently for her arrival. She was all I talked about: "Giselle this, Giselle that . . ." I had called and asked her what her favorite color was (purple) and redecorated the guest room in various shades of lavender. I put a tape player in the room and gave Zoe, Buddy and Eleanor's teenage daughter, a hundred dollars to buy some cassettes she thought Giselle would like. "How do I know what someone from Nebraska would like?" Zoe had protested, but she had done it, secretly pleased—Eleanor assured me—to have been called in as a consultant. Before falling asleep at night, I would create little scenarios—like scenes from one of my family sitcoms—about how it would be when she finally arrived. I pictured us shopping, going to the gym, making dinner, wandering through museums, eating club sandwiches at the Bullock's Wilshire Tea Room. Girl stuff. Growing up with two brothers, I had always wanted a sister. That I was, in fact, old enough to be her mother, I didn't like to think about. Somehow in my fantasy script, I saw us more like two teenage girls whispering and giggling while Clifford brought us dishes of ice cream and smiled indulgently.

A couple of times my best friend, Eleanor, never known for her tact, tried to hint at some darker, more complicated picture. *Don't you worry she'll get too attached?* she had asked. *What about afterward? Are you going to stay in touch? Send her photos? Let her visit?* I could tell Eleanor thought it was a bad idea letting Giselle come live with us. She thought the whole transaction should be quick and businesslike, like a drug deal in the middle of the night in some deserted parking lot. But Clifford argued that it was better this way, our all getting to know each other. It was more humane and personal. In the long run, he felt, it would be healthier for all of us. Eleanor said she just hoped we knew what we were doing. I assured her we did.

But now, as I cut the sandwich in half and dump a handful of Pringles onto the plate, I am not so sure. When I glance outside, the raft is empty. A quick check reveals that the girl is not in the water or anywhere in the yard. Guiltily I imagine her in her room packing her suitcase while I look helplessly on.

ME: *What are you doing? You aren't leaving?*

HER: *I can't take this hostility. (She dumps a handful of underwear into her open suitcase.) I know you're trying to act nice, but I can feel it. It's not my fault you couldn't get pregnant. (The cat sets itself down on a pile of clothes in the middle of the suitcase, and she shoos it away.) I wish I couldn't get pregnant.*

ME: *I don't know what you mean. Clifford and I are overjoyed to have you here.*

HER: *Maybe he is. But you've got a problem. I may be from Nebraska, but I'm not completely insensitive.*

ME:

As I am trying to think what to say, something that will change her mind so that I won't have to explain to Clifford why she suddenly up and left, I hear the toilet flush and the thud of her bare feet tramping down the hall toward the kitchen.

"You were right," she says. "My nose is completely fried." She sits down at the table and I slide the sandwich over to her. "I want to get some postcards when we go out later." She breaks off a little glob of tuna and feeds it to the cat. "Leslie, my best friend, said she was almost jealous. I promised to write to her every day."

Leaning casually against the sink, I tear the foil off a yogurt container and eat a couple of spoonfuls. "What about the boy—you know—the father?"

"Oh, him." She shrugs and frowns down at her thigh, pressing a finger into her flesh to see if she's sunburned. "Forget him."

She seems suddenly to have lost her appetite. She continues feeding globs of tuna to the cat. If she were my own daughter, I would make her stop. Don't feed the cat from the table, I'd say. And no doubt my daughter would frown and sigh and keep right on doing what she was doing. Suddenly the thought of being anyone's mother seems way beyond me, a task for which I am monumentally unprepared and unsuited. Whatever made me think I was cut out for this line of work? "Listen—" I say.

"Wait!" She grabs my hand and places it on her belly. "It's kicking. Feel it?"

I nod solemnly, feeling the tears pushing against my closed eyelids, the tightening in my throat. This whole thing is too, too weird. Crazy. I snatch my hand away.

"Do you have names picked out?" she asks.

I shake my head, toss my yogurt carton into the trash, and hand her the Calendar section of the *Times*. "Pick a movie you'd like to see. I'll be back in a minute. I've got a load of laundry to put in."

Trembling all over, I lock myself in our bedroom and fling myself down onto the unmade king-size bed. I look at the digital clock on the night table. Clifford should be home by the time we get back from the matinee. While the girl is changing for dinner—Clifford promised to take her to a real Hollywood restaurant—I will take him aside and say, "This is an impossible situation. It's creepy. It's like something out of *The Handmaid's Tale*. Believe me, it's never going to work, so let's just call it quits right now. She can call those couples in Tampa and Santa Rosa back. Or we can help her to find someone else. She can keep the money."

Eyes closed, I can see the look on Clifford's face, confused and concerned.

HIM: *If you really feel that way, then I guess—(He shrugs.) But I don't get it. You were the one who wanted it so much. You couldn't wait for her to get here. (He loosens his tie and sighs.) Who's going to tell her? I just don't get it. What happened? (He sighs again and glances at his watch.) We've got reservations at Musso and Frank's at seven thirty. (He whisks his tie off and rolls up the sleeves of his shirt.) I don't believe this. This isn't like you. (He brushes my bangs away from my eyes and holds my face steady between his hands.) Are you sure?*

ME: *I don't know.*

HIM: *You don't know if you're sure?*

ME: *(I nod.)*

HIM: *Great. (He leaps up and paces the room.) This is just great. (Stops pacing.) What if you were pregnant? You couldn't change your mind then.*

ME: *But I'm not. (I start to cry.) Don't you see? That's the point. I'm not.*

On the way to the movie theater in Century City, the girl asks me if I have seen *Terms of Endearment*. When I say yes, she says that it was filmed in Lincoln, Nebraska, not far from her hometown. She was just a kid, but she still remembers her mother driving them to the campus to watch the filming. She asks me if I have read the recent issue of *Vanity Fair* with Debra Winger on the cover. When I say no, she fills me in on the semi-intimate details of Debra's affair with Bob Kerrey, the senator from Nebraska. As we pull into the underground parking structure, she whips out her hairbrush, turns her head upside down, brushes her lank hair vigorously, and then shakes it loose. For a glorious moment, until gravity takes its toll, she looks like any young blond Hollywood starlet. Riding the crowded escalator up to the theaters, she says, "Is your hair naturally curly?" When I nod, she sighs and says in an indiscreet tone of voice, "Too bad the baby can't inherit your hair." If the girl were my daughter, I would tell her to lower her voice, but since she is just a stranger who will be gone soon, I shrug and smile and say, "But your hair is such a pretty color."

Once the movie starts, the girl does not utter a sound. As she sits quietly in the darkness raptly staring up at the screen, I begin to feel more kindly disposed toward her than I have since the moment I laid eyes on her at the airport. The evening she was due to arrive—it seems longer ago than just yesterday—Clifford and I went out to eat at a hole-in-the-wall Italian place near the airport we had discovered years ago when we had first moved to Los Angeles and were dirt poor. I was too excited to eat. I sipped my glass of cheap burgundy and waited for Clifford to polish off his ravioli so we could be on our way to the airport.

We got to the gate twenty minutes early and the flight was due to arrive half an hour late, so we had almost an hour to kill. Clifford bought us a couple of magazines to read while we waited, but I couldn't concentrate. We had stopped by Conroy's and bought a bouquet of pink sweetheart roses, and I was worried they would wilt before her plane arrived. I had this image in my mind of how it would be. She would straggle off the plane, one of the last passengers to disembark, tired and shy. I would walk up and say, "Giselle?" and when she nodded, I would give her a big welcoming hug. There wouldn't be a dry eye in the house.

In fact, it all went pretty much according to my mental script right up until the moment where I give her the big welcoming hug, and suddenly I couldn't do it. Suddenly there she was in the flesh, the embodiment of my own body's failure. A ghost mother hired to author a child under my own name. I felt like throwing a tantrum right there in the airport, pounding my fists and kicking my heels. It isn't fair! It isn't fair! But instead, I traipsed along silently to the baggage claim.

After the movie ends, the girl and I ride the escalator back down to the parking garage and drive home without saying much of anything. It was that kind of movie, the kind that sends you out of the theater wrapped in a dark, brooding cloud that dissipates slowly. When we pull into the driveway, I exclaim, "Clifford's home!" She seems almost as relieved as I am.

While Clifford and I drink vodka tonics, the girl decides to take a nap before it is time to leave for the restaurant. We sit outside by the pool because the cat dander, in just one day, seems to have permeated the house, and Clifford is looking weepy-eyed although his mood is aggressively upbeat. "So how was your day?" he asks me, eager to hear all the details. "Fine, great," I say, giving him a breezy treatment of the day's activities and then deftly switching the topic to business. The deal at Paramount looks good, he says. Demi wants to do it, he says. "Great," I say, "that's great." I think of her on the cover of *Vanity Fair*, naked and pregnant. "I'll have another drink," I say, holding out my empty glass.

Just before it is time to leave for the restaurant, I beg off, pleading a headache and fatigue. Clifford assumes I am just done in from overexcitement and says they will be back early and will pick up a couple of videos on the way home. Great, I think, anything but *The Baby Maker*. "I'll make the popcorn," I say. I stand in the doorway waving to them as they back out of the driveway in Clifford's silver VW, waving until they have disappeared.

In the abrupt quiet aftermath of their departure, I can't think what to do, what it is that I would usually be doing. I go into the kitchen and open a Canfield's diet chocolate soda and grab a handful of Pringles and gravitate down the hall to the girl's room. The door is closed, and when I push it open, I am surprised by how neat the room is. The bed is crisply made, and all her clothes are hanging in the closet. It occurs to me that she must be on her best behavior. The cat is curled up on the pillow. She watches me suspiciously with narrowed yellow eyes and then beats a hasty retreat under the bed. On the night table there is a little stack of paperbacks and magazines, which I sort through. *Mademoiselle*, *People*, a dog-eared copy of Rosamunde Pilcher's *The Shell Seekers*, an oversize paperback entitled *Your Pregnancy: The First Nine Months*, complete with pictures. Sitting on the pale yellow dresser scarf, next to the ratty hairbrush, is a small bottle of cologne, Chantilly—a flash from my high school past. I spray my wrists with the cologne and run the brush through my hair a few strokes. The sweet, familiar scent disorients me. Suddenly I feel tired—terribly, terribly tired, more tired than I can ever remember feeling, as if I have been dragging around an extra thirty pounds. A little nap, I think. I fold back the covers and sink into the bed.

Breathing deeply, I close my eyes, and for the first time all day I feel relaxed. Peaceful. There is a soft thud at the foot of the bed. I open my eyes and see the cat sitting there, watching me. I stretch out my arm to pet her as she makes her way cautiously closer. Across the room, the gauzy golden curtains ripple gently in the evening breeze. I think of wheat, miles and miles of golden wheat swaying in the wind. The cat hesitates for a moment and then nestles up against me. I think of autumn. The harvest. I think of my bedroom back home, the brown leaves falling outside, and me inside, warm and snug, playing with my dolls, bundling them up against the cold, kissing and scolding, pretending to be a mommy. In the moonlit darkness the cat purrs—low and steady, like a finely tuned motor—beside me. Calm and content. As if she has known me forever.

# A LOVE DIVERTED

LYNN LAUBER

,

H ere are some of the things you can do when you give away
a baby: You can deny it, you can dissociate from your body,
you can mistreat yourself or seduce someone to do it for you;
you can overeat, you can drink, you can smoke whatever is ignitable,
whatever you can sear into your lungs.

You can sublimate, you can become ambitious, you can be terrified of ever again being pregnant. You can study faces in shopping
malls, catalogs, over your shoulder. You can talk about your loss and,
by doing so, convince yourself that you are doing something benefi-
cial. You can develop chest pains, you can have a neck lift, a nose
job, a blepharoplasty. You can not show up; you can show up early.
You can refuse to take care of anything, even yourself. You can
dream; you can have nightmares; you can establish unreasonable at-
tachments; you can be attached to nothing at all. You can have an
odd affect; people can say you look sad. Men can say, "Hey, it can't
be that bad." You can start crying and be unable to stop. You can

feel as if you have a straight pin lodged in your face so that it hurts when you smile.

Twenty years after I was pregnant, I found a 1949 book at a garage sale called *Pedigrees of Negro Families*, by an Englishman, R. Ruggles Gates, F.R.S., who wrote of racial traits with the offhandedness of a cattle breeder. I read randomly from page 231: "Kinky or wooly hair is found not only in the Negro but also in the Negrito, Melanesian and Tasmanian. The peppercorn hair of South African Bushmen and Hottentots differs only in being knotted together in little clusters, with bare patches of skull between them." Hottentots!

I studied the photos of these lost subjects, Fig. VI.8 with her tightly kinked African or *cuculaxtl* hair, Fig. 116 with her longer second toe, displayed against a worn Persian rug. I read how violent temper is inherited as a simple dominant without a skip, how inheritance of artistic abilities resembles that of an allergy, that there is a lower frequency of nontasters in the Negro race. I read a quote from a former Justice Hughes who said that "by applying one tenth as much science in mating human beings as we do in mating animals, we would probably add more to the health of our children and grand-children than can be done by all the medical discoveries of the next hundred years."

I studied the interior of Fig. 69's mouth, with his small upper lateral incisors, a disharmony, along with malocclusion, "which oc-curs in racial crosses," the author notes. A strong whiff of disapproval hung over these descriptions, but I was accustomed to that.

In 1969, when I was sixteen, I had given up for adoption my baby by my African-American boyfriend. I had given this child up without a peek or a hug, the method of choice of both the Friends Home for Unwed Mothers, where I had spent seven sodden, lethargic months, and the Methodists' Children's Home, who had placed my child, promptly and peremptorily, with a sniff of righteousness. I had been strongly advised that this was the preferable way to proceed—without sight or sound. Several girls from the home who had resisted and nursed their babies once or viewed them once became troublesome about signing relinquishment papers and developed pesky separation problems. But it had been borne in on me what a heartache and trouble I was, and I was eager to impersonate the pleasant, malleable girl I'd been prior to my rebellion. So I signed the release forms, I had my breasts bound, I did not speak of what I felt or thought. But I couldn't do anything about my face, which had developed during my months of pregnancy a grave and melancholy cast, or the injured point in the center of my eyes.

No matter what you do, pain bleeds through, like a stain. And I still had my imagination. No one could take that.

Deeper in *Negro Pedigrees*, I read about the B family, which began when a Scotsman married a Negro. "When the elder daughter married a Hindu, their five children showed a wide range in hair form." Studying the results of this union, I began to construct an elaborate jigsaw of what my own lost daughter might look like, taking an eye from here, a jowl from there. I knew dark skin was dominant to pale and, according to Mr. Ruggles, that curly hair was dominant to wavy and wavy to straight. I hoped long bones and slimness were dominant, too, for my daughter's sake—my line were long-torsoed Germans with a tendency toward ruddy skin and pastel eyes, but not lithe and lean like my old boyfriend's side.

The photos of the now dead subjects in *Negro Pedigrees* were beautiful to me with their crinkled hair and soft-toned skins. They looked made of chocolate and cream, buttery, umbery. I had always admired the mulatto offspring in my boyfriend's neighborhood, their magnificent curled heads and golden skins. I was aware of formulating a belief that this toss of the races created the most sublime of creatures, the best of everyone.

With my dark tan and wide features, I even impersonated being a mulatto for a time, saying I was adopted, in an amazing foreboding of what would soon actually occur in my life. In what must have seemed to my boyfriend an odd reversal of the usual pattern, I passed for a season as half black.

My boyfriend was another casualty of my pregnancy; three of us were lost, in all. Although he offered marriage, I took this only as a courteous gesture and declined his mother's offer to keep the baby, convinced that it would be the same as keeping it myself. There were hard feelings after that, and a separation; I received a phone call from him occasionally, usually on the birthday of our child. He always believed we would find our daughter, even though I—the one who made sporadic searches—remained doubtful. He prayed for this, he told me; along with his mother, for whom I'd developed a soft spot. He had done what I had done, what you seem to do when you have a child with someone and all is lost—he romanticized our past. That our relationship had only lasted a few months, that he had originally been more interested in a girlfriend of mine than in me, that half the nights I spent at his house were with his mother, listening to her tell stories and eating her cake—these facts became lost to us, glossed over by surplus feelings; the conception of our daughter had gathered around itself a holy, redemptive light. Who had known what a monumental act we were performing behind the shower curtain of his bedroom, when instead of algebra, we turned and studied ourselves. Neither of us could help what we did with such material later. For a long time he constructed a fantasy of what the two of us had been to each other. And for twenty years, using various voices and angles of approach, I wrote about that window of time.

That same year, from two different sources, I came upon another arcane book, *The Game of Life and How to Play It*, written in 1925 by Florence Scovel Shinn. I discovered it first in a house on the Greek island of Santorini where I was staying with friends. The house was hollowed into the cliffs and featured a walled-off courtyard where I sat in the sun listening to a tour of nuns wander by; the sea—and their habits—were just visible through chinks in the wall. I discovered this book tucked in a bookshelf in the bedroom I had been arbitrarily assigned, and I read it through one stormy night, adrift in the sea.

Back home, out of the blue, I received another copy of this same book from a former boyfriend who was by then a neurosurgeon in Hawaii. In *The Game of Life*, Shinn wrote about the power of words and imaginings, how every desire, uttered or unexpressed, is a demand.

She told a little story: "One Easter, having seen many beautiful rose-trees in the florists' windows, I wished I would receive one, and for an instant saw it mentally being carried in the door. Easter came, and with it a beautiful rose-tree. I thanked my friend the following day, and told her it was just what I had wanted.

"She replied, 'I didn't send you a rose tree, I sent you lilies!'

"The man had mixed the order, and sent me a rose-tree simply because I had started the law in action, and *I had to have a rose-tree.*"

There were other such stories, hilarious to me in their mundaneness: of people desiring hats, fur-lined overcoats, houses not intended for them.

Still, one night soon after, I said out loud to whoever might be listening: "I want to find my daughter."

It was this same neurosurgeon who also provided me with the next link in my search, my labor records, which I asked him to request from the hospital and forward to me.

I tore through these faded pages, reading about myself as if I were the fictional character I'd turned myself into all these years—the she, the her, the distant I.

I was amazed by the eloquence of facts, how many clues there were to savor:

The ballpoint words written across the glossy pages: BFA—Baby for Adoption. The signature of the nursery nurse, Frances Lombardi, R.N., who had seen more of my baby then I had. The signature of the delivery nurse, Mary Loomis, R.N., whose wrist I had bitten at one point during my prolonged and ignorant labor. (No one had given us breathing tips at the puritan home for unwed mothers; they'd rather you suffer, better to remind you of your sins.) I read that a sixteen-year-old female, whose leg ached when it rained, had a low-forceps delivery with an ROA vertex presentation and a 400 cc blood loss and that the final diagnosis (for a pregnancy, on these forms, was no more than an illness) was this: next to the word *viable*, someone had drawn the woman sign. This hieroglyph was the only real evidence I had of my daughter. It shook me deep, as symbols can, and concentrated my resolve to find her.


Throughout the years, whenever I tried to imagine my daughter's life, I envisioned her living amidst a family of brisk, competent "professionals," the term that was used to soothe me at the time of her adoption—erudite professors or anthropologists, who wore horn-rimmed glasses and lavished her with World Books and oxblood shoes. I expected this fantasy to be further fueled by the letter I received from the adoption agency a few months later, after I discovered I was permitted to know nonidentifying information about the adoptive family.

In this note, Margaret Eufinger, L.S.W., caseworker of the United Methodists' Children's Home, informed me that my daughter's father was a psychiatrist and that her mother had been a case aide in a psychiatric hospital.

Then she reached into the bag of all she must have known, and pulled out one little narrative to tell me—an emblematic story to stand in for all the rest. It concerned a month spent by the family on a farm with friends where the father helped with the harvest and the mother helped with all the cooking for the farmhands. The mother had described a lovely room with a canopy bed and antique furniture that their daughter occupied when they were there. Their success and family happiness were such that they planned to adopt another biracial child.

I was forty-one by the time I had this little plate of tidbits handed to me, but it did not produce the gratitude I'd expected. And what about my daughter? Couldn't Margaret Eufinger have given me one shard, one descriptive fact, the shade of her hair, or the size of her shoe, something, anything? All along, I had been given to think that whoever was raising my daughter, there were at least two of them, while there was only one callow me. But now that I had this whole panorama of family felicity typed up on cream bond, I felt suspicious. It only enticed me further—my faceless child in a canopy bed!

Of course, by the time the caseworker doled out this thin gruel, she was writing about a vanished version of my daughter, one I had been unable to conjure up in the aftermath of my pregnancy, wandering lost and logy through my late teens. There was something profoundly damaged about me after my pregnancy, as if I had abandoned not only my baby but some central internal organ, a nameless monitor or clearinghouse without which I was running amok. I developed a veneer, a scab, a husk, a hull, and was callous most of all toward myself.

But now I felt something else, a belligerence not necessarily aimed back at myself. Mrs. Eufinger may have thought she was quieting me down with her dull letter, but in fact she was stirring me up.

The letter ended:

"I don't know whether you were aware that since 1985 it is possible for a biological parent to file the form I have enclosed which gives permission for the child to find them. If you want you can fill out the form and send it to the address given. The only problem with this process is that most parents and children born long before it was passed don't know about it. But it certainly wouldn't hurt to send it in."

It certainly wouldn't; and no, I wasn't aware, having not kept up with the nuances of Ohio state law, having escaped, in fact, the state of Ohio as soon as I was able.

But I filled it in; I began filling in many forms.

I discern now what I couldn't then, what we never can make out till later, a pattern; after years of floundering, abortive efforts, I was making inexorable progress.

The next link was simple: a friend gave me a magazine that contained a letter from a birth mother who'd found her daughter in Ohio; she urged readers to call if they wanted further information. I placed the letter on a table and looked at it, then covered it with junk mail, and then found it again. Finally, one evening, I called the number and talked to the birth mother, who told me about a group of women who worked as sleuths, using a computer database, to reunite adoptees and their birth parents. The cost was nominal; she gave me the number.

I called, filled in the forms, and paid the money; I waited weeks, which, after decades, seemed too long. These searchers were house-wives working out of midwestern basements. I didn't know—or care —about their methods. If they were breaking into office buildings with machetes, with machine guns, it was all right by me. In my mind's eye, I envisioned a locked file cabinet bulging with all the facts that I'd wanted to know all these years—starting with my daughter's name—her name! of which I had not an inkling. If I'd had a stick of dynamite, I would have blown it up myself.

The searcher finally called and said she had narrowed it down to four girls who had been born and adopted the correct day and place. She read them off to me, a smorgasbord of possibilities, and I tried to sense some recognition, but there was none. The Deborah sounded the same to me as the Sherryl—none of them were names I would have picked (what would I have picked? It was one of the many things I'd never allowed myself to consider), someone else's idea of a daughter.

The searcher left me to ponder the names; she would get back to me when she pinpointed the girl who had been born at the correct moment on that day in July. I waited again, but with a different taste in my mouth. I knew that I was going to find out now, and I could sense just beyond that knowing the wealth of information that was going to pour out.

And then everything happened at once: the searcher called and told me she'd found my daughter lodged even deeper in the Midwest than I'd been myself—in Missouri, a state I'd never even thought of before. I ripped through the almanac to study its portly shape. Why hadn't I had a feeling about this? On what sublevel had I been living, dumb and numb and factless?

The searcher had been able to locate only the phone number of the adoptive parents. She was going to call them and present the situation; hopefully, they would be agreeable to giving my number to their daughter and letting her decide if she wanted to make the call.

Another day of waiting; and another report. The mother, who turned out not to be the original adoptive one, was willing to talk to me.

Everything was in my throat when I called her: I dimly realized I had to represent myself well or I might lose my daughter again. But

I couldn't hold myself back to prepare a statement, a press release of who I was—instead I rattled off a welter of my professional and personal history and could hear, even as I was saying it, that being an unmarried writer wasn't sitting well in Missouri, a state, I was to learn, where they seem to marry—and divorce—more than they do anything else.

Still, after my recitation, she offered me my first facts, they rolled out of her mouth and into my ear like marbles, so many that I could hardly contain them.

As it turned out, my daughter'd had several mothers in her life before I found her, but no central mother, none who had stayed, starting with me, the original, central fleer.

From a selfish point of view, this lack of a central mother meant there was no major maternal figure who might resent me and withhold access. In fact, the latest wife, perhaps because she had children of her own, was the one who kindly sent me the first views I ever had of my daughter, X ray–like baby photos rolled off the fax machine in my pharmacy, a toddler face bleeding into a glamour shot where she looked like an old-fashioned movie star, bleeding into an honor roll list of 1983—even upside down I could discern one A after another: smart *and* beautiful. Deep in my secret heart, this was exactly what I'd expected.

The next milestone was when my daughter called me: one afternoon in April while I was folding clothes—the simplest of scenes!—the phone rang, and the inevitable happened: Like water seeking its own level, we were connected again. But only by words, and I'd made do with words long enough. Now I wanted the concrete, the three dimensional; I wanted to see the breath in her chest. At the airport, a month later, I searched for her face in the blur of arriving passengers. And then there she was, striding toward me on the most delicate ankles, ankles that had once been folded inside me like a colt's.

That first visit blurred by in a series of concentrated moments—it was almost too much to apprehend her all at once. I looked at her baby

photos for the first time while she sat across the table, studying me.
I left the room and walked back in again, just to see her anew, sitting
there, plain as a lamp in my living room. Her cheek collapsed on the
pillow the first morning was just like my mother's. Heard from another room, her voice was an echo of mine. I couldn't represent this
to anyone—you would have had to be there, you would have had to
be me—but I had already begun developing a brisk, breezy veneer
that belied what was going on inside, a fountain of feelings from the
clogged center of my heart. I'd heard of a reunited mother and daughter who slept together and constantly held hands. But I didn't do
this—I was careful how I touched her, in case she vanished like
smoke. In fact, I felt to my surprise a tug of holding back—the same
holding back I was always so scornful of in Ohio. On one occasion
when she stood in front of me weeping, I hugged my own arms in
frozen inertness; I couldn't do what I longed to, take her in my arms
and hug her back.

The truth was, thrust all at once into the costume of a mother, I
was unsure how to act. I was the one who had always been the
daughter—it had been my most enduring role; encountering her
shook up my sense of myself. It made me aware of how mature, how
solid I was; not having children can keep you adrift in a perpetual
late adolescence. But now I was confronted with the fact I had produced this complex creature, taller and more beautiful than I ever
was, even if I hadn't raised her.

While women around me were going through fertility agonies, I
felt a sense of serenity at what I'd already—however inadvertently—
accomplished.


Seeing my daughter for the first time was like walking into the middle
of my long-ago affair with her father—into the living room of it—that
autumn of her conception: chitlins on the stovetop, Smokey Robin-
son crooning, jumbled bedclothes, a surprising kindness. Out of less
than this are children born.

Why hadn't I become pregnant before? For I had been at this for
some months then—making love in the blind plain way of our old
beagle Missy, who we sometimes caught in the act, her muzzle

averted, looking abstracted at some far-off place. I don't remember enjoyment so much as the powerful salt and liquid of it all. Quickly over, wordless; procreation like in the biology books, which I dozed over shortly—pregnant, more than I had ever been anything. Who would have thought someone so inauthentic, so unfinished, could be something so concrete, so legal—that without a driver's license, a guidebook, I had managed such a serious, elemental state?

I never got over the surprise of my condition and for the rest of my fertile life avoided pregnancy like the dread disease it had once been made to seem. Whatever maternal impulse I might have had was effectively blocked by this experience; to be pregnant without the prize at the end is a cruel trick on more than the body. I rarely lingered over babies; whether I was genuinely uninterested or couldn't afford to, I never knew for sure. In any case, I never considered having another. If I couldn't have her, I didn't want anyone else.

Here are some of the frightening stories you hear about reunification: A child is found, a girl, with bad skin and a reform school record; she slouches into your unmarried life smoking Salem Lights, demanding funds, hoisting grudges that she plops down on your living room rug. There are recriminations, tallying up of old debts, and you are the one who owes. Or this: A young man knocks on your door, a tall dusky man—you answer in your apron, your married life shimmering behind you . . . your appliances, your children, your husband, pale and innocent of your ignoble past . . . Hi, Mom, he says, through corroded teeth. Guess who?

These are the stories you hear of adoptive reunions—only bad stories, because what is adoption deep down but a love diverted?

They are cautionary tales. You don't hear stories like mine without waiting for the twist, the other shoe to drop, as I do.

I worry that my daughter will disappear again—that some words I say will be wrong, that she will all at once express the outrage I fear she feels, deep down—and deprive me of the great privilege of knowing her.

When I don't hear from her for a while, I fear the worst; I have no faith, there being nothing to fall back on. The years between us are not only unaccounted but unaccountable; they cannot be made up no matter how many photo albums I drag from my closet. My face lies flat under plastic, one dimensional, finished—she cannot get to me at sixteen, when I had her, or twenty, just as I cannot reach out now and fathom the scent of her as the infant I never saw. Her baby photos call up in me a well of nonrecognition—there she is beribboned with tiny teeth and eyelet collar loved by someone—while I was where, doing what? Because I did not take her into my arms, there was no early bond, no scent to enrich my torment. It was a plain loss, unexplored, unremarked.

My daughter was twenty-five by the time I met her, a beautiful, pragmatic, efficient young woman. While I, in my forties, work freelance and manage a certain aloofness to tradition, my daughter owns property; she owns crystal; her purses match her shoes.

In these traits, she has jumped a generation to my decorative mother, who was always too much for our hometown. My mother, who is always trying to give me appliquéd gloves and embellished tea towels. These can now go directly to my daughter.

"She's just like us!" my mother cried happily the first time she met her, meaning she was just like her.

I persist in this too; happily counting the ways she is just like me. Unknown to us for so long, we search her face and yearn to find ourselves there, embedded.

Over time, my daughter and I have developed between us a bantering, easygoing manner. I seem to have emerged as an intimate pal, a veteran of life and love, not the role I might have imagined, but what was there for me to be? It was too late for an apron, too late in a number of ways. What could I teach this woman, who already had an M.B.A., who could already choose a stock fund better than I? About novels? Flowers? I did help her plant a garden the third year, bringing nasturtium seeds in my carry-on bag. It was a fine thing, digging in the earth with her under the flat midwestern sun, just as it was good to devour fried catfish with her, to sleep with a fan in the

room with her, to be hypochondriacs together. These are the odd
traits I seem to have passed on to my daughter, but I am thrilled to
have passed on anything at all. It seems now that I spent the whole
first year happily affirming her questions. Yes, I grind my teeth at
night; yes, I pee all the time . . . yes to cheesecake, Laurence Olivier,
Alfred Hitchcock. Yes, yes. Finally.

# ONE IN TEN THOUSAND

L. N. WAKEFIELD

I thought I should have had the amnio results on Friday, which was a week after the procedure, but by the end of the day, I hadn't heard from the doctor's office. I spent the weekend trying to distract myself. Like anyone having this test, I was slightly worried that something could be wrong, but mostly I didn't think it possible. I was thirty-five, not forty. My chances were excellent: 99 percent that everything would be okay; only one couple in a hundred would receive bad news. No one I knew had ever had anything go wrong. No one in my family had ever had a birth defect of any kind. The doctor had said the staff loves to call and tell you the sex if you want to know it, and her words kept replaying in my mind. I could almost hear the cheerful voice of the staffer.

An earlier pregnancy had ended in miscarriage when a sonogram showed only an empty sac. This is also called an "unembryonic" pregnancy, suggesting that it hadn't really existed, and I kept expecting my current pregnancy to just go away as the other one had. Also, my doctor was concerned that my cervix might be incompetent, so with this pregnancy I'd had a cerclage (a stitch that holds the cervix together) put in, and I'd been told that I might be on bedrest later.

But there were many positive signs. At nineteen weeks, I'd already felt movement, and my continuing nausea was more reassuring than uncomfortable. My husband and I had seen sonograms of the baby on several occasions; the amnio was delayed three times due to the position of the baby, and each time, we'd watched it moving and even sucking its thumb. We stared at the white lines on the screen that showed every bone and the outline of a person. Nature was doing it all for me, and I felt part of something larger than myself.

In years of writing about and studying the history of American art, I'd often considered the paintings of Mary Cassatt, and now I felt I had a fresh understanding of Cassatt's images of mothers and children. My husband, who teaches psychology with a philosophical slant, looked forward to gaining a new personal perspective on child development, which had long been part of his work. We had both waited a long time. We were both old to be parents by national standards—he is eleven years older than I am. We'd both had short earlier marriages, and with our recent marriage, we were in a hurry to start our family. We'd watched other friends with their babies and children, and we looked forward to entering their world.

Monday passed with no word from the doctor's office. I think I called a couple of times, and apparently the results hadn't come in. It was eight days. Then on Tuesday morning the doctor's office said they'd contact the lab and get back to me. The call came on Tuesday afternoon. "Hold for the doctor," the receptionist said. I remember the rising sickening feeling as the doctor spoke (it wasn't even my regular doctor—she was out of town). The baby was not okay, the baby had Down's syndrome. Down's syndrome is not something that can be changed. I sat for a while alone in my office. At the time I had an office to myself in an apartment above the art gallery where I worked, and there was no one around. I remember for a moment thinking, well, should I stay and finish my workday? My actions were very cool, very competent—I'm always the competent oldest child. I had to tell my assistant I was leaving, to make phone calls, to locate my husband who was teaching that day, to make some plans, to call the doctor back, to call my family.

My husband and I had only once brought up the question of what we would do if there was anything wrong, and that was a brief moment in a taxi. Now, faced with the situation, we did not have a long and hard debate. We would not keep the pregnancy. I remember making an appointment for what I learned was called a "termination" and feeling glad that I could have an appointment in two days rather than three or four. I tried asking the doctor all the questions about what I needed to do. He was impatient and wanted to get off the phone. I remember going through the motions of the hospital registration, the removal of the cerclage, the hospital itself. I wasn't me. I was pulling a person I didn't know through doors and rooms. I remember the empty feeling of waking up. I remember my husband and my sister beside me and that we tried to laugh.

There was a sense at the time of a paradox. Every aspect of my daily life, from what I ate to how I slept, to my thoughts and emotions, had been focused on protecting my unborn child. How was it possible that I would consciously with free will participate in its death? How could my husband and I have wanted a child so desperately and yet have known relatively quickly that we would not keep it?

While we did not take a long time to reach a decision, there was a background of implicit understanding that we shared and deep ethical issues that surrounded our choice. In choosing to have a child, we were ready to nurture, to give of ourselves generously, to be accepting of an unknown being, who might or might not be like us, who might or might not like us, and who might or might not be grateful to us. We were ready to love unconditionally. We knew that we must not place limits on our love for a child based on its capacities, and we were ready for our child to at times disappoint us, disagree with us, give us pain, sadness, anxiety, misery.

But now it was as if we were saying, well, maybe we weren't quite able fully to accept those conditions. Perhaps there were limitations in our desire to give, limitations in our generosity, limitations in our ability to love. Perhaps we had certain needs of our own that came first. Perhaps there was selfishness in our desire. Perhaps our wish for a child had more to do with our needs than with the child's. Perhaps we were willing to throw the dice, but only on a certain kind of table. We were willing to give, but not unconditionally.

For us the contradiction can never really be resolved, and our decision can never provide satisfaction or be completely explained. It seemed to us that it wasn't a question of generosity versus selfishness, acceptance versus nonacceptance. If we hadn't had knowledge, if the test hadn't existed, and we'd given birth to a child with Down's syndrome, we would have loved that child, done our best for it.

But now we had foreknowledge, data that we wouldn't have been able to get twenty years ago, and with this information we were given a choice that we wouldn't have had in the past. I guess you could say we were lucky. Instead of just playing the roulette wheel, we knew where the ball was going to land, and we could now decide beforehand whether we would play.

The choice was not one of deciding about the life of a child on the basis of the color of its eyes or on the basis of its sex. That extra twenty-first chromosome, that tiny difference between forty-seven and forty-six chromosomes, makes all the difference in the world, assuring that if such a child survived pregnancy and infancy (many do not), his or her mental and physical abilities would be far below those of other children, whether our child was "high-functioning" or not. The child might never have capacities beyond those of a three-year-old, would look like other children with Down's syndrome, would always be a child with special needs. Such a child would never really have an independent life, would always be an extension of our ability to support it.

How could we know that we wouldn't want such a child, wouldn't love such a child, wouldn't be honored and blessed by such a child, wouldn't have pride in such a child, wouldn't do anything in the world for such a child? We didn't know, couldn't know, and given our decision, would never know. We took a chance, gave up an opportunity, a possibility perhaps of finding something out about ourselves.

With my miscarriage I had suffered for a baby that hadn't existed. Now I was suffering for a baby that had, and the fact that I consciously participated in the death of what I wanted most in life made me feel sick with grief. This time my mourning was both for a baby that wasn't and for a baby that was and then wasn't.

There was of course anger as well. Why did we have to make this choice when others didn't? Why were they allowed to breathe a sigh of relief and go on to plan their nurseries, while we had to go through sorrow and guilt? Why were we forced to look at ourselves and decide grand questions of human life? I felt cheated. Why had an experience that was supposed to be one of such joy been turned into such terror? There's no other experience where you can go suddenly without preparation from such extreme happiness to such extreme despair. I remember being indignant; feeling that what happened was not something that could just be called a learning experience. I had gone through too much already in my life to need such a lesson, and this wasn't an experience from which I would get anything that would be of use.

I avoided contact with people. There wasn't anything more to say about what happened, but I had no interest in anything else. I felt anger at other mothers and babies, shame, and I had periods of just feeling sorry for myself, accompanied by bouts of crying that my husband, despite great effort, could do nothing about. I remember being very vulnerable and emotionally fragile. Just about anything could shatter the veneer of control I tried to maintain: news that some distant friend had given birth, news that some movie star was pregnant.

Often when I woke up from a night's sleep, I would for a moment think the movement was still there and feel joy, and then I would have a sensation of falling suddenly and hearing the sound of screeching tires coming to a halt. Because the love for a child is so deep and so intrinsic, I felt that I too didn't want to exist, to be conscious. When there were opportunities to feel happy, I kept myself from them out of guilt.

Generally we received sympathy for our choice and experience, although sometimes people would say insensitive things. There was one instance in particular that was upsetting. This came from an unlikely source, a pregnancy-loss peer support group. When I related my history to a counselor, I was told that I could not join one of the pregnancy-loss groups because I had made a "choice." If I'd wanted to join a group after my earlier miscarriage, I would have been welcome, but now I wasn't. She explained that some group members might be upset by the fact that I could have had a baby. This was like saying that I wasn't allowed to mourn my loss because it had involved a decision, that somehow the control I had exercised negated my right to an emotional response that I could share. I felt more alone after my contact with this organization that was supposed to provide support and solace. I was not only not allowed to share the world of parenthood, I also wasn't allowed to share the world of loss.

The aftermath of termination is very isolating. You're not really part of the infertility club, and you're not permitted to mourn as freely and easily as can women who've had miscarriages. Single and childless friends don't have the same perspective and have different issues. There's no one to identify with, no one with whom to sit and chat and say, "I know how you feel." I created some of my isolation because I didn't really want anyone to say, "I understand," because they didn't, and I didn't really want them to say, "I can't understand," because then what was the point of talking to them.

The group of people who terminate pregnancies seems to be very silent and hidden. There must be a lot of us, though. From ages thirty-five to forty, approximately 1 or 2 percent of women receive positive genetic test results for abnormalities. After age forty, the percentage increases. But maybe because of shame, maybe because of the fear of upsetting people, maybe because it's such an unspeakable thing, this group is invisible; it's as if by not being visible, we can pretend that it never really happened.

Everyone who has gone through a pregnancy loss or termination advises in retrospect: "you need time; you'll feel better after time has passed; give it time." This is, of course, exactly what no one wants to hear or go through. It seems to me that it's only somewhat true. While gradually you start rebuilding your life and coming back to yourself, the pain is still there just under the surface and can be reopened like a partially healed scab.

For me, time brought hope as I began to try to get pregnant again, and then again it brought more loss and grief. We were hopeful when our chromosomal tests did not indicate that we would have any future problems; other blood tests came back in the proper statistical ranges. But then, first I had another early miscarriage (this time, the fetus had been normal), and then when I became pregnant again, I was very nauseous. "It's so good that you're sick," people said, "that's really a good sign." This pregnancy was so bad that it had to be good, but then the unbelievable happened. After a CVS (chorionic villus sampling, a genetic test that can be done between ten and twelve weeks),

I found out that I was again carrying a Down's syndrome baby. The chance of this happening a second time for someone my age are one in ten thousand. This was like winning some sort of devil's jackpot.

We had not let ourselves bond with this potential baby yet, and my husband and I made the same decision we had made the last time. This time the knowledge of how I'd feel in a week, in a month weighed on me, and there was more despair than before. I remember that just to get through the day, I had to try to be depressed, and I worked at it, lying in bed too long in the morning, watching bad TV, obsessively attempting the *New York Times* crossword puzzle. If I hadn't been depressed, I would have been screaming and trying to blame everyone, my husband, the doctor, the hospital, fate, God. I remember that my husband felt helpless because I wouldn't let him console me. But he wasn't allowed his own grief because someone had to be strong.

After this loss I started to try to accept the fact that maybe I was not fated to have a child. Rather than just making errors, for some reason, nature was trying to tell me that I shouldn't have a child. I tried seeing if I could accept this, but I think accepting defeat and continuing to mourn are ultimately harder than maintaining whatever hope might linger. It was not necessarily courage that kept me going.

I remember doctors telling me that there was no reason for what had happened to me and that I should keep trying. I also focused on my work. Since I didn't know what would happen, I had to preserve the sources of inspiration and satisfaction that I did have.

Then, when I was beginning to return to the world, two years and nine months after my first positive pregnancy test, I became pregnant again. This time I was preparing myself psychologically, emotionally, in all ways for another loss. When the CVS result came back and the genetics counselor pronounced "normal" on the phone, we felt a wave of relief, mostly that we would not once again be facing the hospital and the long cycle of sorrow, loss, and self-examination. At least not yet, I told myself.

Throughout the pregnancy I believed that fate was still weighing against us, and I was in disbelief that the weeks and months were going by. I denied symptoms and was sure that the baby had died whenever it didn't move. Every type of anxiety crept in whenever I thought about the pregnancy, which, thanks to a heavy workload, I was able to do as little as possible. I had a cerclage put in again and was on bedrest for six weeks. As it turned out, the pregnancy went smoothly and I delivered several days after my due date. Even during labor I was in denial, and a moment when the baby seemed not to be breathing made me feel that, of course, this baby was not meant to be either. Thankfully, I gave birth to a nine-pound, five-ounce boy, full of strength and vitality. I remember staring at him right after delivery and feeling shocked that he was intact, that he had every toe and finger, that he was absolutely okay. He was not unlike all the other babies in the nursery.

I felt obvious joy as I brought him home. At the same time there was the sensation that my nightmare of grief was over. I could have my life back. The innocent and dependent newborn who couldn't yet hold his head up was responsible for giving us back our lives and adding to their fullness.

In the eighteen months that have gone by since our son's birth, we're overwhelmed with the joy we feel for this child. He's blessed with an exuberant and delightful nature, and we take pleasure in every new movement, every new expression, and every new evidence of growth. He is the child we dreamed about and waited for. He restores our faith that one can have hope in life.

While the elation we feel in looking at our son, in watching him, cuddling him is surely like that of any parent, there is also an element just simply of gratitude, that he's in the world, that we were able to have him. When we feel tired or frustrated, we remember how much we wanted him, how much we went through, and these thoughts give us strength to hold him longer, to give him more attention, to feel our love for him. Although sometimes we try to assess how his development compares with that of our friends' children, as any parent does, our experience brings us perspective and reason. We don't need our son to be an overachiever. It's a blessing just to be healthy without abnormalities.

Perhaps what we went through helps us to become better parents. Our sense of joy is tempered by a greater sense of vulnerability than we once had, the awareness that unexpected things can happen suddenly and change your life. When our son has a fever or falls, we're more afraid than we should be, than we would have been once.

Things can happen suddenly, and your life can be utterly different. Darkness can often press in quickly on the light.

When I see parents of children with Down's syndrome or other "special" needs, I have a desire to express my admiration for their generosity and selflessness and to hug their children, maybe because I would have liked to hug mine.

# SCARLETT O'HARA
# AT THE MOONLIT PAGODA

JENIFER LEVIN

> *ai,"* he says—this improbably beautiful child who, by dint
> of effort and miracle is mine—brown skin, large dark eyes
> that miss nothing, that blaze often with kindness, humor,
anger, sweet crooked mouth always ready to grin, making friends,
luring people closer. *"Mai, tell me a story."*

"Again?"

*"Another. Please, Mai? Now!"*

It's my job—as parent, as writer. And so I will. A story about his
people; for his origins and his life are inextricably mingled with those
of his magnificent, terrible, pitiful country. A land that—like my own,
like myself—I came to fear, then to love.

Here, for my long-limbed beautiful son—a true story:

In one of their wars with the Siamese, the ancient Khmer—rulers
of much of Southeast Asia centuries ago—won, and named their site
of victory Siem Reap: "Defeat of Siam." A name meant to goad as
well as mark triumph, for Siem Reap sits in the hilly jungles of northwestern Cambodia, not far from the Thai border. And modern

Cambodia—a weak nation perpetually trapped between the pincers of the more powerful Thai and the Vietnamese, sapped by French colonial rule, destroyed by American bombing during the war with Vietnam, bludgeoned almost to death under the genocidal rule of the radical Maoist Khmer Rouge—is still proud of the magnificent monuments her brilliant, brutal kings built near Siem Reap, at the ancient capital of Angkor. The giant face of one of these kings stares out today in stone, multiply replicated, facing the world in all directions: dark, smooth, and at the same time raw, his eyes half-closed, epicantheic folds at each corner, broad nose, strong proud chin. If I half-close my own eyes, I can visualize it now; I can see it transform by increments before me, until it becomes the flesh-and-blood face of my son: fierce, loving, sorrowful, handsome, and scarred.

But it was as a childless student of ancient stone monuments that I first entered Cambodia in 1991—before the days of readily obtainable visas, Phnom Penh pizza parlors, fax machines, and UNTAC.* Cambodia was a nation still closed to much of the world. When we arrived at Pochentong Airport (after an error-filled, sweat-drenched journey that had taken us from New York City through Anchorage over the North Pole, to Seoul, then to Bangkok, and finally to Cambodia), we were told that we had obtained the visas incorrectly and would not be admitted. In other words, the price of admission was fifty bucks a head. We paid it, every one, and were ushered under the beer advertisement strung across the entrance to the one arrival/departure building—WELCOME TO CAMBODIA, it read, and the product name. It had been a long trip.

But there, then, just outside Pochentong, on a dirt road where pigs and roosters and water buffalo mingled with people in bare feet, on bicycles, rickshaws, creaking motorcycles, and in rusty Russian automobiles, I began another journey—this one simultaneous with the physical trip I'd already embarked on, but different; for the physical

---

* The United Nations Transitional Authority in Cambodia—a two-year, multibillion-dollar campaign mounted by the UN, involving enormous manpower and a massive influx of resources from around the world, meant to help stabilize the perilous political and human situation in the nation, and to stage, oversee, and monitor fair elections. In light of the most recent developments in Cambodia, one might say that the UNTAC campaign has conspicuously failed.

trip led outward and upward and down, right to the core of an ancient, sunken city; but the other trip led underneath and inside—
inside the skin of my own faulty human existence, past muscle and
bone and borderlines, its ultimate destination not mind or matter but
heart. It was in Cambodia that I would first see the cracked, grinning
skulls of the killing fields piled mountainous high, eat fried cockroach, touch the bas-reliefs of Angkor Wat, and watch Scarlett O'Hara
at a moonlit pagoda. And it was in Cambodia, two years and so many,
many miles later, that I would come face-to-face with my child.


Poverty and grief are good friends. Pals in the land of sickness and
danger, hunger, fear, busted hopes. Trouble breeds trouble. Poor people everywhere in the world often get into trouble. And they're often
in grief. Bad things happen to them. They have no resources to fall
back on, no place of help to turn to. One mistake can take a desperate
turn. Death lingers closely.

Now, in the United States, there is terrible poverty too. But in
corners of the world like Cambodia, poor, powerless places trauma-
tized by war—especially civil war—years of utterly rampant grief and
depression have caused a numbness of affect that Westerners often
mistake for a culturally ingrained impassivity. It is not that at all—
impassivity. It is just that, when you are always poor and in trouble
and fear and pain, you are in a continual state of mourning. There
is nothing you cannot lose—nothing that cannot be taken from you,
including your life—and you know it. You turn a poker face to the
world. Try to cheat the hungry gods.

I believe it was in this spirit that someone brought the infant who
would later become my son to a Phnom Penh orphanage. He had
been born with a minor disability, a cleft lip and palate, and because
of this he probably could not breast-feed; so when he arrived at the
orphanage he was about two months old and in a state of starvation.
It was January 1991. The Khmer word for January is *Makara*; that's
what the orphanage staff named him. In Khmer, *Makara* also means
"lobster." In Sanskrit, however, *Makara* refers to a pincerlike battle
formation intended to flank and crush opposing forces. It is how, in
the great literary epic of India, the *Mahabharata*, the Pandavas and
the Kauravas face each other at the battle of Kurukshetra. That epic,

by the way, memorializes another civil war in which mass genocide took place. One of the most famous bas-reliefs at Angkor Wat depicts the battle of Kurukshetra. Although the battle formation called *Makara* is not itself depicted, it is implied.

At the time of his arrival at the Phnom Penh orphanage, I didn't know of my little boy's existence. I wasn't even in Cambodia yet. That year I would be in the northwestern part of his country in Siem Reap, studying the bas-relief of the battle of Kurukshetra at Angkor Wat, contemplating other Makaras. That first time—although I even visited his orphanage briefly!—he and I would miss one another: proverbial ships in the night. Our karma had not sufficiently ripened. I was in Siem Reap, watching legless men, land-mine victims all, walk on their hands, going out to gather wood in the very fields where their legs had been blown off, under the sun, in the wilting jungle heat. I was watching other children—their bellies hunger-bloated, their hair burnt reddish blond in the dry season—eat raw lizards and broiled fire ants, washed down with cholera-infected water. And I was about to see Scarlett O'Hara one night soon at the moonlit pagoda —although I did not, could not, know it.

On a night of the full moon, when the biggest gecko I'd ever seen crawled along the wall of my mosquito-netted room in the Gran Hotel d'Angkor and obligingly scarfed up the biggest cockroach I'd ever seen; when gunfire sounded from a few kilometers away (Khmer Rouge cadres in jungle holdouts? or the barefoot, unpaid boys of Hun Sen's army getting drunk and firing off ill-aimed rounds?); when the fabulous, crumbling monuments of Angkor hosted only bats; rumors floated among the Westerners at the hotel that traditional Cambodian dancing was about to take place at a nearby pagoda. Traditional Cambodian dance is a rare and delicate art, which takes years of training; most of the nation's learned practitioners of dance had perished during the Pol Pot years. No opportunity to see this magnificent ritual-enactment-in-art-form should ever be passed up. Soon I was out in the merciless heat, the insect-buzzing night, bouncing along on the mud-spattered back of some motorcycle driven by a Maori mine specialist from New Zealand. A variety of other vehicles creaked alongside and behind and in front of us, all heading down the one road that led to somewhere—that led, we hoped, to the pagoda. And then, in the jungle, in absolute darkness punctuated first by the rising white-gray of wood smoke from fires, then by the white-gold of a rising moon, we stopped.

There was a path, lined with candles. A monk, basket held modestly in his orange-robed lap, accepting donations. I put some bills in the basket, started walking, each footprint dissolved in dust. Followed by the soldier from New Zealand, the other Westerners, and many quiet Cambodians. Down the jungle trail, stocky candles. Old women selling balls of rice wrapped in dark leaves. Then we were off the path of flickering light and into a field of darkness, a field of darkness in which loomed the hulking black shape of an unused pagoda, lightless, dancerless.

But beyond the pagoda, in an adjacent field surrounded by jungle growth, were muted sounds and more light—not the light of candles, this, but electronic, modern light, accompanied by a generator's hum. We moved toward it. The moon was up, shimmering through wood smoke, white-gold and full.

There in the center of the field was a television set and VCR, generator-run. In front of it, cross-legged on the ground, sat a rapt crowd of about two hundred, silently watching *Gone with the Wind*, dubbed in Khmer. It was the end of the first reel—I remembered it well—when Scarlett returns to a decimated Tara after the burning of Atlanta, plucks a rotting turnip from the ground, bites into it, vomits, then raises a fist to the sky and cries, "As God is my witness, I'll never be hungry again!" There she was, the young Vivien Leigh of 1939, more than fifty years later: on a generator-run television screen in the middle of a moonlit jungle field near a Buddhist pagoda in war-torn Cambodia, playing the survivor Scarlett O'Hara to a crowd who understood just what she was saying, just what she had been through.

Part one finished to the familiar swell of music. Somebody appeared with a second videotape. Part two was about to begin.

No one danced that night.


I stayed in Cambodia about a month that first time, and many things befell me. But I would most remember how a strange and deep world of emotion solidified inside me. I had long wanted a child, had seriously considered many of the options. For years, the biological option—donor sperm—seemed best, since I am gay. In truth, though, the idea of shooting anonymous seedlings into my body felt a little creepy. I could not reconcile myself to it; for me, it would not have been an act of love. Especially when there were so many abandoned infants and children everywhere. Everywhere. Particularly in war-ruined places.

It was in Cambodia that the idea of adoption took root inside me for real and began to make sense in a compelling, heartfelt way. And it was there—there, and then—that I decided to return one day when the time was right, paperwork in hand, and find and adopt whatever child fate (or karma?) might lead me to.

That would take two years.


*"Mai,"* he'd say later, *"tell me about the war."*

I'd tell him: In your first place, there was a war. There were bombs, and guns, and fighting. Everyone was hungry. A bad guy took over, and he killed a lot of people.

*"Why?"*

To answer the perpetual *why* would be more than his prekindergartner's neural synapses could understand or endure. I would not tell my child yet about the bleached human bones that protrude, still, from the earth, alongside shreds of rag and shoe. Or of the glass pyramid, filled with skulls and bones, that memorializes what happened in one of the largest of the killing fields outside Phnom Penh: each level a series of glass-enclosed display cases categorizing victims by the estimated ages of their skeletal remains. Each case was labeled in Khmer and French: the heads of young men, the femurs of middle-aged women, headless infants, arm bones of children of such and such an age, and so on. Economy-minded, the Khmer Rouge had saved ammunition by bludgeoning people to death. Most of the skulls are fissured.

I would not tell him how, when the Khmer Rouge entered Phnom Penh in April 1975—more than fifteen years before his birth—they were little more than boys and girls themselves, adolescent hillbillies really, indoctrinated by French-educated intellectuals and American bombs, and they wore rubber sandals on their feet and red-checkered *krawmas* around their heads, waved Chinese machine guns, and killed anyone they believed to be an enemy. And nearly everyone was an enemy: soldiers from Lon Nol's pathetic army; officials from Lon Nol's puppet government; Western sympathizers; doctors, engineers, artists, nurses, teachers. How they killed anyone with a college degree. Anyone with a high school diploma. Anyone with soft hands. Killed anyone with glasses. Stormed into the French Colonial–style villas along Monivong Boulevard and drank water out of toilet bowls. Cleared out the hospitals and the prisons. Then gathered everyone together who was still alive, and marched them out into the country to face the impossible task of growing rice on infertile land, destroying every piece of infrastructure they found along the way. They said it was Year Zero. It was time to start over, entirely new. There was no bourgeois West; there was no history, no past. Those suspected of remembering anything before Year Zero were said to have memory sickness. They were sent to harsh reeducation camps, or killed. Many were suspected. In four years, approximately two million Cambodians were murdered, or starved to death, or perished of disease, or disappeared.

I would not tell him, yet, about Tuol Sleng—the Phnom Penh high-school-turned-prison where the Khmer Rouge sent cadres suspected of treason—where they finally turned in against themselves. It, too, is now a memorial to the war. Would not tell him how, as a solitary visitor one day, I stood in a torture cell there, gazing out through rusted barbed wire, shivering. Dried blood smeared indelibly into the floor. Rotting electrical outlet on the ceiling, over the rotting blood-soaked remains of a cot, a bed; and the wire hanging down, hanging down. At Tuol Sleng, cadres were tortured until they signed confessions, then carted out to the killing fields. For good measure, their families and relatives and friends were rounded up, too, and taken to Tuol Sleng, where they met the same fate. In four years, more than 14,000 died there. Seven survived. No one escaped.

I would not tell him, yet, about the war in Vietnam. How Nixon and Kissinger sent American troops over the border into Cambodia and Laos to sabotage the Ho Chi Minh trail; how they sent planes to bomb this suffering little country; how they set up a government there that could not exist without their support; and how, in the end, they left—left Phnom Penh an open city, swollen with refugees and

hunger, ripe for final destruction. How many American people protested; and how some of us were killed. How, because of all that—
and because it reminded me so shockingly, so intimately, of what had
happened to my own people during the Nazi Holocaust—I had always been afraid of Cambodia. And how it was that fear—the repul-
sion and the terror, as well as the fascination and the longing—that
would pull me there, not once, but twice; that would bring him, one
day, into my arms.

I *will* tell him one day; but not yet. I can hardly answer it for
myself.


"*Mai*," he'd say later, "*tell me again.*"

"*Tell you what, sweetheart?*"

"*About how you ask me to be your little son.*"

I'd tell him: In your first place, long ago, I met you. I needed a
little son. You needed a *mai*. I asked you, Hey Mak, will you be my
little son? You thought about it. Then you said, Yes! And I was *so*
happy. I picked you up and hugged you, and we danced and danced
and danced around.

This is his favorite story. In essence, it is true.

And someday I'll tell him the rest of it: How I had wanted children
before Cambodia; but how my first time there showed me the way—
the way of my heart, the way of the world, the way to him. How,
when I returned the second time around, it was after two more years
of American living and working, two years of processing INS ap-
plications and untold other pieces of necessary paperwork, filing
social workers' home visit reports, two years of struggle and of dream.
When I returned, it wasn't to touch or analyze the bas-reliefs at Angkor Wat, or to count and find significance in the number of spokes
of each wheel on each war chariot, as the Pandavas or Kauravas prepared to form a battle-weary *Makara* that would destroy the world it
held in its pincerlike grasp, there on the plain of Kurukshetra. No,
this time it was December 1993, and I went to find him, alone, standing in the dust of an orphanage courtyard. Three years old, anxious
and sad, bright, defiant. Stubby legs, scarred face. A face that might
have been fathered by the king whose visage had modeled for splendid monuments, centuries ago, in times no more or less savage than

these—whose half-closed eyes, carved in stone, facing the world in all directions, turned up at the corners like Makara's eyes. Mak's eyes were wide open; and—although he was otherwise mute—they were the key, searching, grieving, restless. *What?* they asked me, silently, *What will you be to me?* And I said with my own: *Your best friend.* Said: *Okay, little warrior. I'm getting you out. Stateside.* Remembering a line from the original movie version of *42nd Street*: *Stick with me, kid, you'll wash in with the tide.* Later, I spoke with officials, presented some of my U.S. paperwork. They were not encouraging. Adoption in Cambodia was next to impossible. Everything in Cambodia was next to impossible. On the other hand, it was a place where anything could be done—with enough perseverance, with the right attitude, for the right price. The UN had recently cleared out, leaving a shaky coalition government in its wake. The nature of the coalition—between bitter enemies: the Vietnamese-installed Communist government of Hun Sen, and the Royalist faction led by Ranariddh, son of King Norodom Sihanouk—meant that no one really wanted to make decisions about anything, for fear of reprisal from one side or another. Sooner or later, too, it was obvious that such a coalition would inevitably fail.

That afternoon I wandered across the dusty orphanage courtyard from cement-block building to building, wondering how to begin, and saw Mak pass by with a group of toddlers. He spotted me and shrieked the word in his language for "Mine!" and came running for me, kicking and shoving other children fiercely out of the way, and I picked him up in my arms. Here, my son. I'd been chosen.

It was over then, done. The rest just a matter of more paperwork, perseverance, attitude, paying the price. And time.

In the second month of my stay, a government official who was helping shepherd my documents through the political maze of Cambodia's quavery new (yet still somehow staunchly ancient, Byzantine) bureaucracy, had a dream. In it, Mak was floating through water on a boat filled with rice: a lucky omen. Emboldened, we drove on his motorbike through muddy streets to the villa of a top government official—a member of Hun Sen's Communist Party and a former Khmer Rouge cadre, actually, who during the Pol Pot years had personally sent thousands to their deaths. I had no appointment, simply requested an audience. We were let in by an aide, though, and tea was served, and eventually the big man himself appeared. He was plump and quiet, with dark hair and smooth, pale skin. There was nothing remarkable about him. What I remember most is the sight of his hands: they were soft and white, and very small. We sat on sofas and chairs, sipping tea from cups of delicate porcelain. I told him that, although I knew his party was opposed to foreign adoptions of Cambodian orphans, I was there to ask him not to oppose this particular adoption; the child in question was disabled, and Western medicine could improve his life. He was noncommittal. We finished our tea, I bowed and thanked him and left. But in the end, neither he nor his staff opposed us. In fact, many weeks later, they would provide a crucial official stamp and seal on one of the necessary adoption documents. That day—which had started out with more endless trudging through dusty bureaucratic offices in the Phnom Penh heat, occasionally glancing down, while bargaining with some petty official, and noticing eighteen-year-old bloodstains on some of the floors—ended in celebration. Mak and I drove around the city in a bicycle rickshaw, stopping to eat rice by the Mekong, then shrimp soup near the Psaa Tmay; and by the breeze of evening he was so exhausted that his little head bobbled forward and he fell asleep in the bowl. More days and weeks of trudging would follow—but not as many. It's the conundrum of human existence, really: that malice and magnanimity, horror and beauty, cruelty and kindness exist side by side in us all. Nowhere is that more apparent than in Cambodia; and in my life; and in the life of my child.

Something strange would happen to me there, that second time—because of Mak, and because of his country: I stopped being afraid of death.

It happened the way so many big things happen in a life: A steady compilation of experience amounted to something—like crouching on the floor of a Phnom Penh hospital, one mother and child in a long, long line of crouching parents and children, waiting in the heat and the grime, in sickness, in worry, in love, while Makara fought to breathe. A million experiences of grief, unexpected joy and surprise, anguish, terror; and there were all the petty emotions too; and also the flash of guns, the smell of steamed rice and lemongrass, the heatdizzied visions of geckos crowding cracked and damaged and blood-stained walls; of flying cockroaches, of rancid water puddling in the streets—then being able to let all those feelings and sensations go. It happened because, ironically enough, I was also just glad not to be dead. And in Cambodia I didn't feel that any of my particular human identities—as American, or Queer, or Female—really mattered, at the time; I was merely a human being, and not a dead one; and for a while that was enough. I felt entirely high and complete—for a while.

But it is *not* enough.

In the film *Fearless*, an architect, one of the few survivors of a devastating plane crash, struggles to recapture that peak experience of *not being afraid* over and over again. Thinking—mistakenly—that conquering the fear of death is the real key to life. Some of his first spoken words, after the crash, are: "I'm not dead." What he learns, in his emotionally wrenching return to the world, and to his wife and child, is that conquering fear of death is by no means everything. There's a far more difficult task to take on *after* that: He must learn *how to love fearlessly*. When he realizes this, his words are different. "I'm *alive!*" he says. I'm alive.

What Mak taught me, what Cambodia taught me: Between *I'm not dead* and *I'm alive*, the lesson to learn is fearless love. It isn't easy.


There's a photo I took, of Mak looking out the airplane window before we left Pochentong. He never laughed until Thailand—the land his forebears had defeated at Siem Reap, so many centuries ago—hiding behind curtains in the Bangkok airport hotel, running out giggling to open the mini-refrigerator and stare at all the food, pointing mutely to the shower, wanting me to turn the water on, then off, then on. We were both sick with some tropical respiratory virus or another, both on antibiotics, and our noses ran. Still, his magnificent, handsome, scarred little face took on a glow and an allure, then, that I had not seen before.

Through Bangkok, Seoul, Los Angeles, to New York City, through fitful naps and tears, meals, exhaustion, and sunrise and stars. Sometimes I remember the petty anguishes and panics of that trip more clearly than I remember all the months in Cambodia. Brains are selective, protective mechanisms.

We did arrive in America, in the middle of winter; and my tropical child fell out from the heat into oversize down parkas, knee-high boots, many feet of snow. Into a land where people walk dogs on leashes instead of boiling them for dinner. Into a New York City neighborhood—the East Village—where nearly everyone is a different color from their parent, where families come in all varieties and con-stellations of form, where true cultural syncretism happens, where he is never out of place. A greater truth of American family life is rep-resented here: the different forms families *really* take in this country, and—beyond the unimaginative political rhetoric—the many ways we find to expand, combine, recombine our human assets and powers; the multiple ways we find to love. There are no unruffled neigh-borhoods anymore in this country; no middle-class or working-class norm except survival; and people find inventive ways of making it. Our own government officials are plenty unresponsive, especially in matters involving human service delivery. How careless, how thought-less, we miraculously have managed to be in America! And yes, in so many important ways, we are still free. But all in all, I think we are drawing closer to—not farther from—Cambodia. If you can meet Scarlett O'Hara, and civil war, and suffering and redemption at the moonlit pagoda in Siem Reap, you can meet them anywhere. And the great and terrible sufferers in civil war, those who bear the brunt of cruelty and carelessness, thoughtlessness and greed, are not just soldiers but civilians, old people, women, children. Who, like Scar-lett, like my friends in Cambodia—like Makara's unknown biological parents, perhaps?—trek across battle-gouged landscapes bleaker than the moon's barren surface, scouring the ground for food, searching out a vestigial remnant of someone or something familiar. Forever changed, abandoned by the world. Like Scarlett, yearning inside for Tara—Earth—for a home that no longer exists. Waiting, themselves, to be found.

Maybe all of us, all of us, are waiting.

So the world shrinks. My child grows.

Mak? When we first met, he could speak only three words in his language: the words for "Mom" (*Mai*), "mine" (*ahn*), and "car" (*lan*). As we continued to grow together in my own country, he overcame incredulity, forced my heart chakra open, went to school, became the life of the party, grew tall and had lots of surgery, and learned, in time, to speak volumes. The sheer common humanity of the other parents you meet on the pediatric craniofacial wards of major hospitals, where our children's visages are at stake, to be repaired and sculpted and resculpted with knives—and the patience, the suffering, grief, and hope—helps me remember Cambodia. Someday I will tell him exactly how. And someday he and I will go back there together, and I'll show him Angkor Wat, and the bas-relief of the battle of Kurukshetra; and he will show me many things too—as he always does. And we'll go to the other monuments, where more permanent visages are sculpted in stone. And look at the face of a father, a king.

Me? I'm an American writer and single parent, struggling—to do the work, tell the stories; to grow not the economy but the heart. That is what *Makara* means to me, in the end. Because, know it or not at first, fear it or not at first, we may come to accept it when fear is done. This one final, personal, yet universal wish: to be flanked, in the battle of life, by a different Makara—by love's embrace.

# PRETTY STORY

### AMY HEMPEL

,

No one has ever told me that I am good with children. A short time ago, I went to a dinner party. The hostess was setting the table—there were eight of us that night—when her daughter, a barefoot seven-year-old, demanded we play the game.

I had not played the game before. You had to build a tower out of narrow cross-placed pieces of wood, then pull away the pieces one at a time without making the tower collapse.

I am not good at games, and the girl was sure of her moves. Yet somehow I was good at this, and when the girl removed the piece that made the tower fall, she ran to her mother screaming, "I didn't lose!"

A psychic has told me I will have two children. This makes me shake my head. Picture it: I know you are not supposed to leave a baby alone. Not even for a minute. But after a while I would think, What could happen to a baby in the time it would take for me to run to the corner for a cappuccino to go? So I do it, I run to the corner and get the cappuccino. And then think how close the store is that is having the sale on leather gloves. Really, I think, it is only a couple of blocks. So I go to the store and I buy the gloves. And it hits me—how long it has been since I have gone to a movie. A matinee! So I do that too. I go to a movie. And when I come out of the theater, it occurs to me that it has been years since I have been to Paris. Years. So I go to Paris and come back three months later and find a skeleton in the crib.

The appetite of a baby is a frightening thing to me. I watch a mother spoon food into her baby's mouth, then spoon back in what the baby spits out; to me, it is the job of spackling. If I had a baby, I would change overnight from a woman who worries about the calories in the glue of an envelope to someone who goes to the corner for coffee, a nightgown showing beneath my coat, the hem of that gown clawed to shreds by a cat.

A friend of mine tried to get pregnant and found out she could not. I said, "The world doesn't need more babies," and she said she wasn't going to do it for the world.


I brave shower after shower in which the stacks of gifts divide clearly into gifts from moms and gifts from non-moms. The moms give practical items with safety as a theme: a net to keep a crawling child from slipping through the railing of a deck, a mirror that affixes to the dashboard of a car so the driver can see the infant in the car seat behind, a dozen earnest gadgets to "babyproof" a house. Whereas I will have chosen a mobile to hang above the crib, baby animals painted on china disks—a breath sends them swinging against one another with a sound to wake a baby down the block.

Here's a good baby story: it happened in the Caribbean Sea. A woman went into labor after her husband's small fishing boat sank, and the current pulled them apart. He would later be rescued and reunited with his wife, but there was no sign of him yet when the woman's life preserver was not enough to hold her above the water. She panicked, scanning the horizon where she thought she saw a squall, the water churning with storm. It moved toward her, closing in till she could make out leaping forms; it looked to her like hundreds of leaping fish. She bobbed in the waves, enduring contractions, and the school of dolphins moved into formation around her. Later she would learn that they can locate a BB with their sonar, so it was no trouble for them to detect her daughter, about to be born.

The woman screamed when a phalanx of dolphins dove and then surfaced beneath her, lifting her above the level of the sea. But as she pushed her baby out, she saw that they were there to help her, and because the dolphins were there, her daughter didn't drown.

The dolphins held their position, a buoyant grid beneath her, and kept the mother and daughter safe until human help arrived. Had help not come so soon, might the nursing mother dolphin have offered her richly fatted milk to the baby?

"They were sent to me by the Holy Father," the woman would tell her husband. "He wanted our baby to live."

"The dolphins chattered like little children," the woman said. "When my baby was born, the dolphins went wild. They bobbed up and down; their smiles were so beautiful!"

In gratitude, the woman named her daughter Dolphina Maria. The dolphins slipped away through the waves, intercessors supporting humankind on the sea, allowing them to return to land cleansed of sin. Deep inside their bodies float the few bones left from the hind legs they once had on land.

It is such a pretty story told to me by a Cuban woman I met in a bar at the beach. She left the bar before I did; a drunken man took her place. He leaned into me and said, "I see in your dark eyes that you have suffered, and you have compassion, and *I* have suffered, and *I* have compassion, and I see in your eyes that I can *say* things to you—"

"My eyes are blue," I said.

The only time the word *baby* doesn't scare me is the time that it should, when it is what a man calls me.

# WHOSE CHILD IS THIS?

ANN HOOD

,

She is standing in the doorway. I feel her standing there, peering in. She is already dressed, right down to her socks and sneakers. Hair combed. Teeth brushed. Ready. It is 7 a.m.

"Come in," I mumble. I am not a morning person.

She takes a step into the bedroom. Waits.

At her house halfway across the country, everyone is up by now, I suppose. Breakfast is on the table. Beds are made. Everyone is dressed. Ready.

But I like to loll in my bed until midmorning. Or even later. I drink too much coffee. Read the newspaper. Wander around the kitchen in my bathrobe. I have my four-year-old eat granola bars or toast his own English muffin. Even my baby adjusts to this pace. She drinks a bottle, sighs, smiles, and goes back to sleep. I am slow to come to things.

I reach for the remote control and click on *Scooby-Doo*.

"You can watch this," I say, closing my eyes, buying time.

At her house halfway across the country, there is probably no morning TV. Cartoons on a weekday are taboo, I suppose.

When you are a stepmother, all you have are suppositions and assumptions.

When you are a stepmother who is a writer, who doesn't exactly stay home full time and doesn't exactly work full time, a stepmother with a big imagination, you imagine that everything you do, or don't do, is strange and different. Like staying in bed too long in the morning.

My own children are still asleep.

My stepdaughter perches on the edge of my bed.

Is she happy to watch *Scooby-Doo* on a Wednesday morning?

Is she thinking I am a slacker, a failure, a lazy bum?

What does she think of me? What does she think at all? Whose child is this on my bed, completely dressed at 7 a.m.?

I close my eyes.

I need time.

I come slowly to things.


Don't marry someone with a kid.

That was the advice I got from friends of mine who were stepmothers.

Look at your role models, they said. Think Cinderella. Think Snow White.

They told me their own stories with their own bad endings. How they nursed stepchildren through chicken pox and strep throat and the real mothers never even thanked them. How they didn't get cards on Mother's Day. How during a graduation speech only the real parents were thanked for all they'd done and the stepmother was not even mentioned.

You make them birthday parties and take them to Europe and go to them when they have bad dreams; to your husband you don't do enough; to their mother you're the other woman; to them you are a stepmother, that's all. When things go wrong, when the stepchild is angry at her father or lonely for her mother, you will somehow be blamed. You are easier to hate, easier to be angry at. You cannot win.

Still.

You are a woman who falls in love with a man who has a daughter, and you cannot imagine that anything all those other stepmothers say can happen to you and him.


Step One.

This child will love you and you will love her. She has to. After all, you love her father; he loves you. Already the two of you have started to talk about having children together. It feels like this child holds a part of your future in her three-year-old hands. If you can show her father how good you are with children, how easily a child falls in love with you, your life will fall into place. Already he sees you as talented and sexy and smart. Now he will see what a good mother you will be.

You play endless games with her. Go Fish. Spinning like tops. I Spy and Hangman and Stinky Pinky. Secretly you are about to drop from boredom, from exhaustion. But you won't stop. You can't stop. Too much is at stake. If you keep playing, he will love you even more. If you keep playing, she will love you the way he does.

But she doesn't.


Step Two.

You play endless games with her. Whose hand will he hold? Who can go the longest without looking at the other one? Even though you are the grownup, you are suddenly back in third grade when you fought Michele Kinkaid for Gary DiPadua's attention. Back then, you tried to impress him with your collection of Beatles stuff—lunch box, wallet, 45s—your ability to always win at jacks, to explain photosynthesis. Now, your rival is two feet shorter than you and wears Barbie training pants. You have long ago forgotten exactly what photosynthesis is and must resort to larger weapons: you put your hand on your boyfriend's thigh, talk about something in *The New York Times*, drink wine.

Once, you all go to a pizza parlor and you find yourself in a struggle to sit beside your boyfriend. His daughter is smaller, faster, intent on winning. You are across the booth from your boyfriend, and as the evening progresses that small wooden expanse seems to grow to the size of Asia. You start to talk about the presidential election, but he is lost in a story about the Little Mermaid. You narrow your eyes. You are about to drop from tension, from anger. Your boyfriend's daughter whispers to him and giggles the way Michele Kinkaid used to in the playground of your elementary school.

You are forced to eat plain pizza because that is the way she likes it. It tastes like cardboard. You are the adult here. But no one seems to notice you. You could be in another booth, in another restaurant, in another state. You stop trying to interject. Instead you pout and remember this: Michele Kinkaid won Gary DiPadua's heart in the end.


Step Three.

You stop trying. Your future with your boyfriend and his daughter seems hopeless, bleak. The phrase "third wheel" suddenly makes sense to you in a deep meaningful way. When you think about a life with your boyfriend, you see endless arguments. You see yourself always on the other side of the booth eating plain pizza. After trying and pouting and fighting them both, you have gained no ground.

You take long walks alone. You let them sneak off in the morning for hot chocolate down the street. You only half-listen to their stories and their jokes.

Do you even like her? Does she even like you?

Your friends who are stepmothers say, "I told you so."

Then you have your own children, and when she visits it is different. Hectic. Noisy. Busy. There are baby-sitters coming and going. Lessons and camp. Dinner to be made and eaten. Bedtime stories. Bedtime.

Sometimes she looks like a lost kitten and you want to hug her, but she is not a child who invites hugs. At least not from you.

So you don't.


A stepmother has to rely on suppositions and assumptions.

You are always second-guessing.

When you invite her to make pesto with you from the fresh basil someone gave you, she freezes. The smell of the basil fills the warm air in your kitchen. Your son has already started to pluck the leaves from the long stems. Go on, you tell her. Help him. She does, but reluctantly, perched on the edge of the chair, frowning. You don't know what you've done wrong this time. Is her reluctance shyness? Or maybe she doesn't help to cook at home. Or maybe she has never had fresh pesto. Or maybe she doesn't like pesto. You want to ask her what's wrong, but you can't because you are afraid of her answer: maybe she just doesn't like you.

A friend who is a stepmother tells you to remember that you are strange to your stepdaughter. Different. Other.

That's true: I feel my differentness deep in my bones.

What are your strengths that her mother doesn't have? your friend asks.

Play on your differences.

Let her appreciate your uniqueness.


I am a writer.

I tell stories.

When we drive in the car, I tell the children about how when I first moved to New York City, I slept on a door for a bed.

I tell them about the man who put his hand on my butt on the subway, then chased me down the street and jumped on my back. How I gave him a piggyback ride for a block before I could shake him off.

I tell them about passengers I had when I worked as a flight attendant. The man who screamed at me because we ran out of manicotti. The man I fell in love with en route from San Francisco to JFK. The man who rode his bicycle onto the plane.

She loves my stories.

"Tell the one about the man who jumped on your back," she says as soon as she arrives.

Tell the one about this. The one about that.

I am maybe winning her over with my stories.

"Why don't you get dressed when you wake up? Why do you stay in your pajamas so long? Why don't you eat breakfast?"

She is puzzling over these things, trying to figure me out.

I frown and grumble. I am not a morning person, I think, and then I tell her that. "I am not a morning person," I say.

I suppose her mother is. I imagine her mother is one of the mothers I see in the supermarket with their coupons and jogging suits and lip gloss. I suppose her mother wakes up bright and early, goes to the gym, makes a nutritious breakfast, dresses in a skirt and blazer, and goes to work in an office somewhere. I suppose her mother drives a minivan through suburban streets and applies lipstick while looking in the rearview mirror. She has never slept on a door instead of a bed, had a punk haircut, worn two different earrings.

I do not know if that is at all true. But that is how I imagine their life halfway across the country. I imagine that this little girl does not know what to make of me. "Why do you wear bathing suits that show your belly button? Why don't you wear a bra?" Who are you? Who are you? Who are you? she must wonder. And in her wondering, I wonder too. Maybe I *should* get up early, wear an apron, make pancakes. Maybe I should stop buying my clothes at the Gap, put laces in my sneakers, wear a bra. When she isn't here, I feel in charge of my kids, my day, myself. But when she arrives, I start to question all of that.

I click the remote to *Rug Rats*.

"You can watch this too," I say, and bury my head in the *Times*.


I try too hard.

I don't try hard enough.

I don't know where I stand.

There are no rule books for stepmothers. I've checked. There are rule books for everything else: How to get a man. How to keep a man. How to raise self-confident daughters and sensitive sons and gifted children and learning disabled children. How to get a divorce. How to remarry. Nothing for stepmothers though. A few paragraphs here and there. But nothing real. Nothing that makes sense. Nothing I can use.

Part of me feels left out. After all, my husband and his ex-wife plan each visit, discuss how I've acted, measure their daughter's happiness quotient in hushed telephone conversations.

Part of me just wants to understand this little girl who I so wanted to love me. Why is she quiet, frowning, sad? Why is she happy today? I can't stop putting myself at the center of all her reactions. My friends who are stepmothers agree but don't have solutions. Just keep smiling and trying, one says. Just keep your distance, another tells me. But I want to break through. As time goes on, I don't want her to love me as much as I want her to be part of my family, to feel her as an intricate, valuable part. And yes, for her to see me the same way. If I were to disappear tomorrow, a stepmother tells me, my stepchildren wouldn't even notice I was gone.

Before each visit I get tense.

Will it be a good one? Will we giggle into the night over my escapades? Will I pretend to talk Swedish and Italian and Japanese simply by making sounds that imitate the languages? Will I paint her toenails baby blue? Will she kiss me goodnight and hold on tight?

Or will it be a bad one? Will she walk past me without saying hello? Will she call her mother two, three, four times a day? Will she not answer my questions, or cry when I reprimand her, or ask to spend the day sitting in her father's office instead of staying home with me?

Those visits, the bad ones, break my heart. Look, I want to shout, let's figure this thing out! But she's a child and acts on instincts. It is left to me to sort through it all. I struggle to remember stories that she will like. I struggle to act adult, to make this work—not just the visit but the relationship, the family, all of it.

My friends who are stepmothers laugh and say, "Don't worry. Eventually they grow up and go away."

But is that what I want?

I used to want her to love me as a daughter loves a mother. To want to dress like me and tell me who her best friend is, which boy she thinks is cute. I wanted to read *Little Women* with her and cry when Beth dies. I wanted to have her take my hand without thinking as we walked down the street together.

Then I just wanted her to like me.

Then I pretended not to care how she felt about me.

Then what?

I don't want her to grow up and go away without us becoming something important to each other. But what is that something? How do we get there?


I assume she and her mother cuddle and laugh and tell secrets and go shopping and have pancakes together at diners halfway across the country.

Why do you assume that? someone asks me, surprised. Maybe she never talks to her mother about serious things, or funny things, or anything. Maybe she looks at her mother and wonders: Who are you?

I don't know why I assume these things.

But then I realize that is what *I* want to do with my stepdaughter. Normal things. Ordinary things. One day the two of us went shopping for a wedding gift, and we wandered Williams-Sonoma, ooohing over cobalt blue cups and saucers, tasting the samples of jelly, choosing the present together. And I thought, Ah, this is it. This is all I want. Nothing extraordinary.


My good friend and her daughter and my four-year-old son and eight-month-old daughter and me go to Cape Cod for the weekend. I have never traveled with my friend and our children; usually we go away just the two of us.

Right off her daughter needs things. To be entertained. To be fed. She wants our full attention. She wants books and games and answers to her questions, even though the ride is only a couple hours. Even though my son is eager to talk to her and make up songs and games with her, the way he does with his big sister. But this girl has no time for a four-year-old. She wants to talk to the adults.

This is how my family travels: my stepdaughter and my son talk and sing in the back seat, and my husband and I talk to each other or listen in on the kids. They entertain us.

Once, when I told the kids I had packed some blue cheese, my stepdaughter asked, wide-eyed: "Did you get it on the moon?"

Once, as we drove through Vermont, my son ate a muffin without waking up. My stepdaughter laughed so hard, she doubled over.

Once, on a flight to Vienna, my son threw up in my lap on landing. "Oh, Ann," my stepdaughter likes to say, "remember what Sam did to you on the plane?"


It isn't that things go bad on this weekend away with my friend and her daughter and my kids and me.

We stay right on the beach, after all.

The baby sleeps. The other two kids dig for crabs and clams and buried treasure. My friend and I get to read *People* magazine and gossip about movie stars.

Still.

There are issues about sharing, about who pushed who first. My son is worried because my friend's daughter keeps taking his books and he is afraid we will leave without one of them. "Where's *Mike Mulligan*? Where's *Eloise*?" he keeps asking at night, searching his stack of books.

I hear my friend tell her daughter: "You know how he is." And I feel wounded. What has he done? The thing about traveling with my family—husband and stepdaughter and two kids—is that we really do know how each of us is. When the kids get tired, one gets moody and one gets mean. We know who talks in his sleep and who rises early.

Her daughter craves attention. She uses big words, incorrectly, in an effort to impress us. She wants the adults to admire what she's found, what she's built, what she thinks.

Impatient, my son says, "Come on! Let's play!"

Disappointed, he says, "I miss my sister."

I surprise myself by saying, "Me too."

One of my son's first words was my stepdaughter's name, which he said often and with great love. When she comes to visit, we have to stop him from running through the stream of passengers deplaning, down the jetway, into her arms. One of my favorite things to do is watch the two of them walk through the airport hand in hand, my son telling her everything that's happened since he last saw her, my stepdaughter listening patiently.

Now that I have my own children, I see that it is simpler than I once thought it was to have a child love you. There is no need for cartwheels and handstands, real ones or emotional ones. My own children love me *because* I stay in bed late and don't look like a lot of other mothers and work upstairs in the afternoon dressed in boxer shorts and an old sweatshirt. And because I see them loving who I am, I can see my stepdaughter, as she gets to know me, loving those same things. My children's love for each other makes me understand too how easy it is to love, simply by virtue of sharing a life together.

One night, staying at a friend's house, when I went to tuck in my son and stepdaughter, I watched as she read to him, carefully sounding out each word, being sure to show him the pictures before she turned the page. And I went over to her when she was finished and wrapped my arms around her and said, "I love you. Do you know that?" She whispered to me, "Yes, of course I know that." It was the best hug she had ever given me, and I did not want to let go.

The last time my stepdaughter visited, we went grocery shopping together. I taught her how to choose lemons, cherries, cantaloupe, and peaches. Clearly here we take food more seriously than she normally does. But she is no longer threatened or confused by how I do things. Her reluctance, over time, has turned to enthusiasm. Let's go shopping! she says, and she means grocery shopping. After we get back, we sit on the porch and I paint our toenails—mine, hers, and my son's—shiny gold. Then I teach them Mark Antony's eulogy for Julius Caesar. Together we bake a pie and recite poems by Emily Dickinson and William Carlos Williams. That is our afternoon. It is nothing special. It is ordinary. While I cook dinner, I hear the voices of children upstairs. "Let's play husband and wife!" they shout, and my son murmurs, "Oh, sweetie, sweetie, I love you," to his stepsister. It is an ordinary day, and it is perfect.

We have been together for five years now, my husband and me. When we go away with the kids, I like our routines, the way our family has taken shape. We strap our kids into the back seat of my husband's big car—the yacht, we call it—and my stepdaughter reads *There's a Wocket in My Pocket* and *Go, Dog, Go* out loud while my son looks on. My husband rests one hand on my knee. The baby sleeps. I drink coffee from a to-go cup. We are content in our way.

Driving home from the Cape with my friend and her daughter, my son asks me to tell my stories. But they lose something without my stepdaughter's excitement over each one, the way she laughs every time.


When I return from Cape Cod and a magazine that is running a short story of mine calls me for a bio, I say, without even considering it, that I have three children.

My friends who are stepmothers prepared me for many of the things that did happen. The wounds, the insults, the bruised feelings. The confusion that is inherent in the role. What they did not prepare me for was this: that ultimately I would want this child. Not because her father is my husband. But because of how she fits into what has become my family. Because even though her visits sometimes make me sad or tense or frustrated, the truth is, when she is not with us, I miss her. The truth is, our family needs her. For all the times I've wished her gone, or wished her different, or wished myself different, the truth is that without her, none of us in our family is complete.

# SCENES FROM A SURROGACY

## STEVEN BYRNES

,

Them his is the story of how my lover Jamie and I met the mother
of our child:
It is Sunday evening, and we are trudging down the traffic-
choked 405 Freeway, the main artery slicing through Southern California. It is impossibly hot.

Our fellow travelers on the road appear relaxed, probably returning
from idyllic weekend getaways. We are not relaxed. Gears grinding,
headaches building, we can feel every mile as we cross into Orange
County, the notorious conservative suburb to the south.

Although we're unsure of the exact directions to our destination,
the real source of our tension is that we're on our way to meet a
surrogate mother candidate, Tammi, and her husband, Carl. Jamie
and I have been together for nearly ten years, and neither of us has
been on a date since, like, forever. This promises to be one of the
most bizarre blind double dates in history.

We have agreed to meet at the Olive Tree restaurant in Leisure

World, a retirement community that is supposedly equidistant from our respective homes.

Tammi and Carl are twenty minutes late, and we wonder if they're really going to show. While waiting, our stomachs churn, and every minute feels like ten. I go to the parking lot wanting to smoke a cigarette but don't want to make the wrong first impression.

When Tammi and Carl finally arrive, we gingerly introduce ourselves before being ushered to a back table. We are joined by Carol, our chaperone for the evening, who works for the surrogacy program.

If I could've picked the location for our first date, it wouldn't have been this chain Italian restaurant with too much Formica and vinyl, harsh lighting, and the din of chatter and clanging utensils. I would've preferred a private, candlelit table with a body of water in view at a small French bistro. Each of us would share our lives, culminating with the beautiful cosmic moment when we embrace and decide to have a child together.

There are too many strangers' ears nearby, and we are an eavesdropper's delight. But I wonder if any of the people who appear to be listening can keep up with the bizarre details of our conversation.

Because we're paying, Carl asks if he can order two entrées. "Of course," I respond, but wonder how he can eat at a time like this. Tammi orders the "Tour of Italy"—a sampling of the entrées.

Nervous, I repeatedly call Tammi and Carl's son Jacob, Joshua. And I imagine Tammi thinking: "What a jerk. He wants me to have his child, and he can't even remember my kid's name."

Tammi is even more beautiful than the picture we were sent, in which she is squinting into the sun. With a creamy complexion and startling ice-blue eyes, Tammi has all-American good looks. Carl is affable, eager, and solid. Together they're like the Homecoming Queen and the Football Captain, and my first question is why they want to hang out with the queers.

"My mother's like you guys," Carl says, never using the words *gay* or *lesbian*. Growing up with a lesbian mother wasn't something you advertised in suburban Michigan.

Then Tammi reveals that in high school she was "accused" of being a lesbian and ostracized by much of the school. Carl was one of the few who spoke to her.

So Tammi and Carl know what it's like to be different. That we're gay seems to make little difference to them. Mostly, they see us as an infertile couple whom they can help. Once again I get to learn the lesson of how deceiving first impressions can be.

"Why do you want to be a surrogate?" I ask Tammi.

In her early teens Tammi heard about surrogacy on a *Donahue* segment and decided then and there that it was something for her. Some kids want to be astronauts when they grow up; Tammi saw being a surrogate as an equally heroic and noble goal. It wasn't a passing fancy, and Tammi made Carl promise to allow her to be a surrogate before she would marry him.

It's amazing to watch Carl eagerly nod his head, showing how open he really is to the arrangement.

Tammi comes from what we euphemistically call a "broken home." She's had little contact with her biological father and has resentments toward her mother. A molestation is alluded to. Later, we will learn that this is a common history for surrogates. Clearly, Tammi sees surrogacy as a chance to heal some of her wounds.

Tammi and Carl have questions for us: "What's your relationship like? How long have you wanted to have children? Why did you want children?"

Wanting children was one of the things that Jamie and I had in common from the start. But for a long time the dream had been vague and seemingly unreachable. A dream we held so close to the vest that Jamie's parents dubbed it the "bombshell" when we revealed it to them. We had been waiting for the perfect moment to bring a child into our lives. And we might have waited forever if destiny hadn't nudged us in the form of a possible adoption situation. But when the birth mother decided that she didn't want two men to adopt, we embarked on our mission to have a baby by any means necessary. The failed adoption had been only two months before meeting Tammi and Carl.

Our date is coming to a close. Despite the prosaic surroundings—the intrusive waiter, the Tour of Italy cuisine—the evening is undeniably tinged with magic.

On the ride home we are giddy, barreling down the unclogged freeway, wind whipping through open windows. For the first time our dream of having a child, a biological child to boot, seems within reach. And so we laugh at the wind, calling each other "Poppy."

As a couple, Jamie and I relish the postmortems: dissecting a party or a dinner out with friends, rehashing the nuances. Our first date with Tammi and Carl was better than we had hoped for. They seem so completely, well, normal; their marriage solid. Essentials in the fringe world of surrogacy. More than anything, we need someone we can trust.

We had gone into the evening looking for a way to have a child but are surprisingly affected by Tammi and Carl. Young and deep in love, they are struggling and haven't had our opportunities. As Jamie said, "It would be great to help them out with school, et cetera, even if we weren't trying to have a baby with them."

Now the question that lingers is: What do Tammi and Carl think of us?

The next morning we wait for the phone to ring, just like after the other kind of date. Finally, Carol calls to tell us we've passed the audition. Ecstatic, we call Tammi and Carl, who are equally relieved to know that we've chosen them. For the first time I realize how much they were on edge, too, seeking our validation. Now that we've decided to have a child together, we'll have to go about the business of getting to know each other.

With a biological mother in place, we need to pick the biological father, an equally tricky decision. Our first instinct is to mix our sperm, let nature decide. Indecision being the easiest decision. But there would be a decision made, whether we or nature made it, and our surrogacy program encourages us to be assertive and make a logical decision. If for no other reason, at least we'll be sure of the medical history of the father.

I have never been a "baby person," not known to coo over newborn pictures, and have no special affinity for others' kids. When I first wrestled with coming out, having a child seemed impossible. I looked around and saw a nomadic romantic and emotional life ahead, going from liaison to liaison. Sure, gay people were in long-term relationships, but they weren't visible to me. Consequently, my desire to have children had been buried deep, covered with layers of denial. But as the possibility of having a child became more real, my desire to be a father, especially a biological father, grew.

It took a lot of inner work for me to say I was ready to be a father.

Work that most straight people don't generally have to go through, because for them it's usually a less self-conscious act. Few heterosexuals ask: Am I worthy to be a parent? For me, and I suspect most of my gay brethren who have taken the leap, finding myself worthy to be a parent has been the ultimate act of self-acceptance. It is also probably the most important and profound political act that I will ever make. Once I found myself worthy, nothing could hold me back.

Because Jamie had been the engine pushing the baby-making process, and because he made the real money in the family, he would've been the logical choice to go first. But I call a meeting in our living room, leading him by the hand to a couch, and make my own case. I express to Jamie how surprisingly important being a biological father has become to me. Jamie is intimately aware of my struggles with depression, drinking, and drugs. He knows me better than anyone and knows how far I've come. Also, I am going to be the stay-at-home parent. No small factor.

Jamie quietly listens to the case I build, then says, "I'd love to have a little Stevie running around the house. You should go first." It's a moment I will never forget and reminds me of why I fell in love with him.

After our third failed insemination, we are on the phone with Tammi. There is an unstated edge to the conversation. We are all obviously disappointed with our failure to conceive. But strangely, we do not share our disappointment; rather I feel a burden to comfort Tammi. I sense that blame is being cast my way. After all, Tammi's already proven herself to be fertile.

My hunch is right. "Maybe we should try something else," Tammi blurts. That something else would be Jamie's sperm, which tested off the charts. I feel like I'm about to get bumped from the team, and it feels like every unfair rejection I've ever suffered.

I rise to defend my seed and am surprised at the intensity of my feelings. I thought I was immune to silly macho posturings over sperm strength. Obviously, I'm not.

Although tonight I am annoyed by Tammi's attitude, I have generally been surprised by my *que sera* serenity during the insemination process. Previously, Jamie has been the rock—the more stable, calmer one in our relationship. But the trials of failed inseminations are taking their toll, and he is frazzled. I'm not sure where my reserves of strength are coming from. But I am able to stay in the moment and not get carried away by ruminative thought.

We agree to stick with my sperm.

When Tammi calls to say we're pregnant, I mostly feel relief. She threatens to send us the blue positive stick, and I can't tell if she's joking, gingerly opening the mailbox every day, wondering if I'll find it.

It is the tenth week of "our" pregnancy, and as Jamie and I hover nearby, Tammi lies on a table for the amniocentesis. I wince as the needle goes into her belly, but Tammi doesn't flinch.

A few minutes earlier we were in a geneticist's office as she explained the odds of our having an "abnormal birth." We nodded our heads but listened only halfheartedly. Because Tammi is so young, the odds that we will have a problem are extremely low. We're only here because the amnio is required by our always-cautious surrogacy program.

But the amnio is really the opening act for what we all consider the main attraction: a high-resolution sonogram. We've been virtually promised that the gender of our child will be revealed on the screen.

The monitor is set up for Tammi's viewing, and we are assembled behind her. But once the amazing liquid animated vision of our baby comes on the screen, Tammi cranes her neck, nearly contorting, to watch *us*. Throughout the show of head shifting, legs crossing, tiny body tumbling through space, Tammi never looks at the monitor. She is only interested in our reactions, her pleasure vicarious.

When people ask, and they do ask often: "How can she give away her baby?" I think of this sonogram moment when Tammi's motivation crystallized for me. She isn't giving away her baby—she is having a baby for us. Tammi has her own family, and I have never felt that she wanted or needed our baby.

In a final twist to our story, my ob-gyn father delivers Samantha, his first grandchild. Ten years earlier my father wouldn't allow Jamie and me to sleep under his roof. Now he has told me that "Jamie is the best thing that ever happened to you."

The delivery room has a carnival-like atmosphere, with much of my family in attendance. Garth Brooks plays on the stereo, and In and Out burger containers are strewn about. Social workers, nurses, and other hospital personnel "come out" to us and celebrate our adventure. Carl is blown away by everyone's openness.

My father has four other deliveries today, and when the nurse announces that Tammi is crowning, everything moves in a blur, and I'm not sure my father will arrive for the delivery. But he finally enters, slips on a gown, and slides up on a stool to receive his grand-daughter, calmly announcing, "Welcome to the miracle of life."

I look at Carl, manning the videocamera, and see tears streaming down his cheeks. Then I look around the delivery room and see that almost everyone else is crying. Everyone except Jamie and I. We are too stunned, too overwhelmed, to cry. Tammi is also beyond tears.

My parents embrace again and again. One of the few instances I've ever seen them publicly express affection.

I go back and forth between Tammi and Samantha, torn between comforting and celebrating.

After helping to bathe Sammy for the first time, Jamie and I plan to spend the night with her in the hospital. But there are no available rooms. So we leave Sammy behind to spend her first night alone in the hospital nursery.

We arrive at the nursery early the next morning to find that Sammy is gone. The maternity nurse says, "The mother took her at dawn." This was not the plan. We anxiously rush to Tammi and Carl's room, hearts in our throats. Is this the moment we were told to fear? The fear we have not dared give voice to?

Inside Tammi's room all is peaceful, early-morning light streaming through the curtains. "Your baby's waiting for you," Tammi says as she holds Samantha out to me.

Tammi and Carl had wanted to feed Sammy one time; their way of saying hello and goodbye. And Tammi's way of confirming what she already knew—that she could really go through with the final stage of our surrogacy arrangement.

We strap Samantha into her car seat and say our goodbyes, assuring Tammi once again how grateful we are, although words feel pro-foundly inadequate. And as we stand at the door, waving goodbye, Tammi says: "I know she's going to have a better childhood than I had. And that's all that matters."

Samantha is two months old, lying on a sheepskin, while we eat breakfast. Our life has just started to settle into a routine. Then comes the call from Tammi. "If you guys want to have another child with me, we should start now. Because Carl wants to have another baby."

We had talked vaguely about having another child together. But this call feels so out of the blue, it hits us like a stray pitch.

Later, the psychologist in the surrogacy program tells us that surrogates often bond with "their couples" rather than the child they are carrying. The impulsiveness of Tammi's decision seems to indicate that this is her way of preserving a bond with us.

So we start again with inseminations, with Jamie up at bat as the donor. The evening before the third insemination, Jamie and I attend an AIDS benefit extravaganza, the highlight of which is Elton John singing "I Feel Pretty" in drag. On the ride home we talk about our mutual sense that this insemination will take. But when we get home, there is a message from Tammi saying that tomorrow's insemination is off; she isn't ovulating. The next morning Tammi reveals that she and Carl have had intercourse.

I can laugh along with the jokes made by friends and acquaintances—"How dare she sleep with her husband!" But we had emotionally invested in this child, and it feels like a searing betrayal. Doubly so, because we were pushed into having a child so soon. We have contracts with both Tammi and Carl that clearly spell out the prohibition of intercourse before we are pregnant. Trust—the most important commodity in our relationship—has been broken.

Three weeks later, when we learn that Tammi is indeed pregnant, it is an anticlimactic confirmation of what we have assumed. I now have a glimmer of what it's like to share children with an ex-spouse; mixed feelings of anger and connectedness. I hate having negative feelings about the mother of my child. And I know we will be bound together as long as we live.


It's nearly three years later, and we are trudging down another traffic-choked freeway on our way to see Tammi, Carl, and their two kids, who now live on a naval base in Virginia. We have not seen each other in the two years since they left San Diego. After a few half-hearted stabs at finding another surrogate mother for our second child, we reconnected with Tammi and Carl and are now seven months pregnant. We've made peace with our past together and have a sense that everything that's happened between us was meant to be.

We've been prepping Sammy for the visit. She knows that she "came from Tammi's belly" and seems excited. But when they finally meet face-to-face, Sammy and Tammi are both reticent and dance warily around each other—reluctant to get too close. Watching the interaction, I realize that Tammi is like a fictional character for Samantha. She's seen Tammi's pictures around the house, seen Tammi featured in the video of her birth, but in person she's intimidated. Despite clearly enjoying Barney in videos, she has basically this same reaction when she encounters him in person.

I'm glad that Tammi doesn't force herself on Samantha. But I'm once again reminded that Tammi isn't the warm embracing Earth Mother that one would expect a surrogate to be. And I can't tell if Tammi's hurt by Sammy's seeming rejection.

In contrast, Sammy and Tammi's son Jacob are so naturally taken with each other that I wonder if they somehow innately know of their blood link. I take them to the local park where they ride down the slide, limbs intertwined, squealing with delight. Watching them together brings a lump to my throat.

This is not the end of our story. We are still early in the first act. I wonder: What will Sammy's relationship with Tammi be? With Tammi's children? Will they attend each other's weddings? How will they introduce themselves? As "half surrogate siblings"?

Like their respective parents they will come from different worlds. They will be raised in different geographic states; in straight versus gay households; with different approaches to parenting; different economic circumstances. Will there be resentments?

We do not talk a lot with Tammi and Carl about what our future relationship will be. We've only decided on no hard-and-fast rules. "It's up to you guys. I'd just like pictures every so often," Tammi said when we embarked on our journey.

Unstated is the fact that the power will shift in our relationship once the second baby is turned over. Just as we have faith that Tammi will do the right thing, she has to rely on us being good people.

———

At the park in Virginia, Sammy calls me Mommy, and Jacob laughs at her. "He's not your Mommy, he's your Daddy." Language is inadequate to describe the facts of our lives. Sammy has a lot of names for me: Mommy, Daddy, Daddy Steve, and Poppa. Each name reflects a different aspect of our relationship. Of all the names Sammy calls me, I like Mommy the best and can't think of another name I'd rather be called.

# MOTHER OF ONE

LISA SHEA

,

Some months after my husband and I separated, in the fall of 1994, I took the bus to downtown Brooklyn with my then three-and-a-half-year-old son. As we exited the nearly empty bus, I held my son's hand while maneuvering his carriage and a heavy shoulder bag down the steps. At the bottom, I let go of my son's hand in order to open up his carriage. I slung the shoulder bag to the sidewalk, pulled open the carriage, and turned to lift him in. I looked up to see him being led by the hand down the street by a man who had been sitting a few seats behind us on the bus.

In a surge of panic and disbelief, I ran toward them, watching the back of my son's head, his sturdy little legs, his tiny hand enclosed in the large hand of the tall, fleshy man who was walking him so nonchalantly toward the intersection. In seconds I reached them, pulled my son's hand free, and watched as the man continued walking, as if nothing out of the ordinary, nothing at all, had occurred. Was he drunk, on drugs, mentally impaired, a somnambulist? Or was he a real kidnapper who knew that this attempt had failed and was practiced enough to disappear from our lives the same way he had appeared: simply, suddenly, soundlessly?

As I stood with my son in my arms, watching the man make his way down the street, a woman approached me and asked if something was wrong. I told her what had just happened, and she ran to the intersection where the man now stood, seemingly staring off into space. Unbelievably, a blue van full of police cadets pulled up to the curb. The man, who was carrying a beat-up-looking gym bag, was questioned by one of the officers; a policewoman spoke with me; the man claimed that my son had taken his hand; a background check was done (he had no police record); and I was told that I could file a complaint against the man over the incident, which I did on the spot.

Moments later the police got back into the van, and the good samaritan woman said goodbye, and the man with the rumpled gym bag crossed the street and was gone. I put my son in his stroller and buckled him in, and we made our way to our friend's house for tea. Nearly three years have passed since that event, and I still find myself thinking about it, playing the terrible "what if" game, worrying its awful effects, which feel ongoing and indelible. Who was that man, and what was in his mind as he walked my son down the street, and what if he had succeeded in taking my child beyond the twenty or so feet he negotiated before I looked up?

I had come late to motherhood for reasons that were complex and numerous. Some I had celebrated—freedom to write, travel, exist on very little money—and others I had mourned—lack of connectedness, fear of commitment, inability to think about the future. This was the child I had finally had after a nightmare series of abortions and miscarriages, after a slew of both serious and scattershot relationships and one failed marriage, after having been afraid to have a family and then desiring consummately a family of my own. In the calculus of desire, wanting a child had come in increments, slowly accruing as I moved into my thirties and away from the wilder habits of smoking, drinking, casual sex, and other behaviors that had once seemed essential and irreplaceable.

My first abortion, at age twenty, had been terrifying. I almost jumped out of my sister's car on the way to the clinic, convinced that I would die from fright, from being in a state of sin, from the terrible secret of my dilemma. The second time I took myself to the appointment, feeling stupid and sad, against which I acted even-tempered and efficient. The third time I went to the clinic with my then-boyfriend but was unable to go through with the procedure. I waited another week and then chose a different clinic, in a different city, and had the abortion performed, after which I became severely depressed.

In my early thirties I had two miscarriages during a brief marriage that was subsequently annulled. The awful surprise and pain of these events was compounded by the rather dire predictions of two different doctors I saw at the time. One said that when I got pregnant again, I would probably have to spend the entire nine months lying down. The other doctor said that I would be lucky to get pregnant at all, given the septic nature of the second miscarriage, in combination with my already complicated gynecological history.

When, two years into my second marriage, I became pregnant—for the sixth time!—and had my son, my only child, I was grateful and amazed. I still am. At age six my son is thriving. He is reading and writing and performing his own comedy skits. He has many friends, whom he sees for play dates, overnights, parties, outings. He is sensitive and scholarly and stubborn. He is protective of his mother and his father; he is gentle and intelligent and fair. He is my beautiful boy, with his Irish-Jewish blood, his fair complexion, and his dark, dark hair.

It wasn't until my son's father and I separated that I understood my notion of family didn't necessarily include being a wife, and that I may have wanted a child more than a marriage. At the instinctive, animal level, the level of species and gender, I had wanted to bring the others into the world—the early abortions, the later miscarriages—but not with the men who would have become their fathers. While I have never talked to other mothers about this realization, often in our conversations I detect a subtext of delight in motherhood, disappointment in marriage.

Since my own separation, I have acted as confidante and confessor to mothers whose marriages are coming apart or have just ended, who worry that their children are going to suffer (they are!), who dread (or dreaded) both staying in the marriage and being alone, who come to their own and other children's birthday parties wearing swirling peasant skirts, swept-up hair, eye makeup, and lipstick, looking relaxed and sexy, or in baggy sweatpants, sweatshirts, and sneakers, looking exhausted and enraged.

In the past three years, I have been both the mother in the long swirling skirt and the mother in the baggy old sweatpants. Never have I had to call upon such reserves of patience and fortitude and love. Never have I felt such triumphs and inadequacies, such pleasure or such sorrow. Never have I had so little time for daydreaming and letter writing and exercise and socializing and rest. And never have I relished so thoroughly the existence of another person in my life.

When Jonathan was born, I was taken aback at how sober he seemed, how singular and self-possessed. I had always imagined that newborns, with their utter lack of experience outside the womb, by definition were squally, eruptive, chaotic beings. The first time I looked at Jonathan, moments after he was born, I saw a red-faced infant who looked sure of his arrival in the world, about being—body and soul—an entity unto himself.

Even now, in our interactions, I am very aware of how precisely and independently he goes about acquiring knowledge of and experience in the world, how he can take one example of something and make it into a passionate enterprise. One evening about a year and a half ago, to coax Jonathan to pick up his pace as we were walking to meet a friend for dinner, I got his attention by bumping, exaggeratedly, into a light post. He thought this was terrifically funny and ran to catch up with me. That's comedy, I told him. Physical comedy. Remember, I said, anything can be funny. In high silliness we bumped and bonked our way to the restaurant.

Since then, Jonathan has made comedy one of the centerpieces of his life. With me, with friends, with relatives, he creates skits, performs slapstick routines, watches the vintage movies of Charlie Chaplin, Buster Keaton, Harold Lloyd, the Marx Brothers, and Laurel and Hardy, and is making his own encyclopedia of comedy after my months-long attempt to find him one failed. Before comedy, he had immersed himself in the world of dinosaurs, and before that, around age three, he had taught himself to read.

How can anything that has happened to us as a family subtract from what he already is? When Jonathan asks why his father and I aren't together, I say that it is better for us to be apart. I have never come up with a longer, improved-upon answer, if there even is one. It is evident that he wishes his father and mother were together. (In some fixed, primal, unreasoned way, I still want my parents, long divorced, to be together.) His displeasure with having a fractured family surfaces regularly and vehemently, for which I am, mostly, thankful. I would rather have his angry outbursts than periods of sullenness or withdrawal or depression.

When he is upset about our family situation, I hold him or let him have time alone. I listen. I tell him that even though his mother and father aren't together, we are both with him and for him, that he will always have his mom and his dad. He calms down, he runs out of the room to read or draw or play with his stuffed animals, he puts on one of his current favorite CDs—the Beatles' *White Album* or *Abbey Road*—and asks me to dance with him in the living room.

When I am in a low, susceptible mood, I picture in my mind's eye that almost-kidnapper, that scary sleepwalker moving down the street holding my son's hand. I shudder at what might have been taken from me. And I feel a sickly wonderment at the unimaginable fate my son might have experienced when he was too young to know a helping hand from a harmful one. That event, along with the divorce, has shaped in complex and ongoing ways my years as a mother—a mother of one—much as the abortions and miscarriages marked my preparenting years.

Someone I know—a single man, never married—recently said to me about my situation, "Your life isn't bad, it's just difficult." Just? The assessment made me both furious and hopeful. Furious because what did he—a bachelor—know about children and mothering and marriage and divorce? Hopeful because, despite his lack of experience in these powerful arenas, despite his rather thoughtless use of the word "just," the interpretation was essentially correct. It still seems a miracle to me that I have a child at all. And even though motherhood is difficult, beset with burdens, the riches, the rewards are outrageous. How lucky I am to have my one and only child!

# FEAR AND COMPLICATIONS

## MICHAEL BÉRUBÉ

,

Back in the 1980s, I used to know quite a bit about nuclear weapons. I was familiar with high-ranking officials' arguments about ASATs, MIRVs, the EMP, and the TDR—or, for you laypersons, antisatellite weapons (banned under the 1972 ABM treaty but pursued by defense hawks in the Reagan Administration anyway), multiple independently targeted reentry vehicles (numerous warheads on a single missile, a crucial development in cold war nuclear policy), the electromagnetic pulse (triggered by an air blast that would knock out your enemy's telecommunications), and the total destruct radius (an area extending three miles in every direction from the detonation of a warhead, within which every material entity would be instantly vaporized). I read newspapers and quarterly journals diligently, trying desperately to gauge the likelihood that someone, somewhere in corridors of power inaccessible to me or anyone within shouting distance, would decide that a transcontinental thermonuclear war was either winnable or justifiable.

It was 1981 then, and I lived in New York City, on 102nd Street and Broadway—exactly 3.1 miles from Times Square. In those days I hoped that if and when the first warheads hit New York, they would find me on the right side of the total destruct radius, where I could die instantly and painlessly rather than being caught five or six miles from ground zero, where I might be killed by buildings falling on me in the wake of the shock wave. I resolved to myself that if I somehow managed to get any forewarning about incoming ICBMs—which would arrive from northeastern Asia about twenty minutes after launch—I would head for Times Square immediately, in the hope that Soviet aeronautical engineers were every bit as accurate as we Americans were reputed to be.

In the early weeks of 1986 I awoke from the worst nightmare I had ever had. In the dream, I was more or less a camp counselor, charged with overseeing about a dozen small children roughly four or five years old. I supervised group play and crafts and things, and then at one point I was asked to usher the children into a small room in the basement of the building, an institutionally generic cinder-block structure of some kind. The leaders of the camp proceeded to lay the children along the floor and douse them in gasoline, and as they did so I was asked to go back upstairs and bring down another group. I was horrified, speechless, immobile. The scene had precisely that indelible quality of nightmare—*I am fully conscious of something utterly terrible that I have no power to prevent.* But what was more horrible still was the demeanor of my superiors: they were calm, confident, even reassuring. *Don't worry,* they said to me in those distinctively distorted nightmare tones, *everything is under control. All you have to do is bring the children to us. The rest of it is already taken care of.* I woke up screaming and thrashing and clutching at my wife, Janet, who was five months pregnant and didn't need a crazy person as a bedmate. I did not get back to sleep that night. And today I remember the dream not only because of its hallucinatory clarity on that one winter night; I remember it because I had three or four more versions of it in the ensuing months, as Janet and I got closer and closer to the birth of our first child. Nicholas was eventually born twelve days after his due date of April 10, 1986—just in time for the Soviets' epochal nuclear disaster at Chernobyl.

The accident at Chernobyl clarified one thing for me: my fears about nuclear disaster did not hinge on madmen, doomsday machines, or even out-of-control superpower saber-rattling; in a deeper way, they had to do with my simple sense that complex systems generate complex systemic problems that can override the best of intentions. (As many moviegoers have attested, *Fail-Safe* is more terrifying than *Dr. Strangelove* precisely because all the military personnel in the former film are so genuinely good-hearted and grief-stricken at the failure of their fail-safe systems.) And in that sense, my fears weren't even about nuclear mishaps or nuclear war as such—though I remain deeply fascinated by our visual representations of Apocalypse, as in Linda Hamilton's nightmare in *Terminator 2: Judgment Day*, a sublime, awe-inspiring scene that presses all my nuclear buttons (not least because it centers on Hamilton's character's inability to warn or save small children in a playground). Though the cold war gave my fears specific shape and form, my deepest fear was something for which nuclear war itself was but an allegory: like every other parent, I was bringing a child into a world most of whose important parameters were well beyond my control.

Janet and I would do our best, I knew, to love and protect our child and, as he grew, to educate him both with respect to the history of human achievement and with respect to the nature of his moral obligations to his fellow beings. But about the macrostructural variables that would determine his quality of life—from political authoritarianism to environmental degradation to profound socioeconomic injustice—we, as parents, could do next to nothing at all.

There is nonetheless an intricate emotional calculus involved in knowing how much geopolitical trouble your children might get into. If, in 1986, I had sincerely believed that the world was becoming a better place, or a place in which the vast majority of ordinary people could have the ability to determine the salient features of their lives, I probably would have felt less conflicted about wanting a child. But conflicted I was—and guilty, too, every time I realized how much I *did* want the child my wife was bearing. I remember feeling guilty about being a graduate student in English literature when Nicholas was born: surely, given my knowledge of nuclear policy, I could be *doing more* to make the world safer for my baby. But whom, exactly, was I kidding? When Nick arrived, I was twenty-four years (and just under seven months) old. Did I dare to imagine that my informational competence and moral zeal might sway the joint chiefs, might reach to Ronald Reagan, might convert Caspar Weinberger, Rick Adelman, and Richard Perle to the causes of nonproliferation and bilateral disarmament? What in the world could I do?

My nightmares, then, were nightmares about control. At their most searing, they blistered me with the conviction that I had somehow already abandoned my responsibility to my unborn child; and even at their mildest, they told me that some part of me didn't think I was capable of raising sea monkeys, let alone human children. That part of me only got louder and more insistent after Nicholas was born, when my fears modulated from visions of global catastrophe to visions of Nick rolling off the changing table. (I should probably admit that Nick managed to roll off our bed not once but *three times* in his first six months, and we diligently took him to his doctor to "be seen" each time, mortified that we could be so clueless. After the first time he rolled off, we decided to surround him with pillows the next time he fell asleep on our bed. It didn't work. Yep, we were fairly dumb in those days.) But there was something else at work in my nightmares about control too. On the surface my fear was that I wouldn't have enough control over the world in which my baby grew up. But it didn't take a seminar in Freud to tell me that *that* fear, noble and altruistic, was camouflaging another: the rather more selfish and obvious fear that when the baby was born, I would lose control over most of *my* world.

At twenty-three, I didn't have the standard boy-fears about marriage: I knew, or thought I knew, that I'd met a woman with whom I wanted to live the rest of my life, and I didn't imagine that I was depriving myself of innumerable luscious romantic encounters by shacking up and settling down. Nor did I fret that the arrival of a child would deprive me of late nights with the boys at the lodge or long golf weekends. I worried, instead, that we wouldn't be able to finish graduate school, or that we simply wouldn't be able to afford things like health insurance. Until Nick was three, Janet and I worked as many jobs as we could find: we taught courses at the University of Virginia for about $2,500 each as graduate teaching assistants; Janet worked at the hospital as a cardiac care nurse and with the athletic department as a coordinator for the football team's academic tutors; I processed words at a local law firm, delivered pizza, copy edited a pair of academic journals; we both picked up stray editing or tutoring jobs wherever we could find them, especially in the summer. For two full years we held seven jobs between us, and even then we wouldn't have made it without help from friends, family, and the federal government: in 1986–87 we qualified for the WIC program, which gave us coupons to buy formula for Nick after Janet stopped breast-feeding him at six months. (Somehow we managed to avoid falling into the "cycle of dependency" that American conservatives and libertarians attribute to all social welfare programs.) Before Nick was born, I was the kind of person who could survive on a small fellowship stipend and who liked to wake up slowly and luxuriously at some point between nine and noon. *After* Nick was born, I had to become a reliable wage-earner capable of waking up every day at six—and every night at twelve, two, and four—and processing enough words or delivering enough pizza to pay the bills. So whenever I felt that we just wouldn't make it (and I *still* have anxiety dreams about not finding summer work), I consoled myself with the thought that even though my life was no longer my own, I would be only forty-two when little Nick got ready for college. Forty-two—old for athletes, middle-aged by anyone's standards, but still reasonably young for college professors. If, of course, we ever became college professors.

By 1989, when I became a college professor, I was much less worried about nuclear war and babies falling out of beds. Now I had a far more immediate and deadly source of worry—my toddler's severe asthma. One hot, horrible night in June 1988 two-year-old Nick had developed a chest cold, and by the morning he was wheezing alarmingly. We rushed him to the emergency room, where he got two shots of epinephrine—under ordinary circumstances, more than enough to break a bronchiospasm. The epinephrine didn't even touch him. He deteriorated rapidly, beginning to get blue around the mouth; it was hard to tell if he was losing consciousness because he was so sleepy, having been awake most of the night, or because he was dying before our eyes. *But that can't be*, we thought. *He's just a little baby.* But even the admitting physician feared—as we learned much later—that we would "lose the child" (his words). Nick was carted upstairs and put on IV aminophylline; over the course of the day he rebounded at the same bewildering speed with which he'd crashed. He was hospitalized overnight and released late the next day on what Janet rightly called a "boatload" of medicines.

His second hospitalization, three months later, was worse. Worse partly because his stay was three days this time, and partly because the young doctor who was charged with starting Nick's intravenous line couldn't find a vein. Here's what that meant: I had to hold Nick down for almost half an hour while doctors probed the undersides of his wrists with a large, thick needle. (Four years later when I was hospitalized with food poisoning and required IV rehydration, I learned just how excruciatingly painful an IV insertion in your wrist can be—and mine lasted only a few seconds, not twenty-five minutes.) Janet was near hysterics; I began shouting at Nick's physicians to let him go home in peace, asthma or no asthma. All the while, in the futile hope of "distracting" Nick, as if you could distract someone from torture, I was whispering in Nick's ear one of the nonsense singsong narratives I'd made up for bedtime: *You have a green cup, and you have a red cup, and you have an orange cup, and a silver cup, and a brown cup, and a blue cup, and you have an everything cup of all the colors in the world.* Repeat for as many colors as you can think of. It had been one of Nick's favorites. But the singsong became so irretrievably associated with pain and trauma, instead of cuddling and bedtime, that after that day I could never mention it to Nick again—not even four years later, when he overheard me mentioning it to Janet for no good reason, stopped in his tracks with a quizzical expression, and (clearly fighting off a dim and dread memory), said to me, "Dad, I know that poem . . . was I getting a lot of shots?"

Control—it's all about control. We couldn't control his asthma; we couldn't control its causes, either, whatever they were. And so we couldn't control our lives from day to day. At times it seemed like exercise-induced asthma; at other times it presented like an allergy; at still other times it seemed an offshoot of viral infections. I wanted so desperately to fix whatever was wrong, and I couldn't believe that modern medicine didn't have some simple Roto-Rooter kind of device to go in and clean out constricted, mucus-laden bronchioles. It was acutely maddening: even surgery wouldn't help in so subtle a matter as this. No clear causes, no clear cure. At any moment we might receive a phone call from day care or from a baby-sitter; at any moment we might hear a telltale wheeze. Nick was hospitalized a third time, but until he was "stabilized" in 1990, with the help of newly developed inhaled steroids, he was sick much more often than he was hospitalized—sick sometimes for weeks at a stretch. We lived in fear, and we lived in fear for so long that we forgot that it was *fear*.

Perhaps if Nick's asthma hadn't stabilized, we'd never have considered having a child with Down syndrome. Janet had gotten pregnant again in 1988, but we were ambivalent about it at the time, and then, almost immediately, she miscarried—leading her to feel guilty and deeply conflicted, as if (absurdly) our ambivalence about a second pregnancy had somehow caused the miscarriage. But by 1991, when our *third* surprise pregnancy was under way, it seemed that Nick was out of danger and that—when Janet started work as an assistant professor at the University of Illinois in August—we'd have the money to support a second child. (By this point we were making the last few payments on our accumulated medical debt from Nick's hospitalizations, from birth onward.) We decided that if sonograms picked up some severe fetal defect, we'd consider a second-trimester abortion, but that we could handle something like Down syndrome and therefore didn't want Janet to undergo an amniocentesis. (Here, though, Janet's previous miscarriage surely had something to do with this decision: the last thing we wanted was to induce a miscarriage, an event that was more statistically likely than the possibility of Janet's having a child with Down syndrome at age thirty-six.) As I've remarked often in the years since, we really had no idea what it would mean to have a child with Down syndrome, but we were pretty sure we wanted this child. Nick would be five and a half when the baby arrived: the timing seemed perfect. And this time, we'd have solid medical coverage to back us up.

I won't rehearse the details of Jamie's birth that September, not only because I've written about them before but also because Janet has enjoined me from describing her labor to strangers ever again. Suffice it to say that James arrived with a number of complications as well as Down syndrome, but he never required surgery. To this day, remarkably enough, he has no traumatic associations with doctors or hospitals; he doesn't always like going to the doctor, of course, but once he's there, he *does* like weighing himself, taking off his clothes, climbing onto the examining table, and generally comporting himself like the irrepressible little ignatz he is.

Still, Jamie's was a complicated birth, and Jamie is a complicated child. What would we have done if we had known for a certainty that Jamie would be born with Down syndrome? In one way, we'd already answered that question in a hypothetical mode during the third and fourth months of Janet's pregnancy, simply by refusing amniocentesis. *We will have this baby,* we thought, *regardless of whether he or she has Down syndrome.* But as I've said, it wasn't really an informed decision. We had no sense of *how* complicated this child would be. Just to take one important area of complication: we were utterly ignorant of how many agencies and therapists and Individualized Education Plans we would have to schedule, juggle, and negotiate; how many appointments we'd have to meet on top of the usual raft of soccer games, tae kwon do classes, and swim camps scheduled for Nick; how much law we'd have to learn just to make sure Jamie is treated fairly by schools and municipal recreational programs. As I write these words, Jamie is two months away from kindergarten, and he's very excited about going to a "big school" like Nick. But we weren't at all sure, this past spring, that we wanted him to go to kindergarten in his "home district," so we had to look into the possibility of appealing to the Powers That Be to allow him to go to another school—just as the Champaign School Board was considering a host of redistricting proposals that included, in turn, a variety of plans for creating "schools of choice" within the public school system. In other words, just getting Jamie ready for kindergarten involved weaving through a maze of local regulations—a maze that was itself being redesigned as we tried to make our way through it. At the same time we were also dealing with the federal and state stipulations under the Individuals with Disabilities Education Act that would suggest an "appropriate" placement for Jamie (with an in-class aide in a "regular" classroom for 1997–98). How tricky is all this? Let's put it this way: Jamie's extensive battery of tests in spring 1997 placed him in the "educable mentally handicapped" (EMH) range, with developmental scores (including IQ) somewhere in the 60s. His "social skills" scores suggest that he's in some ways quite mature for his age, just as his memory skills equal those of some of his peers; but, we were told, we should be happy that none of his scores "spiked" over the 70 mark in the end, because if they had, Jamie would have to be classified as "learning disabled" (LD) instead of EMH, and he would accordingly become ineligible for certain social services.

Back when I was worrying about whether my children would be annihilated by ICBMs or the EMP, in other words, I could have been worrying whether they would eventually be classified as LD instead of EMH.

Actually, I don't resent the classification system, any more than I resent my school board's redistricting plans; every system needs general guidelines to go by, and this one's more humane than most. Certainly it's a vast improvement over the regime in which children like James would be classified as either "idiots," "morons," or "imbeciles." It's just that all boxes are square, and people are somewhat more complicated than that.

But although we didn't know how complicated this child would be, we didn't know how wonderful he would be, either. We never imagined that by the time he was five, he would be able to operate a computer and entertain himself with the CD-ROM version of *Green Eggs and Ham*, complete with a "play page" on which he can devise a matching game with foods as ridiculous as green eggs and ham—like yellow lamb chops, black carrots and rice, and turquoise pizza. (Every time he matches a pair, his daddy is supposed to say, "Turquoise *pizza*? Yuck!" and adopt an appropriately dramatic expression.) We had no idea that this child would someday create a game called Animals on the Bed, in which we ask him whether there's a tiger/gorilla/shark/chicken/snake/elephant/kangaroo/zebra/dog/whale/duck/bear/monkey/giraffe on the bed, and he does his imitation of each animal before throwing himself on the pillows. For "giraffe" he makes the American sign language sign: he holds out one hand in front of his neck and makes an up-and-down motion as he walks, signifying "long neck"; for "zebra" he improvises a hand gesture in front of his face to suggest a horse's head; for "elephant" he swings his arms together as a trunk while galumphing in a circle; for "gorilla" he walks on his knuckles, he really does. And then there's an imaginary animal called a "schlum" (as best we can make it out) that he insists on imitating, except that (of course) we can't tell how faithful his rendition is. We think it's a sea creature. Sometimes it swims, sometimes it jumps. It would seem that the "schlum," like Jamie himself, eludes any easy classification.

And just as we had no clue as to what shape our fears would take, we had no idea that we would come to love James—or Nicholas— with this overwhelming, bone-crushing, life-transforming, complicated feeling of wonder.

None of Janet's three pregnancies was planned, which is another likely reason my fears about child-rearing have been fears about things being out of my control. Accordingly, by the time Jamie was two or three, we began worrying about whether our reproductive systems would present us with another little surprise. Would we be able to have another child? Would we want to? Would it be fair to Jamie— or to Nick?

We reasoned that Nick had a pretty formidable big-brother job already, and that we might not want to draw yet more parental attention away from him. But then we reasoned that Nick loves babies and would just cherish another sibling. Nick had said so himself— and we wondered whether he wasn't also saying that he would like to have a "normal" sibling as well as Jamie. We knew we couldn't afford a third child; we would need a larger house, to start with. But most of all, we couldn't imagine taking care of an infant while also taking care of Jamie during his extended toddlerhood. We told ourselves that our first obligation was to the living, and that we were strained to the limit with Jamie. We argued that a third child would actually impair Jamie's development by cutting into the amount of time we could spend on his "special needs." And yet every time one of our friends had a child, or every time she held an infant in her arms, Janet would turn to me and say plaintively, "I hear my ovaries calling me . . ."

But I was very much against having a third child, and not just because of James. There were other considerations at work as well. I had gotten tenure in 1993, but Janet was still in the middle of her six-year "probationary period." If Janet finished her book and got tenure, I thought, many of our worries about job security (and health care, and Nick's college costs, and retirement) would be over. Given everything else we had on our plate, I didn't want a third child to be the thing that stood between Janet and the publication of her book, between Janet and tenure.

I had my selfish reasons too. Nick was still a decade shy of moving away to college, and Jamie's future was thoroughly uncertain. Did I want to be a full-time father until the age of fifty, until my wife was fifty-seven? Exactly how long could I wait before my love and I could take a long vacation together alone? By the time we could travel together as a couple, would we be too weary for anything but shuffleboard on a Caribbean cruise ship?

Eventually we made a decision. I had a vasectomy in the early summer of 1994, the day after my long-suffering New York Rangers had lost game five of the Stanley Cup finals to the Vancouver Canucks. I remember this weird juxtaposition so well not only because I'm a former hockey player and lifelong Rangers fan, but also because the doctor who performed the vasectomy *just happened* to be the coach of the Illinois hockey team (small town, no?), and we talked hockey all through the procedure. Whatever fears I entertained about having a hockey coach mess with my vas deferens were offset by the happy chance that the previous night's surreal game provided us with a lot to talk about and thereby helped me not to dwell on the fact that I was undergoing my very first surgical procedure and that smoke was rising from between my outstretched legs.

I have no regrets about the vasectomy. But I do still wonder about having a third child. For now, as it turns out, we *can* afford another child—and now we're thinking that maybe a little baby would *enhance* Jamie's development rather than impair it. He's so solicitous of small children, so careful in playing with them, and such a chatterbox around babies, that maybe we'd be doing him a favor, all things considered, if we brought another little ignatz under our roof. Nick, for his part, demonstrates his talents as a big brother every day; we *know* he'd be just great, yet again, shepherding a sibling through the world. And Janet turns to me every so often and says, "Boys, boys, I'm surrounded by boys," casting her arms in the air and crying, "Where are my daughters?" This is of course a direct indictment of my reproductive practices, since it's my Y chromosome that's done all the dirty work.

Janet and I have been together for fourteen years; we've learned to raise children, we've learned to deal with hospitalizations, we've learned about federal disability law, and we've confronted almost all of our fears. And it doesn't look like our planet is anywhere close to a global thermonuclear war.

So now, we think in the rare idle moment, now maybe we should adopt.

# FINALIZING LUKE

JESSE GREEN

Though he has been through this before, Andy cannot get himself calm. He yanks his tie in and out of alignment, mops his forehead with a ragged handkerchief; it's January, but it's hot down here and we've just had Mexican food for lunch. He hands Lucas to me so he can shuffle fruitlessly once again through his date book, which offers the fact of the appointment—"Finalization 1:30 p.m."—but no instructions as to where. Lucas, having started walking on his first birthday, a month ago, wants to climb the steps to the courthouse, so I let him down; he is already up the two stone flights and pawing at the massive doors by the time Andy gives up on his search. "Never mind," Andy says. He remembers that the courtroom (the same one in which he finalized the adoption of his older son, Erez, a year and a half earlier) was on the sixth floor, and except for the fact that the building, when we enter it, has only four, he could be right.

A panicky call to the adoption agency leads us to their lawyer, a crisp woman with extremely dark and lacquered hair in the manner of Lady Bird Johnson. She is waiting for us at the second-floor elevators—or waiting for Andy, really; by now he holds Luke and I hover behind, a nonspeaking extra man, an unspoken *eminence mauve*. As far as the law is concerned, I don't exist. Nowhere in the country is it possible for an unmarried couple to adopt a child together, let alone a gay couple, unmarried of necessity. As such, I'm just the friend with the camera, the pal along for the ride from New York, which is something of a comfort, actually. But lawyers are not the law. When Andy, making introductions, says to Lady Bird, "Maybe you remember finalizing my other son's adoption, he's almost two now," she gives me the quick once over and dryly responds: "Oh, now, he looks older than *that*."

Lady Bird clacks down the hall in her stout black patent leather pumps, informing us, rather too casually it seems, that the agency has misplaced the relevant papers and that she needs to tend to another matter just now. "But don't y'all worry," she continues without looking back, "the whole thing is basically pro forma. Anyway, you'll be in good hands with Maggie." And now she hands us over to a different lawyer—this one, herself an adoptive mother, as blowzy and warm as Lady Bird is crowlike. Maggie introduces us to Sylvia, another client finalizing that day, who shows us pictures of her *four* adopted children, some with "special needs" and some with needs that are presumably more ordinary. "This one's from Colombia, this one from Ecuador . . ." After the tour Sylvia introduces us to the woman of unexplained provenance at her side: her friend with the camera? We raise eyebrows at each other, inconclusively.

Andy waits in the hallway, playing with Luke, while I sit in courtroom 218 listening for our case to be called. Presiding at the front of the room is District Judge Edna Buchanan; Her Honor has a blond flip, a pointy face, and sharp blue eyes behind frameless glasses. Pinned to the lapels of her robe are several dozen miniature gold charms: hearts, flowers, musical instruments, bees. But she is no pushover. However many years she has been handling family court cases, she is not sentimental beyond her wardrobe. As I enter, she is addressing a twelve-year-old girl without condescension: "Are you here willingly? Were you under any type of duress?" The girl looks confused, for she is wearing slacks. "Not dress, *duress*," says the judge, stretching the syllables. "Did anyone *make* you?" The girl nods uncertainly, yes then no.

The courtroom must have been handsome once but is now somehow both overpolished and undermaintained, like the pocky, silver-haired southern lawyers waiting their turns in the pews. The pews themselves, half filled with various clumps of hopeful or hateful families, are scratched with the markings of decades of children's bored feet. Despite the penitential furniture—and the dark paneling and the pageant of flags—this is not a place of awe; it's less like a church than like a church kitchen, with brown linoleum floors, buzzing overhead fluorescent fixtures, and frequent but totally ineffectual shushings. The families come and go at will. Some are toting cameras, some videos, some a dime-store picture of their child in lieu of the child himself; others, here not for happy events like adoptions but for inevitable events like divorces, have only grim, sarcastic smiles to show for themselves. A bored, angry teenage Latina slumps in a middle pew as if watching an insufficiently lurid daytime drama; nevertheless she vigilantly maintains a body-length distance between her and her father, who does the same between himself and his wife. A divorce, I assume—or is it? The divorce cases, when called, are palindromic in their recrimination: *Zabloski v. Zabloski, Iming v. Iming, Ortega v. Ortega, McCloud v. McCloud.* After the gavel comes down on one of them, a lawyer leads a man and a woman back down the aisle away from the judge. "Well, that's done," mutters the new ex-wife, as if it were the first task she ever got her husband to complete on time.

The adoption cases are called according to a kinder if quainter legal formula: *In the Interest of Baby Boy, a Child.* When the bailiff utters this curious phrase, it takes some sorting out among lawyers and judge to determine which baby boy here is currently of interest. Eventually, it is Luke; Maggie directs me to fetch him and Andy from the hall and then to stay put in a pew at the back of the room until the judge indicates it's time to take pictures. I nod eagerly, trying not to think too much about how I've come these thousand miles to record a happiness not my own. But that isn't right, that's the law speaking; my happiness or lack thereof is not the court's to adjudicate and will take place elsewhere anyway. I'm a *special needs* parent. I may have thought that as a gay man I would never have children, I may even have convinced myself that I therefore did not want them, but here they were, want them or not. They came with Andy. Whatever the law said, they were now mine too—and yet: As Luke enters the courtroom in Andy's arms, smiling his usual jolly smile and looking around at these interesting new surroundings, he sees and then reaches to me in my pew, and I feel I must wave him past.


If adulthood and parenthood are, for most of us, synonymous, that may be because most of us were raised by parents. Almost all of the adults we knew when we were young had families—and as far as we were concerned, that is *all* they had. The marriage, the mortgage, the professional machinations were matters sequestered behind the Oz curtain, and what was left in front of it was us; happily we believed we were not just the center but the whole of their lives. We defined them: If children were what adults took care of, then adults were those people (and only those people!) who took care of children. Oh, sure, there was the occasional unmarried great-uncle, but great-aunts spoke of his condition with the sad sympathy otherwise reserved for teenagers with acne, as if being childless were a developmental mishap. He proved the rule, as did my brother, who never seemed much of a grownup to me until the day his first child was born—at which point society suddenly conferred upon him the respect it reserves for those who have "chosen" adulthood. That he was no less (or more) childish on that day than he had been the day before was irrelevant. He was now a parent, thus no longer a child.

Formulated this way, adulthood becomes a tricky concept for those who don't procreate, or who wait longer and longer to do so. For gay men especially—but for more and more heterosexual women too— the question of what forms a mature identity has been left, since the first days of the sexual revolution, unanswered. And often unasked. Throughout my twenties I contented myself to observe the obvious: No matter how much I doted on my niece and nephew, no matter how many godchildren I might walk to school, I felt more like them than like their parents, and I startled when the classroom door shut me out. The world did not confer its accreditation easily; uncles were only uncles, and however many babies I changed, none had changed me in return. Only later did I realize that this observation implied a challenge: I was going to have to create some idea of adulthood without the concept of parenthood to give it form—or not become an adult at all.

Not becoming a real adult, by which I mean a traditional adult, remains a viable option for gay men; they can become faux adults instead. Banished from the precincts of Dreft and Kwell—as I have come to call the five-year landscape defined at one horizon by baby laundry detergent and at the other by toddler lice shampoo—some gay men who remain single make a kind of life's work out of adolescence, their days filled with breathless gossip, fantastic crushes, self-beautification. Others, particularly those in couples, cultivate an eerily parallel world to the world of families. They buy and renovate charming three-bedroom cottages in the country, turning nurseries into guest rooms and installing pergolas on the site of rusty swing sets. Down come the cowboy-wallpapered walls (or maybe not) and up go the flea-market chandeliers. Oh, their taxes still help to finance local schools, and their Halloween decorations are the wittiest in town, but few children knock at the door for their homemade candy apples (if Halloween happens to fall on a weekend), and the pre-empty nest stays empty.

Or they garden: comprehensive assemblies of every legitimate iris, tomatoes shameless on their stakes, and months of sauces from them. Or they collect: Roseville ceramics from the drought month of July 1947, when the celadon glaze acquired a valuable peachy aura. Or they make children of their pets, or pets of each other. "Kiss! Kiss! Papa wants a kiss," I remember overhearing a friend once croon, while I froze in embarrassment in the doorway where I stood—but was it his human partner or his spaniel being addressed? It was his spaniel.

Or they travel or they cook or they prune and pump until their big hairless breasts resemble the breasts of women. Or they stay at the office even after the heat is shut off, doing the job of two family men and saving their ungrateful employers the expense of adequate staffing. Or they go on the road for thirty weeks with a bus-and-truck tour of *Paint Your Wagon*. Time is what they can offer the world instead of offspring, and with it, they make the world interesting or efficient and occasionally even beautiful.

But it is in the nature of substitution manias that the substitutions never suffice; since the fundamental conflict remains unresolved— how do I make an adult identity in a world that constricts the concept so narrowly?—the distractions just grow more importunate. The garden can always be quainter, the body leaner, the lover even lovelier in a madras shirt from Barney's. Any job can be done even better: can be and must. Which is why, for gay men, process is all. Without children they can afford to be perfectionists. Or do I mean: Perfectionists, they cannot afford to have children.

I was one of them—though I had no dog, no garden or Roseville, and barely ever a lover near enough to impose himself on my neatly made bed. I *did* have a mania, though. Every night for years, when any sane person would long since have been dreaming, I watched back-to-back reruns of *The Mary Tyler Moore Show*, with my best friend on the other end of the telephone line, anticipating together the punchlines we knew by heart and laughing harder for the foreknowledge. I could not fall asleep without its familiar squall, without the nattering nanny of television watching over me in its bland, impartial way. But our choice of shows was no accident, either, for the theme of the series was that a single person could make a kind of family out of her work and could become an adult by treating herself as one. As I reached my mid-thirties, this was an ever more comforting message, for by then I realized I had unknowingly entered into an alternative contract with the world—a contract that paid me a living wage of respectability in return for exorbitant amounts of labor. Work was my only child, and I fretted over it in much the same anxious, proud way my mother, it seems, had fretted over me.

I was Mary Richards, and so be it. All I asked in return was a neat, efficient life with not too much dirt at the edge of the rug and, if not a shelf full of Roseville, a few unbroken things. I understood that a world so fine and clean and safe could never withstand a live-in child, or a live-in parent for that matter. This seemed a shame, but at thirty-five I believed I had finally come to understand the truth about myself: I wanted a house, not a household. The never-abandoned, never-faced notion of becoming a parent had seeped out of my heart through various holes when I wasn't looking; good riddance! I would not have a child.

And then I met Andy.


Andy takes the oath, though I can't hear him; what I can see is that in order to raise his right hand he must shift Luke into his left. There then ensues a kind of litany, which I can only make out as mime, in which Maggie reads a list of questions to be answered by Andy and approved by the judge. Later Andy will tell me that the questions are like these: *Are you Andrew M—— of Brooklyn, New York? Have you been caring for this baby boy known as Lucas since January 12, 1996? Do you understand that the adoption that is about to be completed is irrevocable? Do you attest that you want it to be permanent, for the rest of your natural life? Do you understand that though you may disinherit your birth children, you may never disinherit your adoptive children?*

This last must be the question that elicits from Andy a look of surprise and a few blinked-back tears, for he does not remember from Erez's finalization how the state puts a higher responsibility on adopting parents than it does—or can—on biological parents. The reason is hard for me to fathom: It is not because adopted children are felt to be more precious, but because they are often felt to be less so. In short, the state does not want them tossed back in the lake. The procedure is therefore constructed to formalize a compact not of ownership but of attachment, and in this the law seems very beautiful. And symmetrical, too: What are the divorces that precede and follow us but Zabloski detaching herself from Zabloski, Ortega from Ortega? If the room lacks intrinsic sacral gravity, the counterpoint of divorce and adoption provides it. Up at the altar they seem to feel it: Maggie tilting her head with each question, Andy nodding yes, the judge turning from one to another and starting the cycle again. Even without hearing the words, I find it a very moving dance.

Of course I have always been more comfortable watching others dance than getting onto the floor and doing the hustle myself. To all my twitching college friends, I was the forgiving uncle on the sidelines—forgiving if dour. Even at twenty, as if I were sixty, I watched their marvelous gyrations (and now I don't just mean at a mixer) with a wholly unwarranted sense of regret. These were the dancers, the procreators; they would have lovers—already did—and, one day, lapfuls of gyrating children. Whereas I, I had lost so much already (though I couldn't say what) and had borne it so bravely; if I were to be a parent, it would only be to my own rue. Call me Mother Discourage, and yet I would never have believed, had you told me then, how much more there was to lose and, even stranger, how much to gain.

For the blinked-back tears I can just make out in Andy's eyes as the court records his affirmations are my tears by proxy. This is the joy of watching the person I love become more fully who he is—a father—but it is something else too. Erez was already fourteen months old when I joined his life; I treasure him but was not a part of his conception. Luke I chose. Perhaps not while in my right mind: He was offered to Andy at a time that seemed singularly inopportune for me, for us, and especially for Erez. But it was, perforce, the right time for Luke. And so we moved the furniture around, unearthed some baby clothes from the basement, and tried to prepare Erez for the boy who would be arriving in—oh my God!—just five days. Can we be forgiven if in our haste we did not notice that we had mistakenly prepared him not for a baby brother but (much the same in his childish lisp) a baby umbrella?

Many tears have rained down on Luke since the wet night Andy first showed him to me near the baggage claim at Newark Airport. I gave him his name, in honor of light, and held him down as the mohel taught him a lesson he will never forget, or remember. The mohel taught me a lesson too: There are pains more real than adolescent rue, and the realer they are, the more lightly they hover. *To be real!*—the phrase from an old gay disco tune haunts my parenthood. A child makes you real, if you meet him halfway: if you come to him when he comes to you. Which isn't to say there aren't other methods of inhabiting one's outlines. But as Andy keeps answering *Yes Yes Yes* I finally realize that this is my method. Finalizing Luke means finalizing me. Becoming a parent—the pun can't be helped —means becoming apparent. Not to the law; the law can never make you real, though it makes the process seem much easier. Apparent to myself, I mean.

Three minutes after it began, the procedure is over; the judge claps her hands together and says, loudly enough to be heard where I sit, "Okay now, lemme have him." Luke is duly transferred into her arms; she has clearly done this hundreds of times and knows how to hold an infant. Luke obliges with a giggle and a leer. Only now does Maggie motion for me to approach, which I do, content in the role of cameraman. "Smile," I say, my only line, as the judge instructs me from long experience which angles work best in the harsh overhead light. Even so, only one photo eventually develops, and neither Andy nor I is in it: just a jolly baby and a woman with gold charms.

"I want to see this one again," she drawls.

"We'd like him to come back," Andy says, leaving that *we* to hang in the air. "Maybe we'll send him back for college."

"But not for law school. We don't need any more lawyers here." The lawyers in the gallery laugh obligingly if bitterly, and another case is called.

We hasten from the courtroom and stand vibrating in the hallway. Luke needs his diaper changed, but we have forgotten how to move. The only thing I can think to do is to keep playing my supporting role: I ask Maggie to take a picture of the three of us before the moment passes. "I guess there's no danger now," I venture to add as I hand her the camera.

"There was no danger before, either," she replies.

And indeed Edna Buchanan, tough old bird, knew the score. *Everybody* knew the score. The agency, the social workers, the lawyers, the clerk, the studiously nonjudgmental reservationist at the motel. They need only have looked at us—and not cared. No lie was spoken. Everything proceeded pro forma, as Lady Bird predicted it would; but how could a gay man find it less than profound to become a parent *according to form*? If the system required of us a little discretion in return, of whom does it not? In our hearts we are enough indiscreet to cherish the child discretion gave us. That certain politicians and preachers may not be so kindly disposed to our happiness is moot for the moment. It can't be ignored—which is why I've changed everyone's name in this story, except our own. But it can't be allowed to be decisive either. As far as adoption goes, process finally is nothing; we're all de facto in our homes. If the law is a ass, it is sometimes a nice one.

Maggie knows this. She retrieves some papers from her bag and holds them toward us. "These are the forms from which the new birth certificate will be produced, so I think it's important that you look them over carefully and make sure everything's spelled properly, because the clerks are not necessarily the most careful spellers. A lot of lawyers don't do this," she adds pointedly, "but I think it's important that you look these papers over carefully and make certain you've seen that everything's right." She hands the buff-colored forms to me first. "Look carefully," she repeats.

I immediately see why she's placed so much emphasis on our studying these papers. It's not the spelling, which is fairly straightforward. It's that they list quite plainly the names of the birth parents—names we are not supposed to know, names we could never learn later. I immediately feel my temples dampen as I look at the neatly typed information, which includes, I now notice, not just their names but their cities of origin. I hand the bundle to Andy and say, "Look at this. Carefully." And as casually as I can, I take out my notebook.

Unfortunately, my hands are shaky; the next day I am unable to make out what I wrote. Elaborate graphological experiments later suggest several viable candidates for the birth mother's name—Delores Bel Reese, Belinda Rodriguez, Olivia Beria, Doris del Rio—and that she's from somewhere in Mexico that begins with a Q. However I combine and recombine the letters, she sounds like an aquatic movie star, or an ill-paid, kerchiefed *maquiladora*, when in fact we had learned at the time of the placement that she is a young woman with a college degree in—can it be?—tourism. I content myself not to know what I am not supposed to know anyway, but one day months later, I suddenly do crack the code of my scrawl and decipher the names and the hometown too. A quick look at my atlas shows how the tourism student must have traveled some five hundred miles to cross the border—not, like her clients, for a swanky vacation, but so her child could be born in the United States.

Back in the courthouse we do not dare to look at each other. We feel, we both feel, that we have been shown something dangerous,

fissionable; why else would it normally be locked in steel safes forever? And yet we are grateful to have seen the names. Somehow,
instead of making us feel that we have been trumped by biology, it
makes us feel that we have been handed the deck. This is not an
entirely comfortable sensation, especially for me; shadowy as I am in
the transaction, I am more sympathetic than Andy to the fate of the
woman now to be erased from the record. I can almost feel her dis-
appearing, becoming invisible just as he becomes visible, in a way
*permitting* him to become visible. For the state enforces its legal fiction to the last degree; the three copies of the birth certificate that
arrive by certified mail two months later are inexpertly doctored to
render *father* where *mother* once had been, and Andy's name is typed
there. As for the birth father, the court decree includes a heart-
stopping paragraph entitled "No Existing Parental Rights"—parse it
how you will: "The Court finds that the child has no living parent,
and no living alleged or probable father whose paternity has not been
adjudicated, whose parental rights have not been terminated by final
judicial decree."

We gasp at its brutality, but not every gain achieved in the world
is accompanied by an equivalent loss. Adoption has given Lucas's
birth parents, no less than Andy, something they apparently wanted
dearly: the right not to have a child at this time. Perhaps it was a
hard decision, motivated by unfortunate factors of religion or eco-
nomics, but would the pregnant woman who hied herself five hundred miles to cross the border really have balked at the paragraph
entitled "Adoption Granted"?

> IT IS ORDERED AND DECREED that the above-described child the
> subject of this suit by Petitioner is GRANTED and that the parent-
> child relationship shall henceforth exist between the child and
> the Petitioner. IT IS FURTHER ORDERED AND DECREED that the
> child the subject of this suit shall henceforth have the legal
> name of LUCAS . . .

We'll never know. Almost as an afterthought, the decree states that
"all other papers and records, including the minutes of the Court, in
this case are ordered sealed"—and with that swipe of legalese, Lucas's
first birth disappears into the state's machinery. Back home in Brook-

lyn, Andy is elated; he clasps the manila envelope with a blush of pride, as if it contained a cum laude diploma. But I am ambivalent. Could not an instrument so arrogant, so unreal, abrogate me as easily as it did Delores?

However arrogant, however unreal, the gesture doesn't seem to have fazed the judge, who has been through this a million times and accepts without cavil the dirty business of joy. She has signed the document, just her first name and last initial, with loopy flair, it would seem almost girlishly.

# SWIMMER IN THE SECRET SEA

## WILLIAM KOTZWINKLE

'

J ohnny, my water just broke!"

Laski rose through a sea of dreams, trying to find the surface. The sea was dark, and iridescent creatures came toward him, one of them suddenly exploding into brilliance. Laski woke, sitting up in bed. Diane had her hand on the night lamp and was staring down at a water stain spreading on the sheets.

"That's it," he said. "Get ready." The first wave of shock was already over him, speeding his pulse, turning his skin cold, making him shiver.

"I'd better put a napkin on," she said. "I'm getting everything all wet."

He took her arm and helped her to the stairs. She too had begun to tremble and they were trembling together as they passed the window and saw the forest, covered with snow. The stillness of the woods calmed him, and he paused with her on the landing, drinking in the white nectar of the moon. His trembling subsided some, but hers continued, and he walked with her toward the bathroom. She went stooped over, her arms across her mountainous stomach, where her earthquake had its origin. He helped her onto the toilet seat, then went to the closet and brought a blanket. He wrapped it around her and rubbed his hands up and down her arms, trying to generate some warmth.

She looked up at him, her teeth chattering. He hadn't expected it to be like this, the two of them caught and shaken like rag dolls. They'd studied the childbirth manuals carefully and performed the exercises regularly, and he'd thought it would be merely an extension of all that, but there'd been no transition. Suddenly they were being dragged over a bed of rocks. Her eyes were like a child's, astonished and terrified, but her voice was calm, and he realized she was prepared, in spite of fear and chattering teeth.

"I can control the water now," she said. "I can keep it from running out."

"I'll get the truck warmed up." He went outside into the snow. Beyond the shadowy tops of the pines the vast sky-bowl glittered, and the half-ton truck sat in the moonlight, covered with brightly sparkling ice. He opened the door and slid in, pulling on the choke and turning the ignition key.

The starter motor whined, caught in the icy hand of the North. "Come on," said Laski softly, appealing to the finer nature of the truck, the trusty half-ton that never failed him. He listened for the little cough of life in the whining, and when it came, he quickly gunned the motor, bringing the truck completely to life. "You're a good old wagon." As far north as they were, any motor could freeze up, any battery suddenly die, and it was fifteen miles through the thickest forest to the nearest other vehicle. He'd seen fires built under motors, and had heard incredible cursing float out on northern nights, while hours had passed and all ideas had failed and nobody went anywhere. He kept the choke out, so the motor ran fast, then turned on the heater and stepped back out into the snow. The truck's exhaust was the only cloud against the brilliant moon, and he went through the swirling vapor, back toward the cabin that sat like a tiny lantern in the great tangled wilderness.

Diane was still shivering in the bathroom, her stomach bulging under her nightgown. He helped her back toward the stairs and up to the bedroom, where she started to dress, going through all the regular motions, but trembling constantly. It seemed to Laski there were two distinct Dianes—one who was shaking like a leaf, and another who was as calm and decisive as any old midwife. He felt the same split in himself as he picked up her valise and carried it toward the stairs. His hand was trembling, his heart pounding, but another part of him was calm, unshakable as an old tree. This calm quiet partner seemed to dwell in some region of the body Laski couldn't identify. His guts were jumping, his brain was racing, his legs were shaking, but somewhere in him there was peace.

He stepped into the snow. The truck was running smoothly now, and he eased off on the choke until the engine was gently cooking. Turning, he saw Diane through the upstairs window of the cabin, her stomach huge in front of her. She moved slowly and carefully, and he knew that she was going to wear exactly the clothes she'd planned on, finding them just where she wanted them. His own life was a bundle of clothes flung in all directions, shoes dancing in unlikely places, nothing where he could find it.

He went back in, joining her in the bathroom. "How're you feeling?"

"The contractions have begun."

"What are they like?"

"I can't describe it."

He helped her down the stairs to the door and looked around the kitchen. She's got everything in place, there's no more to be done here. He locked the door behind him and led her to the truck. She slid inside, and he covered her with a blanket.

The truck was warm and moved easily up the snow-packed lane, through the tall pine trees. At the top of the lane he turned onto the narrow road. They'd walked it all winter long, and they'd played a game, pretending that the baby had already been born and was swinging along between them like a little trapeze artist holding on to their hands, and they'd swung him that way, up and down the road.

The road went past a vast snow-covered field, in which an old wagon appeared, on its own journey to nowhere, rotting away, its spoked wheels half-buried in the snow.

"I'd feel better if you didn't go so fast."

He slowed down. One minute, ten minutes saved, makes no difference. We know how long the first stages of labor last.

There was ice beneath the snow, and the wheels of the truck did not have perfect traction, but he knew how to play the road, easing through the turns, never using much brake. Both sides of the narrow road had been deeply ditched to carry away the waters of the spring runoff, but now they were covered with snow and it would be a simple matter to slide into the ditch and be there all night. Every winter he'd helped pull travelers out of the ditch, with much swearing, skidding, heaving, and hauling. It was great fun; but not tonight.

At the bend in the road stood the one-room schoolhouse, forgotten in the moonlight. He geared down, taking the turn in second, thinking of little boys with caps and knickers on, and little girls in gingham dresses, long ago, coming up the hill toward the schoolhouse. Then he was through the turn, leaving the old ghosts behind him, on their endless walk through a buried century.

The road went straight through pines that formed a high wall on both sides. "Old Ben is up," said Laski, nodding toward a ramshackle farmhouse in the midst of the trees. Most of the windows were broken out, and it was like all the other abandoned farmhouses in the settlement, except for a flickering light inside, from the one room the old lumberjack had sealed off against the elements.

Diane looked toward the light. A hermit herself, she liked old Ben. He had a bad reputation in the village, living as he did, so contrary to the ways of the world. But he could make anything out of wood —fiddles, boats, snowshoes—and he'd spent a lifetime in the woods. Laski saw a shadow moving in the darkness—old Ben's dog, sniffing around in the snow. Then the truck was into the next turn, near the river that came out of the darkness, its icy skin shining in the moonlight. Laski followed the river until it slipped back into the trees, where it wove a silver thread through the dark branches.

Another clearing appeared, and a small board shack. It was a camp for "sports," as the backwoods Canadians called the Americans who came to fish and hunt and rough it for a week. Laski remembered a time, a long time ago—he and his father were fishing in Canada, steering a motorboat along on a bright morning over a wide and winding river. Laski had suddenly felt like he was the river and the trees and the sun and the wind.

He touched Diane gently on the shoulder. She was trembling inside her heavy coat, and he knew enough not to ask her how she felt.

The camp for American sports fell back into darkness. The villagers had thought of Laski and his wife as sports, with no visible means of support, until it was learned they were artists. Never having had such strange creatures around, except for old Coleman Johns, the mad inventor who had built his own automatic milking machine and promised to make a trip to the moon with a magnet in his pants, the country people left the Laskis alone. There was some talk that Laski, with his thick beard and wire glasses, resembled old Coleman enough to be his twin brother. Whenever Laski drove past the ruined foundation that had once been Coleman's home, he was overtaken by a strange nostalgia, as if he and the mad inventor had shared the same vision of this vast land, which made men build strange objects beneath the moon.

Laski's sculpture was certainly odd. Likenesses of Diane filled the forest, her strangely beautiful face gradually appearing on tree stumps or on rocks. Old dead trees with gray bare branches had become Diane dancing, like a priestess of the wood. Eventually the ceaseless weaving of the weeds had made gowns of green for the statues, bright berry beads and buttons entwining the arms and legs, marking them as part of the endless dream of the deep pines.

"The contractions are ten minutes apart."

Laski laid a firmer foot on the gas pedal. Baby's in a hurry.

A ghostly light flashed ahead of Laski, leaping out of the darkness of the country graveyard where Coleman Johns lay buried and where Laski's headlights had caught the top of an old tombstone. The truck wheels spun on the turn, rear end lashing like a tail before coming straight again. Then darkness claimed the graveyard once more, and the road was again lined by heavy forest.


"Maternity?" smiled the receptionist. "Do you have your papers with you?"

Diane took them out of her purse. An orderly came across the waiting room with a wheelchair and Diane sat down in it, still wearing her shaggy forest coat. Laski looked at the receptionist.

"The orderly will take her up, and you can follow in just a few minutes, sir. I have some papers for you to fill out."

Laski touched Diane's hand, and she looked at him, smiling but distant, as the orderly turned the chair and wheeled her off.

The receptionist put a form into her typewriter and asked Laski questions about age, address, insurance—lifeless items holding him in his chair.

A drunken young man, face cut and swollen, swaggered into the waiting room. Glassy-eyed, he approached the desk. The receptionist looked up. "If you'll have a seat please," she said coldly.

The young man leaned on the desk, but the receptionist ignored him, even though he was bleeding from a wound over his eye.

Laski looked into the young man's eyes, expecting hostility. He found a frightened child making brave. The nurses will give him a hard time, thought Laski. Then the doctor will stitch him and he'll be turned back out into the night. But he was once the baby on the way, and everybody rallied around him. The great moment was once his.

An older man entered the waiting room and looked around for a moment, until his eye caught the young man's figure. He came over slowly, his walk and manner similar to the young man's.

"What happened?"

"Nothing much," said the young man, striking a confident pose.

"I haven't seen you for a while."

"I've been around."

"You interested in working?"

"Yeah, sure."

"You can go to work tomorrow."

"Oh no," said the young man, shaking his head and touching his bruises. "I can't do anything tomorrow."

The papers were completed. The orderly returned, and Laski followed him down the hallway to an elevator. They rode together in silence, to the floor marked MATERNITY. The hall held a couch and two leather chairs. Beyond it was a door marked DELIVERY—NO ADMITTANCE.

The orderly walked away. Laski sat down. This is where all the fathers wait. He stood and walked slowly up and down. Now I'm pacing the floor like an expectant father.

The sounds of a floor-waxing machine came along the hallway, somewhere out of sight, whirring, wheels creaking, coming along. Laski listened to its approach, and then it appeared, pushed along by a uniformed maintenance man. "This is your big night, eh?"

"Yes."

The waxer nodded and waxed on. He's seen it all, thought Laski, seen them come and go, seen them every night—pacing back and forth on his waxed floor.

An elderly nurse came out of the delivery room. Laski looked at her, but she gave him such a blank cold stare, all questions dissolved in his throat. He listened to her footsteps going away down the hall, and then he walked over and peered through the porthole window in the delivery room door. The hall beyond the porthole was dimly lit and empty.

He paced back again, past the leather chairs. The alcohol-medicine smell of the hospital filled the air. The floor was squared tile; he stepped between the cracks with each foot. His boots were still wet with snow. The dark tips of them looked back at him, worn down and scarred from the forest.

He reined himself around, came back the other way along the floor. The door swung open again. A young nurse appeared, smiling. "We're just getting your wife ready," she said. "You'll be able to join her in a few minutes."


Diane was sitting up in bed. He went quickly to her, searching her eyes, which showed the same mixture of fear and calm he'd seen all night.

"The baby's upside down," she said.

The air seemed dreamlike, a dream in which he could make things take any shape he liked. But he was standing in a hospital room and their baby was upside down. "It'll be all right," he said, touching her folded hands.

"Dr. Barker says he doesn't want you in on a breech birth. I told him I understand, and that I hope he'll change his mind."

Her face suddenly changed as the contraction came on, and she began her breathing as they'd practiced it, inhaling rapidly and evenly. She closed her eyes, her brow in wrinkles as she grimaced with pain. He stood, powerless, watching the hand within her clenching itself tightly, until her face was one that he had never seen before, a screwed-up mask of desperation that suddenly and slowly relaxed, wrinkles fading, eyes opening, as the contraction subsided.

She looked up at him and smiled. "He must have turned around last week. Remember the bump we felt high on my stomach? That was his head."

"We'll be swinging him down the road soon," said Laski.

Her smile suddenly disappeared as the next contraction came. She went into her rapid breathing, and he willed her his strength, trying to make it pass out of his body and enter hers.

The nurse came in as the contraction subsided. "How're we doing?"

"All right."

"Let me have a look." The nurse lifted Diane's gown for a moment, then lowered it. "You're dilating beautifully."

Diane's smile was once again ruined by the return of a contraction.

A young intern entered and stood at the foot of the bed, waiting as the contraction worked toward its peak. He looked at Laski and asked politely, "Would you mind stepping outside a moment while we examine her?"

Laski went out into the hallway. What do they do to her that I can't be there? Does he think I've never seen my wife's body before? Don't send bad vibrations. They're running this show. He walked up and down the hallway, feeling like the odd man out.

The door opened; the intern came into the hallway and nodded at Laski, who went back in and joined the nurse at the foot of the bed.

"You're fully dilated," said the nurse to Diane. "You can start pushing anytime you want."

Diane nodded her head as the next contraction hit. Laski went behind her, lifting her up from the back, as they had practiced. He lifted, and she hauled back on her knees with her hands, bending her legs and spreading them apart, pressing down within herself. He held her up for the length of the contraction and then slowly let her down.

"Very nice," said the nurse. "Keep up the good work." She smiled at them and left the room.

"Would you wet a washcloth and put it on my forehead?"

Laski got a washcloth out of her bag and wet it in the bathroom sink. He wiped her brow, her cheeks, her neck. "Where's the doctor?"

"He's sleeping in a room down the hall. They'll wake him up when it's time."

"How do you feel?"

"I'm glad to be pushing."

The contraction came and he lifted her again, his face close to hers. The wrinkled brow and tight-closed eyes formed a face he'd never dreamed of. All her beauty was gone, and she seemed like a sexless creature struggling for all it was worth, laboring greatly with the beginning of the world. Their laughter, their little joys, their plans, everything they'd known was swallowed by this labor, a work he suddenly wished they'd never begun, so contorted was she, so unlike the woman he knew. Her face was red, her temples pounding, and she looked now like a middle-aged man taking a shit that was killing him. This is humanity, thought Laski, and he questioned the purpose of a race that seeks to perpetuate itself in agony, but before he had his answer, the contraction had passed and he was lowering her back to the pillow.

He took the washcloth, wet it again, and wiped her perspiring face. "Relax deeply now. Get your energy back. Spread your legs—relax your arms." He talked softly, smoothing out her still-trembling limbs until she finally lay quiet, eyes closed.

The wave came again and carried them out onto the sea of pain, where he wondered again why life ever came into the world. The loveliness of the highway night, when all the stars seemed watching, was now drowned in sweat. The most beautiful face he'd ever seen was looking bulbous, red, and homely.

The tide that drew them out into the troubled waters once again spent itself, and they floated slowly back, resting for a minute or so, only to be dragged out again. He held her up while she contracted and pushed inside herself, trying to open the petals of her flowering body. He'd thought that such a miraculous opening would somehow be performed in a more splendid fashion. But she was sweating like a lumberjack's horse after a summer morning of hauling logs.

He lifted her, trying to free the load she was struggling with, but she was straining against the traces, getting nowhere, her eyes like

those of a draft horse—puzzled, frustrated, and enslaved. He could
see the strain pulsing in her reddened temples, just as he'd seen it in
the workhorses when he thought they would surely die of a heart
attack, racing as they did through the woods with huge logs behind
them, jamming suddenly on a stump, the reins almost snapping and
their mighty muscles knotting against the obstacle. Who would
choose this, thought Laski, this work, this woe? Life enslaves us,
makes us want children, gives us a thousand illusions about love, and
all so that it can go forward.

He felt the supremacy of life, its power greater than his will. I just
wanted to be with you, Diane, the two of us living easily together
and here we are, with your life on the line.

*She was coming down the staircase of a brownstone building. She
wore a long purple cape with a high collar turned up around her neck.
The cape flared out as she touched the sidewalk, and he stood rooted
and stupid, struggling to speak. She must have felt it, for she turned
and looked his way.*

Her face contracted again, her eyes closing tightly and her mouth
bending into a mask formed by the pain that came on her again. He
held her up, feeling the strain in her muscles and the fever in her
skin. The short ringlets of hair at her neck were soaked and glistening.
A wet spot was spreading across her back.

The intern and the nurse returned while they were out upon the
waves, struggling together, pushing together, sweating together to
bring the thing to completion, and when the contraction ended, the
intern did not ask Laski to leave while he made his examination.
"You're showing some progress now."

"You can see the baby," said the nurse.

Laski looked down, and in the shaved and sweating crack he saw
something pink and strange, a little patch of flesh he could not com-
prehend. All he knew were the waves that took them out again, where
they were alone in love and sadness that none else could share, alone
and clinging to each other in the reality they had long prepared for,
for which no preparation was ever enough.

*"I've seen you before," he said, stopping her on Broadway.*

*"Have you?" she said, the slightest touch of flirtation in her voice, just enough to keep him coming toward her, out of his deep embarrassed nature.*

Back they drifted, to the green room in the sleeping hospital.

Hardly had they rested when the waves carried them out again, like a nightmare that repeats itself over and over through the night, and over and over again through the years. Back and forth they went, and he feared that her strength could not hold. He had no confidence, not in himself, nor in her. He felt like a helpless child, and Diane seemed helpless too, their long struggle getting them nowhere, only repeating itself—contraction, release, contraction again. But the nurse and intern seemed unconcerned by it all, were cheerful and confident. And the doctor is down the hall, sleeping. He's not worried. If there were anything wrong, he'd be here.

*She dressed by the window of his tiny room, slipping slowly into tight knit slacks and sweater. Her short hair needed no combing or fixing, and she was the most natural thing he'd ever seen, unlike his previous loves, who'd always thrown him out of the room while they dressed and primped or put curlers in their hair.*

Her gown was wringing wet, her hair plastered down, as if the sea had broken over her. She closed her eyes and crow's-feet came there, lines he'd never seen before, lines of age, and he knew that ages had passed. "Again," she said, her voice almost a sob now, but not a sob, too tired for tears. And he lifted her up as the tide carried them out again, into the wild uncharted waters.

He held her, his love for her expanding with every tremor of her body. It seemed he'd never loved her before, that all of their past was just a rehearsal for this moment in which he felt resounding inside him all the days of her life, days before he'd known her, days from the frightened child's face he saw before him, and days from the wise woman's ancient life that came calling now to give her unknown strength. All the frustration of Diane's thirty years was present, and she seemed to be making a wish in the well of time, that everything should finally come out all right, that finally something she was doing would be just as it should be.

*"I can't have a baby," she said, "because of the shape of my womb."*

"*Bullshit.*"

"*He's a Park Avenue gynecologist.*"

Well, thought Laski, it took us ten years, but we finally made one. He lowered her back to the bed, wiping her brow with the washcloth. She smiled, but it again was a mask, formed by momentary release from her anguish. In it was none of the flirtation, none of the peace, none of the things he usually saw in her smiles. But he knew she'd made this smile for him, to ease his worry. *She's seeing into me too; maybe she sees all the care of my days, as I am seeing her.* He felt them together, then, on a new level, older, wiser, with pain as the binder in their union. *We came more than fifty miles tonight; we've crossed the ocean.*

Her smile suddenly drew itself up beyond the limits of smiling, becoming a grimace, and he lifted her up. *We're not across the ocean yet.*

"*Gee-yup, Bob!*" *The great horse pulled, his hooves scraping on the forest floor, sending moss and sticks flying. The tree creaked and swayed and fell and Bob-horse ran with it, dragging branches and all.*

"I guess we can get Dr. Barker now," said the intern.

The nurse went out of the room. Laski wiped Diane's brow, and the intern stood at the foot of the bed, watching. "You've been pushing for nearly three hours," he said.

"That's too long, isn't it?" she asked.

"It's because the baby's weight is up instead of down."

And suddenly they were out again, in the tempest. Laski held her up, pouring himself through his fingertips into her, as she lifted her legs and pushed.

The nurse entered with a tall young man in a white uniform. He stood at the foot of the bed with the intern as Laski and Diane held on, out upon the sea, love-blown sailors lost in fathomless depths of time and destiny, coming now slowly back to a room of strangers who seemed eternal too, in a never-ending play. "If you'll just step outside a minute," said Dr. Barker.

Laski went into the hallway and gathered himself together in a single prayer without words, offered to the ocean.

The door swung open. The young doctor stepped out and said, "Things are developing now. We'll be taking her down to the delivery room."

Laski went back to Diane. She was bent up, contracting alone, and he went to her.

"Your baby's on the way now," said the nurse, smiling cheerfully at Laski.

He suddenly remembered the baby, the little swimmer in the secret sea. He's struggling too, struggling to be with us, struggling just like we are.

Laski's heart became an ocean of love, as nine months of memories flooded him, and the baby was real again, real as in the night when Laski felt tiny feet kicking inside Diane. Our baby, our little friend, is being born!

And this, thought Laski, is why we labor, so that love might come into the world.

The contraction passed, and he and Diane were washed back, limp like sea-plants when the waves abandon them on the shore. "It looks very good," said the intern.

The nurse came in, wheeling a stretcher. "All set?"

"Yes," said Diane. They slid her from the bed onto the stretcher, and they all walked beside it down the hallway toward the delivery room. Dr. Barker was being put into a white gown. Laski leaned over and kissed Diane.

"Aren't you coming in?" she asked, her voice filled with longing.

The nurse continued wheeling her into the delivery room, and Laski stood in the hall outside. His will, his speech, his guts were gone. Barker stepped over to him. "The nurse will give you a cap and gown, and you can watch from behind the table."

Laski's strength came back in a whirlwind as a great smile crossed his face. We're going all the way together! He stood, watching the doctor and intern wash their hands in a nearby sink, washing them again and again, in a slow methodical manner. The nurse came to him and held up a gown. He slipped his arms into it and she tied it in back. She gave him a white cap that he fastened over his ears. Then he and the intern went into the delivery room, where Diane lay on the central table, her legs in stirrups, her wrists strapped down.

"You can sit here," said the nurse, setting a stool behind the table.

Another nurse fixed the mirror that was above the table, so that Laski could see the area of birth.

"A clear picture?"

"Perfect."

One of the nurses then brought a little sponge soaked with surgical soap and wiped Diane's vaginal area.

"Oh, that feels good."

"Has she had any anesthetic?" asked the other nurse.

"No."

"Well, now, isn't she wonderful?"

Dr. Barker came and sat on a stool at the other end of the table. "I'm going to drain your bladder."

He inserted a tube into her urethra, and a moment later her urine ran out of it, into a bucket at Barker's feet.

"I have a contraction," said Diane.

"Go ahead and push."

Laski could not reach her, and she lifted herself, working alone. When the contraction subsided, Barker said, "I'm going to make a small cut. First I'll give you something to numb it." He inserted a needle at the edge of her vagina, making three injections. Then he pinched her skin with a tweezers. "Do you feel that?"

"No."

He made an incision, cutting sideways toward her thigh. "Check the heartbeat."

The nurse laid her stethoscope on Diane's lower belly and listened, timing the baby's heartbeat with her watch.

"Normal."

"All right—push again." Barker inserted his finger into Diane's vagina, feeling for the baby. When the finger came out, Laski saw more of the strange pink skin, and a thick dark substance.

"Don't let that worry you," said the nurse to Laski. "The baby's just had a bowel movement."

"Push," said Barker. Diane pushed, and Laski could see the baby's rear end, at the doorway of the world, ass-backwards, thought Laski, but coming!

"All right, dear, push again," said Barker.

She pushed, and he put his long fingers into her vagina, moving them around and spreading her lips. Suddenly a foot appeared, followed by a long limp leg. Barker quickly brought the other leg down, and Laski looked at it in wonder, at the tiny toenails and the perfectly formed little feet that had been developing all along within her, about which he had dreamed so often, envisioning them in countless ways, and now the first step of those little feet into life had come before his eyes.

"It's a boy!" exclaimed the nurse.

Laski's heart filled with joy. Staring at the entranceway, he saw the tiny penis and a second later it squirted a jet of urine.

"I felt him pee on me!" cried Diane in wonder.

"Push," said Barker. "Push with all you've got."

As she pushed, he guided the tiny body out, all but the head, which remained inside. Laski stared in fascination at the dangling little creature, the skin gray and wet—his little son, come at last.

Barker inserted the forceps. "Once again."

Diane pushed, and Laski tensed as he watched Barker forcefully pulling with the forceps to release the head. My God, thought Laski, they handle them hard. And suddenly the head popped out, and the child was free.

Barker's hands moved with incredible grace and swiftness, turning the baby in the air, holding him up like a red rose. Laski saw a face filled with rage, yet triumphant, the god of time and men, whose closed eyes looked straight into Laski's and said, *See, see, this!*

"Cut the cord!"

The intern severed the cord, and Barker carried the child with utmost delicacy in his two hands, moving quickly over to a table by the wall.

"The aspirator," he said, sharply.

The nurse handed him an instrument that looked like an old car horn, a rubber bulb fitted on the end of it. He put it to the baby's face and squeezed.

The child lay perfectly still. Barker worked the pump, then touched the limp wrist, lifting it for a moment and laying it back down. One nurse massaged the feet, and the other handed Barker a length of fine hose, which he inserted into the baby's mouth. He breathed into it, and Laski watched his son's chest rise and fall with the breath of the doctor moving inside him.

Barker stopped for a moment, wiped his brow, returned to the blowing-tube. Laski looked on, watching the lungs rise and fall again. The rest of the body lay perfectly still. How long his legs are, thought Laski—just like his mother's.

Barker removed the tube and put his mouth to the child's, blowing into it with his lips pressed against the tiny mouth.

The nurse continued to massage the feet. Laski looked at the clock on the wall: four thirty-five.

Barker stepped back, wiped his brow again, and Laski remembered moments from his own life, when he'd worked on things and found them puzzling and unyielding, and he'd wiped his brow that way. Barker put the aspirator back on the still little body and pumped it, a little sighing noise coming from the rubber bulb.

"Is that the baby?" asked Diane.

Laski looked at her, and looked away, drawn back to his little son, to the little arm that rose and fell so limply in Barker's hand.

"Where's the baby?" asked Diane.

"He's over there," said Laski softly.

Barker removed the aspirator and put his mouth to the child's again, blowing in and out, gently, evenly. He stepped back, wiped his brow, turned to Laski, and shook his head from side to side.

Laski nodded.

It was over.

He turned and sat down on the little stool beside the table. The intern was stitching Diane's opened vagina.

"Does that hurt?"

"No," she said, laughing nervously.

Laski looked at her flat stomach. How can she possibly hold together in the face of this? How do we tell her?

He turned to the table by the wall. The baby had been lowered into a glass case, and he was on his side, eyes closed. Laski saw resignation in the little face, the expression of work completely done, like a man who has rolled over to sleep at the end of the day.

"Are you all right?" asked Barker.

"Yes," said Laski.

Barker stepped over to the maternity table and looked down at Diane.

She raised her eyes to his. "I know," she said.

"I'm sorry."

"It's not your fault," she said, a sob breaking from her throat.

"The baby looks perfectly normal," said Barker. "There's no reason why you can't have another child."

Laski listened numbly. He thinks that's what has been at stake, our wish for a child, any child, not this particular child who swung down the road between us. They can't know how special he is. They point to the future. But we're here, forever, now.

The nurse slipped Diane onto the wheeled table. "I have a needle for you," said the nurse.

"No," said Diane, still refusing any anesthetic.

"It's to dry up your milk," said the nurse, gently.

"There are no private rooms," said the other nurse. "We can put you in a semiprivate."

"I can go to a ward," said Diane. "I only wanted a private room so I could keep the baby with me."

"It would be better for you in a semiprivate. All the other babies will be brought into the ward for feeding, and they'll make you feel bad."

"I wouldn't mind the babies," said Diane, crying softly. "But I'd probably make all the other mothers feel bad."

They wheeled her through the dimly lit hallway, and Laski walked beside her, to a room with two beds, both of them empty. They helped her into the bed and drew the covers over her.

"May I stay?" asked Laski.

"Yes, certainly," said the nurse. "Do you want to sleep on the other bed?"

"No, I'm not tired."

"If you want to," she said, "just flop down on it." The nurse leaned over to Diane. "These things happen. I'm sure you'll have better luck next time."

Laski looked at the little handbag beside the bed, in which Diane had packed two baby washcloths, one pink, one blue, and he saw that it was the blue one he'd been using to mop her brow.

She looked quietly at him and stroked his hair with her hand. He laid his head down on the bed beside her, as the full weight of his own weariness took him. The nurse came in again and said, "Are you sure you won't lie down?"

"All right," he said, and walked over to the other bed.

"Let me slip this sheet over it. I'm lazy. I don't want to have to make it again."

He crawled onto the top sheet and lay looking at the ceiling. Beneath his head he felt cement blocks. He drifted, into kaleidoscopic sleep, so filled with images he could not sort them into any recognizable dream, and they rushed over him like water.

He woke and saw Diane looking at the ceiling. He got up and sat beside her again. The dawn was breaking. Through the window he saw another wing of the hospital, and beyond that the street, on which the gray light was falling. He watched the street as the sunlight fell upon it.

In the hallway the sound of dishes began. "They're bringing breakfast," she said.

The breakfast carts came closer, and an elderly woman entered, carrying a tray. She smiled at Laski. "Well, it's a lovely day, isn't it?"

Diane ate cereal and toast, and sunlight found the room.

"They'll want me out of here soon," said Laski.

"Yes, the mothers will be feeding their babies."

He saw the sorrow break over her for a moment, like a wave upon a cliff, but the wave washed away, and there was the cliff, which sorrow could not drown.

"I'll be back this evening," he said. "Visiting hours are at seven. Is there anything you want?"

"No, just you."

He leaned over and kissed her, her tears going slowly down his cheek.


Laski drove over the bridge and out of town. As he crossed the railroad tracks that ran through the slum on the edge of the city, a delicate film of light came across his eyes, as if a shimmering translucent veil were covering the morning, and he knew that it was his son's spirit, riding with him. And then he saw himself running with his son, through the fields, leaping the old broken fences. They walked to the stream and dove into it, then danced upon it, then ran to the trees, climbing up above the mist.

Laski drove toward home with tears streaming down his face, his spirit racing with his son through time, across the morning of the world, from place to place, in cities and in the lovely valley. The moment of their meeting was endless: they took a boat, and took a train, and saw the sights, and grew up together. It seemed to take years getting to the forest, and as Laski climbed the hills into the abandoned settlement, he felt the spirit of his son spreading out all around him. Spreading out as it did, into every tree and cloud, he felt it losing personality, felt it dissolving into something remote, expanded beyond his powers to follow. He's going now, thought Laski. He's grown up and leaving me. Goodbye, goodbye, he called, looking out to the beautiful eastern sky where the sun was dazzling the trees.

You're free in the wind. You're great with the winds and sun.

Then it was over and Laski was alone again, bouncing along the old winding road through the forest.


Returning to the hospital in the evening, he got lost in the corridors beyond the lobby, none of it familiar to him anymore. He stood looking toward a staircase he could not remember climbing before. A strong voice came at his shoulder. "Where are you headed for?"

"Maternity."

"Follow me," said a powerfully striding man in boots and ski sweater. He took the steps as if they were a mountain trail and Laski kept the pace.

"What did you have?" asked the man, not looking back, keeping his eyes on the trail.

Laski hesitated as fragments of explanations rose in his mind—*the baby died, we had nothing*—but then he felt the spirit of the child again, suddenly surging in his heart, and he said, "A boy."

"Congratulations," said the mountain man, as they reached the top of the mountain staircase, at the hall marked MATERNITY.

"And you?" asked Laski.

"A boy," said the mountaineer, his voice filled with wind and stone and wild joy. He turned off to the left, and Laski went straight ahead, down the hall to Diane's room.

She was in bed, her eyes red, her face pale, the shock of the night still on her. He sat down beside the bed and took her hand. "Was the doctor in to see you?"

"He said he examined the afterbirth and found that the cord had been connected to the edge of the placenta instead of the middle. It was a weak place, and at the last minute the cord tore. The baby bled."

Laski slowly nodded his head and looked toward the window. Through the other lighted rooms of the hospital, he saw distant figures moving.

"He'd like to perform an autopsy," said Diane.

"Is it really necessary?"

"It's up to us."

"Do you want to let them?"

"I guess they always do it."

Beyond the windows of the hospital, he could see the sidewalks and the snowy street. In the maternity hallway, at the desk, the nurses were chatting and laughing together.

"He's in the morgue," said Diane.

A nurse entered the room, smiling cheerfully. "Time for your heat lamp." Then, turning to Laski, "Would you excuse us for a minute?"

Laski stepped out into the hall. The doors of the other rooms were open, and he could see women in their beds, visitors beside them. He lowered his eyes toward the floor and followed the sound of the waxing machine and the elevator and the visiting voices, all of it flowing like a stream in which he seemed to be floating. The second hand on the wall clock over his head was humming, round and round. The laughter at the nurses' desk continued, and he realized it was New Year's Eve. *In a room on Ninety-first Street in New York City, in the darkness of a little bed, while the bells rang and the sirens called, he held her.* The waxing machine appeared, its long whiskers whirring around and around over the tiled floor.

A snowstorm had begun in the city. The night was cold, and he was filled with tired thoughts. Twenty-five miles away, out in the woods, the house was waiting, empty and cold. A hotel would be warm and bright—a single room, a table with a lamp on it, a bed. I could get some sleep and hang around town tomorrow until visiting time.

The traffic light turned green through the veil of falling snow, and he drove down the main street of town to the street of the hotel, where he parked the truck. The snow was coming harder. He walked along toward the hotel. It's not the best and that's all I need, just a flop for the night.

His body ached and his eyes were tired. The shops on the street were all closed, the merchandise on display beneath dim nightlights, and he passed by it all on weary legs. The hotel had a single door leading to a cramped little lobby, into which he stepped, looking toward the night clerk's desk. The clerk, reading a newspaper, did not look up. A television set was going, and two men sat before it, smiling at some flickering image Laski could not see, but he sensed the loneliness of the men, and their desperate fight against it, huddled together before the television.

As if turned by a magnet, he went back out through the door into the street. The snow fell on him as he walked back to the truck and climbed into it, driving out of town and over the white highway toward the woods.

He entered the cabin reluctantly, as if it were a cave of ghosts. The stove was low and he stirred it up. When the surface was hot, he slid on a frying pan and cooked himself supper. He ate slowly, staring out the window at the whirling snow. When his meal was finished, he washed the dishes, not hurrying, but working slowly, with concentration, leaving no room for morbid thoughts, ghosts, fears. There was only the hot water, the dish, his hands, the soapy rag.

The stairs to the second floor looked dark and foreboding, and what's up there, amidst the baby clothes and crib? There's nothing up there, he said, and he walked up the stairs and undressed in the small bedroom. He kept the light on for a few minutes and then, resigning himself to darkness and sleep, switched it off.

Alone in the dark house far out in the woods, with a storm blowing on the outside and the shadow of death on the inside, he crawled beneath the covers. Specters rose up behind his closed eyes, weird and menacing. He watched his mind play out its age-old fears, and trembling, he fell into dreams, finding himself outside the cabin, walking through the dream-forest. Beside a tree he saw a cloaked and hooded figure. The figure turned, and the face beneath the hood was

The night visiting bell sounded. "I'll be in first thing tomorrow afternoon," he said, kissing her lightly on the lips. Then he went down the green hall, toward the street, the highway, and home.

The steel roof of the cabin was bright in the moonlight as he parked the truck in the drive. He opened the door to the shed, where his lumber was piled. How am I going to do this? he asked himself, looking at the long pile of pine boards, and at his tools. He was overcome by a feeling of dread about making the coffin; he had no wish to build it, or anything, ever again.

He fingered the smoothly planed surface of the boards; the heavy feeling in him remained, as if he were in a dark cloud, but he grabbed a board and hauled it out of the pile.

Carrying the sawhorses into his studio, he spaced them out evenly. Across them he laid the long clean pine board. Then he brought his toolbox in and set it down. He pulled the metallic rule out of its case and stretched it along the wood, imagining the size of the baby's body.

He laid his T-square on the mark, drew a straight line, and sawed along it, thinking of the old days when men had always built the caskets of their loved ones, and he saw that it was a good thing to do, that it was a privilege few men had anymore. He marked the next line carefully and sawed a matching piece to form the floor of the casket.

He joined the two pieces and then cut the sides and ends for the box. The time passed slowly and peacefully. He worked, sanding the edges of the pieces so that they would join well, to form a box that no one would see, but which had to be made perfectly. He drilled holes and countersunk them, and screwed on the sides and endpieces.

Squatting on the floor, sawdust on his knees and a pencil behind his ear, he turned the screws slowly, biting deep into the wood. He sanded along the edge of the box, making another fine cloud of sawdust, which filled his nose with a memorable smell. I built a house for us, with a room for him, and now I'm building his casket. There's no difference in the work. We simply must go along, eyes open, watching our work carefully, without any extra thoughts. Then we flow with the night.

a smiling skull of stone. Death held out his walking stick, and Laski took it in his hand.

Late afternoon sunlight streamed through the hospital window, and he sat down beside her again. She looked stronger, and the storm was over.

"We have to bury the baby," she said. "They don't want him in the morgue anymore."

"We can bury him in the woods."

"That's what I told the nurse. She said it was highly unusual, but that it would probably be all right. She had a lot of forms. We'll have to have a witness."

"How about the autopsy? Won't the baby be . . . ?"

"She said they put him back together again."

Dr. Barker came into the room. They both looked at him in silence. He stood, tall and uncomfortable at the foot of the bed. "The autopsy showed your baby was perfectly normal. There's no reason why what happened should ever happen again."

"Do you think she can go home tomorrow?"

"How do your stitches feel?"

"They burn a little, that's all."

"I suppose you can leave, if you'll feel better at home." He turned to go, then turned back to Diane. "I know it's difficult to lose your first baby when you're thirty."

The last light of day went along the brick wall of the hospital. Laski sat by the window, watching as night came on. Diane, wearing a bathrobe, entered the room. "I told the nurse we'd be taking the baby home tomorrow afternoon."

"I'll build a little box for him tonight."

"Will you be able to dig a hole in the frozen ground?"

A nurse peeked her head inside the door. "There are some fluids in the hall if either of you want any."

Laski went out and found a tray of watered fruit drinks. He poured some orange into two glasses and returned to the room. "Fluids," he said, handing her the thin orange drink.

The little box took shape, and he resisted feeling proud of it, for pride was something extra. I do it quietly, for no one, not even for him, for he's gone beyond my little box. But he left behind a fragment of himself, which requires a box I can carry through the woods. And the box needs a lid, and I've got to find a pair of hinges.

He rummaged around the shed and found an old rusted pair, small and squeaky but serviceable. Making the outlines for the hinges, he chiseled out their shape, so they slid snugly down into the wood. He tried the lid and continued setting the hinges, until the lid finally closed solidly. He worked the lid up and down a few times, enjoying the smooth action of it, until he remembered what it was for, and he saw again that there should be nothing extra in the work.

He put away the sawhorses and his tools and swept up the dust. Then he sat down in a chair and quietly rocked, back and forth, looking at the coffin. A vague dissatisfaction stirred in him, growing slowly more clear and troubling.

If we bury him here, we'll be attached to this land permanently. I can have him cremated at a funeral home, and his ashes will be put in a little metal box, and we can carry it around with us when we travel. And when we get to the middle of the ocean someday, we can throw his ashes there.

That's exactly what we should do. I'll take him to the funeral home tomorrow and they can cremate him in the little coffin.

A feeling of freedom came to Laski—freedom from land and houses and graves. And keeping this thought in his mind, he went upstairs to bed.

When he entered the hospital room, it was into a new atmosphere— the other bed was now occupied. As he went toward Diane, out of the corner of his eye he saw a young girl lying in the bed he had lain in. Beside her was a young man and two older women. They pulled a curtain around themselves, and Laski sat down beside Diane.

"She lost her baby," whispered Diane.

Laski glanced toward the closed curtain, behind which soft shadows were moving. "I think we should have the baby cremated in town this afternoon."

"But why?"

"If we bury him on the land, it will just be another tie for us, that this is the place where the baby is buried."

Her eyes filled with tears again. "If you think it's best . . ."

"I don't know what's best," he said. "Maybe there isn't any best. But the thought was very strong, and I'm trying to flow with it."

"What will you do?"

"I'll go over to the funeral home now and find out if they can do it right away."

He stood and went past the other visitors. Down the hall once more, and down the stairs, his thoughts were racing now—to get it over with and set them free.

He crossed the parking lot quickly and started the truck. Vaguely remembering the whereabouts of a funeral home, he drove through town. They'll deal with the whole thing, and we won't have to get involved.

Snowplows were still working, clearing the streets, and here and there people were shoveling out their sidewalks and driveways. Laski turned a corner and saw the old colonial manor with the black and white nameplate on one of its large old pillars. It was an enormous place, with many windows, and he looked through the front window, down a long hallway lined with flowers and muted floor lamps. The parking lot was filled with cars. Three large limousines were heaped with flowers, and a crew of professionally somber men in black were standing beside a fourth limousine, hung with gray velvet curtains. The side door opened, and the front end of a casket came out, made of dark wood polished to a high gloss and trimmed with silver and gold filigree. Clinging to its shining brass carrying-rails was a crew of professionals, wax-faced and silent, bearing the huge gaudy coffin toward the hearse, where the back door was opened smoothly by a driver, who helped to slide the coffin into the richly curtained interior.

Laski drove on, horrified. What in hell did I almost do?

His hands were trembling on the wheel. Tears in his eyes, he looked down at the little pine box on the seat beside him and laid his hand upon its plain smooth surface.

Circling back through town, he returned to the hospital; once again through the corridors, once again up the stairs, once again past the nurses, and past the people visiting in Diane's room.

"Let's go," he said softly, taking Diane's hand. "We're going home together, and we'll bury him down by the stream."

"But what about the funeral home?"

"Just something I dreamed up to protect myself from the truth of death."

She got up from the bed. "I just have to get dressed," she said, taking her clothes into the bathroom; he sat on the edge of the bed and heard the voices of the visitors talking to the young girl behind the curtain.

"You mustn't think about it anymore."

"Tomorrow's another day."

"Yes," said the girl. And then again, "Yes," softly.

"That's right, dear. You should always look to the future."

"What a pretty nightgown."

"I got it at the Kmart."

"They'll have the sales there now."

"Everything will be half-price. After New Year's."

Smoke drifted over the curtain. Laski went to the window. The previous day's paper was on the windowsill, and glancing at the headlines he saw war, scandal, inflation. We'll bury him by the stream. This moment dies and is followed by another moment that also dies. Moment to moment I go.

"I'm ready," she said. He picked up her bag, and they went to the desk. An elderly nurse spoke to them. "I've told them to have the baby ready for you down at the reception desk. He'll be all wrapped nicely."

Another nurse appeared with a wheelchair.

"I can walk," said Diane.

"Rules," said the nurse. "You get to ride."

Diane sat in the chair, and they went to the elevator. The nurse wheeled her into it, and Laski stood beside her as they rode down to the lobby.

The usual crowd was there, reading magazines and staring at the pale yellow walls. The nurse wheeled them to the reception room. "The Laski baby," she said.

The receptionist went into the room behind her and returned with an orderly, who carried a small linen bundle.

Diane, still in the wheelchair, held her arms out, a sob breaking in her throat. The orderly stood puzzled, not knowing what to do.

Laski reached out and took the cold little parcel, cradling it in one arm and carrying Diane's suitcase with the other. They went up the exit ramp toward the door. He looked down at Diane and saw her still crying.

"I'll bring the truck to the door," he said, and went out across the parking lot, with the baby still in his arms. He could not feel the outline of the body, only the small weight of it in the cold linen wrapping. From a refrigerator, he thought, and then he opened the truck and slid inside.

With the baby on his lap, he opened the pine box and laid the linen-shrouded child into it. He closed the lid and latched it shut. The nurse was waiting at the sidewalk as he drove up to the entrance of the hospital. They helped Diane out of the chair and into the front seat of the truck. "You'll have better luck next time," said the nurse. She waved to them, standing for a moment beneath the hospital awning, and then as they pulled away, she turned with the empty wheelchair.

"It's a lovely box," said Diane, her voice calm now.

The box was between them on the seat, and for a moment Laski smelled the sweet perfume of death, or was it the smell of the wood? The delicate odor continued to come to him as they went along the highway, by the fields and the river. The day was unseasonably warm, with wisps of gray mist above the water, and the snow was changing to slush along the shoulder of the road.

"It's just us again," he said.

"Yes," she said, their hands touching on the lid of the pine box.


He wheeled the truck up into the wooded hills, along the old road toward their home. Above an abandoned farm a crow went through the January sky, black wings beating slowly on the gray heights.

Laski turned down the lane to the cabin and into the drive. He got out and opened the door for her. She stepped into the snow, leaning on him. The sound of melting snow as it dripped off the trees filled the air, and the smell of the trees came strong on the moist warm breeze.

"What a beautiful day," she said, suddenly crying again.

He walked with her slowly up the shoveled path to their door. She leaned on him into the cabin; he had the couch made up for her and settled her onto it. Then he stirred the fire and went back out to the car for her bag, and then back again, for the pine box.

He placed the box down on top of the table, and it remained there in the last light of the afternoon, while they sat quietly on the couch.

"I'd better go see old Ben and ask him to come here in the morning." Laski went out again, and he saw her watching him through the window.


Ben's collie dog came bounding up to Laski's truck, and Laski got out and petted him, rolling him over on his back and scratching his stomach. He knelt in the snow for a moment, his hand on the dog's belly. In the sky the crow was still calling, circling on the wind, and Laski felt as if he were the crow and the dog and the sky, as if he were transparent and the day was passing through him.

"Come into my castle, friend."

Laski looked up and saw old Ben standing in the doorway of the broken-down farmhouse. Ben led him through the labyrinth of boards and falling rafters, into the innermost room of the house, where an old iron stove was glowing with heat and everything was neatly in place—table, chair, water bucket, and a small single bed behind the stove. The hermit sat down on the edge of the bed and tossed a chunk of wood into the fire. "Well, what can we do for you today?" he asked, taking out a package of tobacco.

Laski hesitated, holding his hands out over the heated top of the stove. "The baby died," he said.

Ben stared at the cracked old firebox of the stove, where tiny sparks were dancing.

"Will you help me bury him?" asked Laski.

"You'll have to get a lot number from the cemetery," said the hermit, trying to roll a cigarette, the tobacco sticking out at both ends.

"I'm burying him in the woods."

Ben hesitated, looking at Laski across the stove. "Do you have a permit?"

"It's okay, Ben. They filled out the papers at the hospital. I put your name in as the witness." He stared back down at the stove. How scared we are, he thought, to even bury our dead, unless we have permission from the government. "I'd like to do it first thing in the morning."

"I'll be there," said Ben.

Laski went back through the winding tunnel of debris and out into the snow. The dog jumped up to him, licking his hand, and Laski saw all the sad wisdom of dogs flickering in the collie's dark eyes.


The sun was gone, and they sat quietly, looking toward the box. Finally she said, "I'd like to see him."

"All right," said Laski, his stomach going weak. He had a fleeting image in his mind of the baby he had seen, a powerful face looking at him in the moment of death. What will he look like now, thought Laski, dreading the opening of the box.

He slowly lifted the lid and touched the linen bundle. It was still cool. He felt as though he were in a dream again. "You'd better let me look at him first, in case he's too badly marked." He turned back the clean crisp linen. Beneath it was a faded, dirty piece of sheet, its edges torn and frayed. He unfolded it, expecting to suddenly see the little face, but beneath the sheet were old pieces of rags laid on top of each other, and beneath the old rags was a green plastic garbage bag.

He untwisted the piece of wire that held the garbage bag closed. Slowly pulling down the edge of the bag, he came to the proud little head, now gray and cold. Gently, he rolled down the rest of the garbage bag and looked into the open cavity of his son's chest and stomach.

"They left him open," he said, his hands trembling on the bag.

"It's all right," she said. "I saw."

Laski unfolded the garbage bag until the baby was completely visible, his torso a hollow of skin right to the backbone, holding a little pool of blood, like a cup. Drifting in the blood was a plastic stick with a number on it.

A fire raged through Laski's body, swelling his chest with blood and burning his throat. "This is death!" he cried, tears bursting from his eyes. "There's nothing strange about it!"

He moved his eyes down the long legs where the little feet were tucked together, one atop the other, and death was upon them, holding them still as stone. He looked again into the open hole in the baby's body, to the framework of the backbone. They took out his lungs and his stomach, took out all his guts. They even took his little heart.

Laski was engulfed again by love for the little boy who lay before him, all cut up. He took the right hand in his own, opening the stiff little fingers and gazing into the tiny cold palm. The fingers held firm against his, with death's unbending grip. How tiny his fingernails are, and so perfect.

He looked at the face of his son and saw that it had undergone a strange transformation. The features had completely matured, the face now that of a man of many years, as if the single moment of life when he was spun upon the doctor's hand had been a lifetime from beginning to end. The triumph and rage, the gain and loss, all this was gone from the face now, and the closed eyelids radiated serenity.

"He's so lovely," said Diane, her tears falling on the exquisite little head, finely sculpted as that of a Grecian statue. "He struggled so hard to be born . . ."

Then the ocean of sorrow took her, and she was crying wildly, like a seawind that drives the water into terrible waves. And through the storm the little pine box floated calmly, with its strange passenger, the infant who was also an old man.

Laski opened the little eyelid and saw a blackened jewel, gone far into the night. He closed it and put his mouth to the little ear, into which he whispered, "Don't be afraid." Then, looking at the high broad forehead and the noble eyelids, and seeing again so clearly the wisdom they embodied, he knew the being who had come to them and left so quickly didn't need any advice. And he felt much younger than this infant who lay before him, this infant with the head of an age-old sage.

"He never got to live at all!" cried Diane, howling in the seawind.

Laski touched the little cheek, and it sagged beneath his touch, the lifeless flesh like softest putty.

"Oh no, don't," said Diane, her voice suddenly soft, as she gently pushed the flesh of the cheek back into place. Bending her head over, she laid a kiss upon the little forehead. "He's just like marble."

Laski slowly brought the garbage bag up around the little body.

"I could look at him forever," said Diane, but she wrapped the bag in the old rags and the dirty sheet, finally pinning closed the clean white linen. Laski lowered the lid of the box, and again it seemed like a dream that could move in any direction he willed. But then he felt reality moving in only one direction. The baby was born and he died, and I'm closing the lid of his coffin.

Diane wiped the baby's blood from Laski's face and from her own lips, then went slowly to the couch and lay down. He sat on the floor beside her. There was nothing to say. Neither of them wished to escape the passing of the hours, and they were powerless to change the winding stream of the night; there was nothing to do but sit in the stillness.

He fell into reverie, and he fell into fantasy. He was back in the labor room, seeing the baby's skin pushing at her vagina. *He's right there—he's waiting. Get him out of there—don't waste any more time.* But the doctor slept down the hall.

Finally his thoughts faded, and there was only the sound of the winter night outside. He felt Diane with him in the deep strange quiet, and holding to it, dwelling in that stillness, he saw life and death merge into one calm and shining sea that had no end.


He woke before dawn and made them breakfast, then carried the pine box into the shed. Through the east windows the first gray light came as he laid the box down and brought hammer and nails. Then slowly and carefully he hammered the lid shut, and the pounding of the nails rang out like solemn drumbeats in the winter dawn. As he drove the last nail in, he heard Ben at the shed door.

Laski opened the door for the old man standing there on snowshoes, a ragged cigarette in his mouth. "I'll be right with you," said Laski, gathering up his pick and shovel and his own snowshoes.

"We should dig the hole first," said Ben. "And you can come back for the box."

Laski nodded and walked ahead, over the hard morning crust of snow that crunched beneath their snowshoes. He went into the woods, past the skeleton of an old barn, where a porcupine had made his own beat in the snow, and Laski's path crossed it, and went down, into the deeper trees.

He followed an old logging trail through the pines, and Ben kept close behind him, smoking and coughing in the still morning air. The trail went through alder bushes, and down, to the larger trees, where no lumber had been cut for many years. Laski went on, through the old trees to the high bank above the stream. There the bank sloped down, with thin firs growing on its sides. Below was the stream, frozen but still flowing, and the sound of its flowing came up to his ears. He stopped in a square of four small spruce.

They shoveled off the snow, clearing a space of earth in the little square. "The ground doesn't appear to be frozen," said Laski.

"No, it'll be good digging," said Ben, raising the pick. When he'd loosened the dirt, Laski shoveled it and threw it into a pile. The sky remained gray, and the hole took shape and grew deeper, Ben chopping and Laski shoveling out the loosened earth.

"Don't appear to be many roots," said Ben.

"No, it's not bad."

"Has to be wider though," said Ben. He broke more surrounding earth, and Laski shoveled it off, so that he was able to climb down into the hole and work at the walls.

"How deep do you want it?" asked Ben.

"So an animal won't dig it up."

"Nothing will touch it," said Ben, but they shoveled deeper until Laski was in up to his waist, throwing the dirt out.

"You go and bring the box back down," said Ben. "I'll get the hole squared up."

Laski climbed out of the hole, put his snowshoes on, and followed the beat back up through the pines. The dampness of the morning brought many smells into the air, of dead wood and leaves, and from time to time he caught a faint trace of the musk of some animal who had passed by. All around in the snow were rabbit tracks weaving in and out through the trees, and there were also the tracks of a bobcat going in his gracefully curving line deeper into the forest, to the cedar bog, where the deer stayed.

The old barn came into view, and Laski went past it, toward the cabin. At the shed, he removed his snowshoes and stuck them in the snow. He entered the shed and laid the toboggan down on the floor, placing the little coffin on top of it. Then he roped it down.

When it was securely fastened, he went into the cabin. Diane was sitting up on the couch. "Did you find a nice spot?"

"On the high bank above the stream," said Laski. "I'm taking him down there now." He returned to the shed and carried the loaded sled out into the snow. He put his snowshoes on again and took the rope in his hands. The load was very light and went smoothly over the crust.

On the slope behind the old barn, the toboggan moved on its own and he ran alongside it, guiding it with the rope through a stand of young spruce. The arms of the little trees touched the box, shedding some needles upon it, and a few tiny cones.

# EX UTERO

## JILL BIALOSKY

,

## One

This is about the history of my beautiful child. My son. It begins in 1954. I am not born yet. My mother is a nineteen-year-old child bride. I love looking at the pictures of her and my father when they were so in love and the future was in front of them. I love my mother's fifties haircut, her stirrup pants, bobby socks, and black penny loafers, and the way her head is tucked in the fold where my father's arm meets his shoulder and they are side by side on the tweed couch. Nothing has happened yet to jeopardize their future.

I can only imagine how my mother must have felt when she told my father she was pregnant. She would have been waiting for him to come home from work at the real estate office where he was selling houses. She would have been beside herself with excitement. Sometimes she would tell me the story of how my father couldn't stand to be away from her. He would often come home for lunch just to see her. So you can imagine how awful it would have been for them, when she lost her baby. Her firstborn. And you can imagine how much her doctor would want to offer her hope, to make sure this would never happen again. I know his name. His kind face. He was also my doctor. Years later, when my mother was in her fifties—he had long given up his obstetrics practice—he was the one who held her hand when we found out she had breast cancer. But that's another story. Another history. He was the doctor who gave me my first Pap smear.

I can imagine them, my mother and father. On the tweed couch, my mother in tears because the baby they had made together, the baby whose cells had long begun to multiply, whose genes were part hers, part his, was not going to have a chance to be their child, and sit at their dinner table, and drink apple juice from their cup. Isn't history about loss?

When my mother became pregnant again, her obstetrician prescribed DES (diethylstilbestrol), a powerful synthetic hormone that was then known as the "miracle drug." It was supposed to prevent miscarriages by thickening the lining of the uterus. The irony is that DES was given to an estimated 4.8 million women in the United States from 1938 to 1971, despite reports from as early as 1953 that the drug was ineffective for preventing miscarriage.

My mother and father had three daughters, one after the other, a year apart. Nine years later another daughter would be born. I am the middle daughter. Her miracles. We drank from her cup.

## Two

It is October 1989, and I am just married. There is a look of loss in my eyes in our wedding photos, but it is tempered by the lucid and grateful knowledge that luck has come to me in the form of my husband, David. It is the look of a daughter who lost her father when she was two and misses him on her wedding day. And it is the look of a young woman who knows she has a chance now. It is the look of a young woman who has said goodbye to one life and has entered another. But most of all it is a look of hope. In the photo I am looking into the eyes of my husband, and in my mind is the thought that he will be the father of my child. I am breathless.

## T h r e e

It is New Year's Day, and we are lying on the couch in our one-bedroom brownstone on Columbus Avenue, and I'm watching the light just now coming into our picture window facing the courtyard, where each morning I'm grateful not to be looking at the dirty city streets, but at this perfect few square feet of land. In the summer there are climbing flowers that make me intensely happy. And in that moment of watching light fill up a dark sky, feeling hungover and no longer angry at my husband—we had drunk too much at a party and had fought coming home—I am seized with the desire to have a baby. And that morning, the first in the new year, our daughter was conceived. I'm sure of it.

## F o u r

In another photograph I'm wearing a winter-green Ann Taylor jacket I bought just before we were married. I'm standing in front of the Pig Hill Inn, in Cold Springs, New York. My baby is four months inside my womb. It is my birthday, and David has taken me out of the city for a weekend in the country. We bought antique lace white pillow cases in an antique shop for our bed that day, and I remembered thinking, my baby will lie on these pillows. In the picture my baby has taken the color out of my face. I look bloated. For four months I've been nauseous day and night, and because I've been so sick, my husband has planned this weekend. The night before, he threw me a surprise birthday party. I remember making a wish, and it's terrible to think it, but I felt a fatal chill run through me. It's an old Jewish thing. Another kind of inheritance. The evil eye, looking down on us when we are happy. I tried to will the feeling away as I blew out the candles on the devil's food cake.

Sometimes I go into the trunk in my bedroom and take out this picture and stare at it. I was really pregnant. My baby did exist.

## F i v e

I am sixteen weeks pregnant. I know the exact date from where I marked it on the pregnancy calendar my great-aunt Harriet gave me when she found out I was pregnant, to record the unborn's early milestones. My mother is in town, and we spend the afternoon at the Frick Museum. I remember looking at the Rembrandt. The painting of those two ethereal girls in their dress-up clothes. I remember hoping I would have a girl. I remember going into the bathroom and seeing a spot of red blood in my white Calvin Klein underpants.

We rush into a cab and immediately head for my doctor's office. After he examines me, I learn that my cervix has begun to dilate, a sign of premature labor. Within a half hour I am checked into the hospital for surgery to stitch my cervix, and a course of medication to control the contractions.

## S i x

After the surgery all I remember is vomiting from being under general anesthesia. My cervix is sewn up. My doctor tells me I have an "incompetent cervix." For the rest of the pregnancy I am confined to bed. Am I incompetent too? For the next three months I come in and out of this hospital trying to hold on to this baby, trying to stop the contractions. Each time I'm hooked up to a fetal monitor and given a course of medication through an IV.

My baby will be fine, I assure myself, because when a woman is pregnant for the first time, she is completely innocent and euphoric, she feels nearly immortal. Nothing possibly can go wrong. The contractions come and go, but still there is a queer feeling inside me; it seems as if the baby is telling me something I don't want to know.

I take pills that ironically give me the shakes, as if I've drunk too much coffee, but they are designed to relax my uterus. I feel my baby kick, and I reach my hand to greet her. I'm confined to my bed, on bedrest. For days on end, for hours, I sing for her. Sometimes I take off my headset and put it against my belly. Did I mention she is a baby girl?

*The Golden Bowl* takes me through another month of bedrest. I want to savor every word, and Henry James is difficult. Then *Portrait of a Lady*. I'm so enamored of Isabel Archer that I decide my baby must bear her name.

For twelve weeks I do not leave my apartment except to go to the doctor's office. Each time my husband carries me down three flights of stairs in our brownstone walk-up. The only time I leave my bed is to lie on the couch and eat my meals and relieve myself. Did I mention that in spite of this mad kind of solitary confinement—it *is* a kind of prison when your life is restricted—I am happy. I don't want to get too dramatic, but I do think about Camus a lot during the day when I am lying on our Workbench couch that we paid for on credit. Did I mention that whenever I am grouchy, everyone reminds me that there is a goal I will eventually reach? A prize in the form of human life!

## Seven

I am thirty-two weeks pregnant. A landmark. Every day of this pregnancy I awake each morning and cross off another day in the pregnancy calendar. It tells me everything that is happening: how my baby is growing; when she will sprout hair; when her lungs have developed. I still have this calendar, in a trunk at the foot of our bed, on top of a baby book. Inside the baby book is a picture of my baby. A lock of hair. A tickertape monitoring the contractions. A sonogram picture. The unopened lime-green lollipop the nurses gave me to suck on during labor.

It is Saturday morning, and I am lying in bed, where I've been for the last three months, and David has gone to the gym to let off steam. All of a sudden my bed is filled with water. Does this mean my water broke? I'm not sure. Earlier that week I had been leaking fluids, but this time there is a gush of water. Part of me is terrified. It is two months early, this isn't supposed to be happening now. But still a part of me refuses to *not* be happy. I have heard so many stories of women giving birth as early as twenty-six weeks, and the babies survive. I am supposed to be past the danger zone. At twenty-eight weeks the lungs are supposed to be developed.

I am going to have my baby, and I call up my husband at the gym, and they page him, and I remember thinking this will be a part of my child's story, how I had to page her father at the gym.

At the hospital my doctor ruptures the membranes completely to avoid infection, and as the waters gush out, the balloon of optimism that I have been carrying to protect myself pops too. I am dead sober. My doctor looks worried. The best course of action is to try and control the contractions and see whether the labor can be stopped. The doctor wants to give the baby more time in the womb. Every day is important, he says. And so I'm in bed in the hospital for another ten days. Something doesn't seem right. How can the baby live without any amniotic fluid? The doctor tells us that the fluid replenishes itself, and so I try and feel reassured. Still, the fluids continue to leak. Each time a new nurse or intern or resident makes the rounds, I bombard him or her with a litany of questions. Is there enough amniotic fluid? Shouldn't we do a sonogram? Is the baby all right? How long before I go into labor? I count the hours before the nurse comes in with the machine she hooks up to my uterus to hear the sound of my baby's heartbeat magnified. It is a kind of music I could listen to all day.

At night, after my husband has gone home, and it is dark, I pray.


*E i g h t*


On day ten in the hospital the contractions start again. This time the labor has progressed too far to be stopped. The baby is in a transverse lay. I am rushed to surgery for a C-section. There are complications during the delivery. At one point they take my husband, dressed in his proud scrubs, aside and make him leave the delivery room. All I can see are the bright hospital lamps that look like lights on a movie set, only this is real. The doctor, residents, and surgical nurses are in a panic. I hear my doctor, that round, sane, warm Fred Flintstone look-alike, swear. Yet I feel as if I'm floating outside it all, detached, unaware that everything in my life before has now changed forever. I will never look at the world so innocently again.


## N i n e

I am holding my baby, and she is beautiful. David says she has my forehead. We are intensely euphoric, marveling at our daughter. Our flesh and blood. And she is dead. I still curse the fact that I did not hold her longer, that after ten minutes we let the lovely neonatal nurse take her away.

I will always remember the nurse. She is like a nun, or something close to holy. She is so quiet. She holds my hand while my doctor tells me my baby has died. She sits by my bed and lets me sob for hours. She says our daughter is a miracle. She urges us to see her, to say goodbye. She allows her to be real.

We have a Polaroid snapshot of our baby. Sometimes it is painful to look at, but I look anyway because of this terrible fear I have, that eventually the image will fade, and I'll have nothing to remember her by.


## T e n

God or science (whatever you believe in) has played an awful trick. The drug that my mother ingested while carrying me, while I was inside her, protected by her womb, to supposedly stop *her* from miscarrying *me*, damaged my reproductive system. It is only later that I learn that I am a DES daughter. That 50 percent of the daughters whose mothers ingested DES while their babies were in utero have reproductive damage. I feel like a character in some kind of Greek tragedy. The daughter must pay for the mother's sin?

Our daughter weighed four pounds and two ounces. She was a fully formed baby. She lived for ten minutes, before the resuscitation effort failed, and her lungs collapsed.

During the postmortem at the hospital, when the team of doctors sits us down to explain how they are not culpable, one doctor says that my uterus crushed my daughter and put pressure on her lungs. There wasn't enough amniotic fluid to fully cushion her. All those ten days in the hospital when I was trying to keep her inside me, I was damaging her. For months I obsess over this: would she have lived if they had delivered her the day my water broke? After a while you learn how to let go of what you can't change. Still, I believe I failed her.

I can't help but wonder what thoughts were in her mind. Of the world, what would she know? The sound of my voice? The echo chamber my husband's hand set off when he touched my pregnant stomach to feel her kick? The lull of water, the bright lights overhead, the metallic smell? It was so cold in the surgery room.

### Eleven

I am given a medical workup. Laparoscopy, colposcopy, hysterosalpingogram, endometrial biopsy, you name it, I've had it. I want to find out if there is still a chance I can carry a baby safely. The doctors reassure me that now that they are aware of my condition, certain precautions can be taken. I have an incompetent cervix, a t-shaped uterus, a thin uterine lining—classic DES anomalies. During the pregnancy the baby's placenta grew into my uterine lining, a condition called placenta acreta. When they removed the placenta from the uterine wall, the placenta had grown into the lining to compensate for its thinness. As they tried pulling it away, I began to hemorrhage. I lost so much blood that they almost took my uterus to stop the bleeding and save my life. There is a 50 percent chance of recurrence in a future pregnancy. But still, you can have another baby, I'm told. There's still hope.

Don't worry, friends and family say, to console us while we are grieving, you'll have another baby. How do *you* know? I want to shout. And what about *my* baby? Everyone wants to pretend she never existed. I want to talk about her so much that instead I barely speak. How do you explain that once you've felt life inside you, the child has been permanently imprinted on the soul? When I report the remarks friends tell us to make us feel better, my therapist assures me they are just trying to help us. Her job is to help me recognize my anger. But what good is anger? I want to shout at her. It won't bring my baby back.

### Twelve

My baby. Her little pine coffin would break your heart. In the cemetery in Westchester there is a place where they bury the babies. She's in the earth, on a piece of land overlooking a magnificent stand of pines. Did you know that in Japan there is an entire cemetery for lost babies? We come to visit the grave every year on her birthday. We bring a bunch of baby's breath and scatter it over the headstone. It's the perfect flower.

### Thirteen

What is this burning desire? This need for a child? I remember wishing they could extract it out of me, the way they extracted my child, when they had to cut me open too soon. Even though one baby does not replace another, there is still the taste of baby in my mouth. This taste of life. Nothing washes it away. And still there is this need to mother. I cannot live without it.

### Fourteen

Without bringing a live baby home, the recovery from the C-section is slower. There's no reason to get out of bed. No baby to feed. No diapers to change. No one-stop shopping at Bellini's to push me out the door. Only reminders of my failure in the outside world: Mothers pushing strollers, pregnant women, children tearing through the grocery stores looking for the cereal aisle when I'm buying candy bars to numb the pain.

It takes me a good year to heal, to feel even the smallest pleasure, though I'm not sure you ever stop grieving. There are moments when I am stopped short by my loss. When I hear the name Isabel, goosebumps cover my arms. It is such a beautiful name.

## Fifteen

Hope saves me. Without that insane emotion, where would we be? We decide to court danger one more time. Please, just give me one live child, I pray. I'll sacrifice anything. By now I've made so many pacts with God, I'm certain he thinks I'm crying wolf. I wonder if my mother had known there was a risk in taking DES—that I could be damaged—would it have stopped her? Look. I am willing to risk another child's life, to bargain with science. After Isabel dies, I ingest infertility pills, so afraid I'll never conceive again, as recklessly as if they are candy.

## Sixteen

It takes us a year to get pregnant again. I worry each month that I've depleted my supply of eggs. I am so familiar with the science of my body—the sounds, rhythms, and smells, the wax and wane of my cycle that tells me when I'm fertile, when the egg has been released, when my period is coming—there is no chance of forgetting myself. Of forgetting I need to get pregnant. It is inside me, the need. No amount of rational thinking, mind over matter, wills it away. Still, I'm afraid. Once I'm pregnant, will I be able to carry a child safely? And for how long? But medicine is seductive. It gives me the hope I need to get up in the morning. The hope that one day I too will push a stroller in the park with the self-possessed and purposeful look mothers wear.

It's like being on drugs, the intense highs and lows of trying to conceive. The war between my want and my fear. And after months of basal thermometers, ovulation kits, and frantic sex, I am pregnant again. When the blue line appears on the pregnancy stick, I don't believe it. I rush out to the store and buy three other kits, each a different brand. I lay out the sticks whose pink and blue colors announce that I'm *with baby* on the dining room table, as if it were a feast for when my husband comes home.

## *Seventeen*

My son looks like a frog and is barely as big as David's hand. David stands next to his isolette for nearly twenty-four hours, while I am still coming back from the anesthesia. Every part of his little wrinkled, translucent body, with not an ounce of fat on it, is hooked up to a machine. You can see his heart beating under his skin. He is born at twenty-six weeks. The smallest living birth at the hospital.

One morning I didn't feel him moving inside me. The kicks slowed down to mere flutters. It scared the hell out of me. My doctor immediately asked me to come in for a nonstress test. As I sat in the doctor's office waiting to be called in, all the other pregnant women in the waiting room seemed to be carrying so much larger. After that everything happened so fast, it was as if my life were racing past me. I was rushed into surgery and cut open again. It felt as if my baby were being stolen from me. One minute he was snug and safe in my womb, or so I thought, the next gone, only I could still feel him there, the flutters, like a shadow limb, haunting his empty place. We would learn later that the placenta wasn't functioning properly because of my thin uterine lining. Imagine learning your baby wasn't being properly nourished. Imagine knowing he was no longer safe in your womb.

Even in his tiny face you could see my husband's distinctive nose.

## *Eighteen*

If you've never had a C-section, you may not be aware that the scar it leaves is in the shape of a smile just at the top of the pubic bone. When I look at myself in the mirror, it is as if my own self is smiling at me. The body has a mind of its own. It seems to say to me, it isn't your fault.

## *Nineteen*

Samuel Max lives for three days. After such a struggle to survive, his kidneys finally quit. When the doctor comes in to tell us, my husband is sleeping next to me on my hospital bed. It is nearly dawn. They bring our baby in, bundled in a flannel hospital blanket, wearing the smallest cap I have ever seen. He lies between us. He has such an old name for such a young soul, my husband says.

Now I'm aware that a day can be a lifetime. In the three days that mark our son's life, he held his father's pinkie. He felt his mother caress his face. A team of nurses and doctors knew every inch of his body. He weighed a little less than a pound. I remember waking up on the second day of his life, and it was snowing. It was January 20, and I felt relieved somehow when I saw out the window the mass white confusion. I so desperately wanted to lift him up out of the isolette and take him to the window. It was so pure against the dirty New York hospital buildings. And now each time it snows, I see his face. I pray that this global warming is nothing to worry about, though haven't you noticed that it's only snowed twice this year and already it's February.

## *T w e n t y*

Two babies in the ground, and the carrot is still dangling under our noses. Only this time it's my life I'm worried about. After two C-sections and a uterus that is filled with scar tissue, the chance that I'll hemorrhage is so great that they tell me that if I give birth again, they'll have to be prepared to perform a hysterectomy to save my life.

My mother's mother died during childbirth. Somehow I seemed to have forgotten the fact that I could die. My mother's brother survived the birth. He is his mother's living witness. Childbirth can be dangerous, and life is not to be taken for granted. Do you understand where I'm going now? What I'm getting at? I cannot even imagine it. A mother who did not live to see her child feed from her breast. Who did not get to feel those beautiful, perfect toes. Then it dawns on me. This is not about wanting a child. This isn't about manipulating science or medicine. This is about life and death being so close together it is as if they are holding hands.

It is my body that finally quits. I stop producing estrogen. My period trickles from a four-day flow to barely a half a day. My body is protecting me from losing another child, I'm sure of it.

## Twenty-one

David and I are the luckiest people in the world. Listen. In the other room I hear my son and my husband. It is Sunday morning, and the kitchen smells like Zabar's coffee, and the windows have steamed up because with wind-chill it is below zero outside. In my son's bedroom, sitting together on the blue and white checkerboard chair, they are singing Elvis's rendition of "Blue Christmas," and when they get to the hubba-hubba-hubba, my son breaks out in a fit of laughter. There isn't anything I'm not capable of doing as long as they are in the other room, my husband and my son. It is such a warm, protective feeling in our house now that we have our child, sometimes I'm scared to leave. I still feel that disaster is lurking around a corner. That even my son, this perfect child, will be taken from me. Post-traumatic shock syndrome, the shrink calls it. It takes time.

This one was born ex utero. Bless his heart. The woman who labored him is my definition of a Messiah. Born from another set of sperm and egg, and yet sometimes I feel as if he were born out of my head—my imagination. He is all that I've ever imagined.

On Isabel's and Sam's birthdays, we now take our son with us to the cemetery. He likes to pull up the overgrown grass around their headstones. He likes to smell the baby's breath. Without Isabel and Sam, our son would not have come into our home. Be our son. Their losses created a space for love. They existed; they matter.

# CONTRIBUTOR NOTES

Michael Bérubé is professor of English and director of the Program for Research in the Humanities at the University of Illinois at Urbana-Champaign. His most recent books are *The Employment of English: Theory, Jobs and the Future of Literary Studies* and *Life As We Know It: A Father, a Family, and an Exceptional Child.*

Jill Bialosky is the author of a poetry collection, *The End of Desire.* Her poems and essays have appeared in *The New Yorker, Redbook, Partisan Review, The Antioch Review,* and other journals. She is an editor at W. W. Norton & Company.

Sophie Cabot Black's book of poetry, *The Misunderstanding of Nature,* received the Norma Farber Book Award from the Poetry Society of America. Most recently, Black was a fellow at the Bunting Institute at Radcliffe. She divides her time between New England and New York City, where she lives with her partner, Diane, and their daughter, Fiona.

Steven Byrnes lives in Los Angeles with his partner, Jamie Mandle-
baum, and their two daughters, Samantha and Elizabeth. He has
written for TV and film and is currently working on a book about his
experiences as a gay father. His one-person show, *Swinging Wild*,
opened recently in Los Angeles to critical acclaim.

Kevin Canty is the author of *A Stranger in This World*, a story collection, and *Into the Great Wide Open*, a novel. His short fiction has
appeared in *The New Yorker*, *Esquire*, *Story*, and *The Missouri Review*,
among other places.

Peter Carey is the author of two short story collections, *The Fat Man
in History* and *War Crimes*, and five novels: *Bliss, Illywhacker, Oscar
and Lucinda, The Tax Inspector*, and *The Unusual Life of Tristan
Smith*. Recipient of the New South Wales Premier's Award, the National Book Council Award, the Miles Franklin Award, and the
Booker Prize, he is a fellow of the Royal Society of Literature.

Rita Gabis is the author of *The Wild Field* and the recipient of a
Connecticut State arts grant for poetry. Her work has appeared in
*Poetry, Columbia*, and other journals. "Oracles" is an excerpt from a
memoir she is writing about infertility.

Jesse Green is an award-winning journalist whose articles have appeared in *The New York Times Magazine*, *New York*, *Premiere*, *GQ*,
*Philadelphia*, *Out*, *Mirabella*, and *7 Days*, among others. His first
novel, *O Beautiful*, was published in 1992. "Finalizing Luke" is
adapted from *The Velveteen Father*, a memoir that will be published
next year.

Amy Hempel is the author of three collections of stories: *Reasons to
Live, At the Gates of the Animal Kingdom*, and *Tumble Home*. She
teaches in the graduate writing seminars at Bennington College and
lives in New York City.

Ann Hood is the author of six novels: *Somewhere off the Coast of
Maine, Waiting to Vanish, Three-Legged Horse, Something Blue,
Places to Stay the Night*, and *The Properties of Water*. Her new novel,

*Ruby,* is forthcoming. She has published her short stories, essays, and book reviews in *Parenting, Mademoiselle, Redbook, Seventeen, Story, Self, Cosmopolitan, McCall's, Glamour, The New York Times, The Washington Post, The Chicago Tribune,* and *The Los Angeles Times.* She lives in Providence, Rhode Island, with her husband, stepdaughter, son, and daughter.

Tama Janowitz is the author of a collection of stories, *Slaves of New York,* and two novels, *A Cannibal in Manhattan* and *By the Shores of Gitchee Goomee.*

Barbara Jones is a senior editor at *Harper's* magazine. She lives with her husband and daughter in New York City.

William Kotzwinkle is a novelist, poet, and screenwriter. He is the author of such enduring and varied classics as *The Fan Man* and *Fata Morgana,* as well as the best-selling novelization of the movie *E.T., the Extraterrestrial.* His most recent novel, *The Bear Went Over the Mountain,* was published in 1996. He lives with his wife on an island in Maine.

Lynn Lauber is the author of a collection of stories, *White Girls,* and a novel, *21 Sugar Street.* She lives in Piermont, New York.

Jenifer Levin is the author of four highly acclaimed novels: *Water Dancer,* which was nominated for the Pen/Hemingway Award; *Snow*; *Shimoni's Lover*; and *The Sea of Light,* a Lambda Literary Award nominee. Her short stories, widely anthologized, have recently appeared in the collection *Love and Death, and Other Disasters.* She has written for *The New York Times, The Washington Post, Rolling Stone, Mademoiselle, Ms., The Forward, The Advocate,* and other publications.

Phillip Lopate is the author of three personal essay collections (*Bachelorhood, Against Joie de Vivre,* and *Portrait of My Body*) and editor of *The Art of the Personal Essay* and the *Anchor Essay Annual.* He teaches at Hofstra University.

Agnes Rossi is the author of two collections of short stories, *Athletes and Artists* and *The Quick*, and a novel, *Split Skirt*. She is currently working on a new novel.

Helen Schulman is the author of a collection of short stories, *Not a Free Show*, and two novels, *Out of Time* and the newly released *The Revisionist*. Her short stories, essays, and reviews have appeared in *GQ*, *Elle*, *The Paris Review*, *Ploughshares*, *The Los Angeles Times*, *The Antioch Review*, *The North American Review*, *StoryQuarterly*, and *Food and Wine*, among others. She has received a Pushcart Prize and a New York Foundation for the Arts grant. She is the author of several commissioned screenplays and teaches in the Graduate Writing Division of Columbia University.

Bob Shacochis is the author of the novel *Swimming in the Volcano*, a finalist for a National Book Award, and two short story collections, *Easy in the Islands*, winner of a National Book Award, and *The Next New World*. He received the Prix de Rome from the Academy of Arts and Letters.

Lisa Shea is the author of *Hula*, a novel, for which she received a Whiting Writer's Award. She is currently writing a second novel, *The Free World*, and a collection of poetry, *The Thief of Strawberries*. Her essays have appeared in *Joyful Noise: The New Testament Revisited* and in *The Writer's Journal: Forty Contemporary Writers and Their Journals*. She writes regularly for *Elle*, *Newsday*, and *The New York Times Book Review*.

Marly Swick is the author of two short story collections, *Monogamy* and *The Summer Before the Summer of Love*; a novel, *Paper Wings*; and a forthcoming novel. She teaches creative writing at the University of Nebraska.

L. N. Wakefield is an art historian who lives and works in New York City.